10   3ᵍ

£3.95

2070346155
        6318

Terror
in the Arctic

Terror
in the Arctic

Bjarnhild Tulloch

Matador
9 Priory Business Park,
Wistow Road, Kibworth Beauchamp,
Leicestershire. LE8 0RX
Tel: (+44) 116 279 2299
Fax: (+44) 116 279 2277
Email: books@troubador.co.uk
Web: www.troubador.co.uk/matador

ISBN 978 1848768 079 (pb)
978 1780880 297 (hb)

British Library Cataloguing in Publication Data.
A catalogue record for this book is available from the British Library.

Typeset in 11pt Adobe Garamond Pro by Troubador Publishing Ltd, Leicester, UK
Printed and bound in the UK by TJ International, Padstow, Cornwall

Matador is an imprint of Troubador Publishing Ltd

This book is dedicated to the memory of my father, Bjarne Wian, whose loyalty to his family and his country never wavered.

… for my sons, their children and grandchildren

… with love

Contents

Prologue

The Altmark Incident.
Events leading to the German invasion of Norway in April 1940.

In January 1940, the *Altmark,* an auxiliary warship, was battling her way through heavy seas in the North Atlantic with 299 British prisoners on board. To avoid the British Navy, the *Altmark* sailed as far west as possible, slipping around Iceland before heading for the North Sea, and hopefully, the relative safety of the Norwegian coast.

Following Germany's invasion of Poland in September 1939, Britain and France had declared war on Germany. As early stirrings of war were unfolding during the closing months of 1939, the pocket battleship *Graf Spee* was attacking, and sinking a number of British merchant ships in the South Atlantic. The *Altmark's* orders were to stand by and assist the battleship, and to pick up survivors.

When three British cruisers closed in for attack, the *Graf Spee* sustained serious damage in what became known as the 'Battle of the River Plate' and sought refuge in Montevideo in Uruguay. The *Altmark* escaped with the British prisoners and was now heading north. By using the deception of Norwegian and other neutral flags and with an adjustable funnel in place, Captain Heinrich Dau was hoping to avoid detection.

On the 14th of February 1940 *Altmark* reached neutral waters near Trondheim. Norway had been alerted by Britain that there may be British prisoners onboard, but did not want to be drawn into the conflict. *Altmark* was boarded and superficially searched. The German officers in charge denied carrying British prisoners. The prisoners remained undetected. An escort was provided to follow *Altmark* out of Norwegian waters.

In the meantime, a British plane had spotted what was thought to be the *Altmark* as it neared the Norwegian coast. The hunt was now on.

Two days later, British Navy ships appeared on the scene, led by the destroyer HMS *Cossack*. When an attempt was made to board the *Altmark*, the Norwegian escort protested. Refusing to stop, *Altmark* fled for shelter into the nearby Jøssingfjord, 110km south of Stavanger.

That evening – on orders from the British Government – Captain Philip Vian took HMS *Cossack* into Jøssingfjord with an assault team ready to board the *Altmark*. In the battle that followed, four Germans were killed and five seriously wounded. Two hundred and ninety-nine British sailors were liberated and HMS *Cossack*, its mission accomplished, set course for Britain.

The two Norwegian motor torpedo boats in the fjord had protested, but their orders were not to open fire on a British ship. Both Germany and Britain had violated Norwegian neutrality. The German soldiers killed in the skirmish were later buried in Norway.

After the outbreak of war between Britain and Germany, Hitler at first seems to have supported the neutrality of the Scandinavian countries. But the *Altmark* incident raised doubts in Nazi Germany about Norwegian neutrality.

At that time a small movement in Norway called 'Nasjonal Samling' (NS) was sympathetic to Germany. The movement was led by Vidkun Quisling, who had been minister of defense in the Norwegian Parliament in the early 1930s. On a secret mission to meet the German leaders, he requested assistance to attempt a coup in Norway. Quisling would take command and introduce National Socialism, working in conjunction with the German government. He also had two private meetings with Hitler in December 1939.

These meetings resulted in Hitler ordering an investigation into how Norway could be taken. A closer contact between the German

National Socialist Party and its Norwegian counterpart was also to be encouraged.

But Hitler hesitated. Invading Norway at that time was not on his agenda. His plans were to advance west to Holland, Belgium and France. An invasion of Britain, 'Operation Sea Lion', was also in the making. But the *Altmark* incident made headlines around the world and changed Hitler's mind. Due to British intervention in a neutral country, Germany had lost face and Hitler was furious. To him this was a defeat for Germany and could not be tolerated. Norway had been unable to protect its neutrality. Hitler's doubts melted away. Norway had to be secured before the British and French moved in.

One of his generals, Nikolaus von Falkenhorst, was ordered to work out a plan for the occupation of Norway and Denmark and was answerable directly to Hitler himself. The top secret plan was code-named Weserubung (exercise on the Weser – the name of a German river).

Although the war in Europe was looking increasingly serious, the general opinion in Norway at the time was that the country was not at risk. However, the Norwegian Navy had been mobilized to patrol the coast, guarding the country's neutrality. Both Norway and Sweden wished to remain neutral, having resisted requests from Britain and France to bring in their troops.

Meanwhile, movements of British and French troops and ships were reported regularly. To Hitler it looked increasingly likely that there could be a British/French invasion of Scandinavia. He wanted to beat them to it.

Hitler decided on a 'Blitz Krieg' – a swift combined attack by the Army, Navy and Air force. Secrecy was of utmost importance. The attacks would take place simultaneously at all main ports around the Norwegian coast as far north as Narvik. The date of the invasion was set for 15th March 1940, but had to be postponed due to sea ice in the Baltic. The final date was set for the 9th April. Merchant ships with troops and equipment concealed onboard had been sent to various ports in Norway in readiness for the combined attack. Surprise was the key factor. The Germans had great respect for the British Navy and knew they had to get there first, before the British government realised what was afoot.

Under cover of darkness, late in the evening of 8th April 1940, German warships sailed stealthily in towards Oslo fjord. The Norwegians were nervous; the guard boats patrolling the coast had orders not to let foreign ships pass.

The German ships were led by the 12,247 tons heavy cruiser *Blücher*, the newest of their larger warships, with heavy cruiser *Lutzow* and the light cruiser *Emden* close behind. Three torpedo boats and eight small minesweepers completed the fleet.

The Norwegian patrol boat *Pol III,* on discovering the ships heading towards the entrance of Oslo fjord, fired warning shots. This was followed by flares to alert the coastal batteries. The German Commander ordered one of the torpedo boats, the *Albatross,* to take care of the Norwegian 'intrusion'.

During the attack which followed, Captain Leif Welding-Olsen was wounded. As *Pol III* was burning, the lifeboat was launched. Weakened by loss of blood the Captain was unable to get into the lifeboat and died before midnight on the 8th of April – the first Norwegian casualty of the impending war. The Norwegian crew was taken prisoner, and the *Pol III* was confiscated by the German Navy.

When word came through of skirmishes at the entrance to Oslo fjord, all lighthouses were ordered to extinguish their lights. As the ships moved in through the fjord they were attacked by shore defenses – but the invasion fleet turned on their search lights, blinding the defenders. Luck was with the invaders, as thick fog rolled in through the fjord, hiding the ships. Assault troops from the bigger ships were transferred to the minesweepers, to be landed and take control of defense posts along the fjord – including the Navy base in Horten. The warships continued their journey in through the fjord.

Towering over the Drøbak sound, where Oslo fjord is at its narrowest, stands the old fort of Oskarsborg (built during the nineteenth century). The armament in April 1940 consisted of 32 old guns of various sizes. Night illumination for the guns was provided by searchlights. A floating boom defence blocked a side-channel.

Before midnight the garrison knew that foreign warships were moving in. Colonel Birger Eriksen, the commander of Oskarsborg, decided to attack, but was unsure of the nationality of the ships. However, confirmation came at 0030. The defenders prepared to fight, but were few and lacked experience, as Norway was not on a war footing.

The main battery of the fort had three old cannons. One of them was named 'Moses', because it had once fallen into the sea and had to be fished out again. The other two had been nicknamed 'Aaron' and 'Joshua'. At 0421 on the morning of the 9th of April, *Blücher* was about 1800m away from the fort. The order was given to engage, and two shells from Oskarsborg exploded into the warship. 'Moses' and 'Aaron' had spoken!

The smaller cannons on the east side of the fjord now opened up and at such short range *Blücher* didn't have a chance. Then two torpedoes from Oskarsborg hit the side of the ship. Fire spread to the ammunition magazine, which exploded. Like a grand floating torch, lighting up the sea and the landscape ashore, the *Blücher* slowly sailed on – and as she began to sink, the order to abandon ship was given. Within a short space of time, more than 1000 men lost their lives. Locals along the shore put to sea in an attempt to help the screaming sailors, who were splashing around in the freezing, oil-covered sea.

The heavy cruiser *Lutzow* had also been hit, and the Commander decided to turn back. The remainder of the German flotilla followed *Lutzow*. Their troops were put ashore further south that morning and were ordered to move overland towards Oslo.

The attempt to take Oslo by sea had failed. Instead German troops were flown into Norway, landing at Fornebu Airport near Oslo later that day. More were landed at other airports in Norway, to support those already there.

Just before midnight, members of Parliament had been alerted to the fighting in Oslo fjord and made their way to the Foreign Ministry for an emergency meeting. Messages began to arrive, and it became clear that a German invasion of Norway was unfolding. Members of the Government present took the decision to mobilize the nation to resist the invasion.

Curt Bauer, a diplomat who had been appointed German envoy to Norway on the 14th of November 1939, presented himself at the Foreign Ministry at 0430 in the morning of 9th April 1940. He was met by foreign minister Halvdan Koht. Due to power cuts their meeting was conducted by candle light.

Bauer had come to put forward the German demands. He said that the Germans had not come as enemies but to protect and defend the Norwegian people, and to make sure that the Western Allies stayed out of Norway. Contacts with foreign powers must stop; censorship of military news would be introduced. Any resistance was futile and would be crushed. The Norwegian Government must order the people not to resist the German occupation. An immediate reply was expected.

Koht was stunned. He told Bauer to wait while he consulted his colleagues – assembled in the next room. The response was unanimous – voiced by Trygve Lie, who became the United Nations' first Secretary General after the war:

"No, this we cannot accept."

Curt Bauer got his answer and said:

"Then it will be war," whereupon Halvdan Koht replied:

"But the war has already begun."

King Haakon VII and his Cabinet knew that they had to escape. They decided to board the train for Hamar – a small town to the north of Oslo. (The other members of the Royal family had already left for Sweden).The first result of their 'No' to mighty Germany came when the train stopped at Lillestrøm to change locomotive. German bombers came in and bombed the airport near the railway station. The passengers were ordered out and into the shelter under the station. After the bombing raid, the planes swept low over the train but did not attack.

At Hamar the German ultimatum was discussed again at length. Germany was a great power – what could little Norway do to oppose such a force? King Haakon got to his feet. Looking around at the assembled ministers he stated that should his Government decide to accept the German demands, he would abdicate. After serving the country as King for 35 years he could not accept the German ultimatum. The decision was then taken that theirs would be a King and Government in exile. Sweden had been their first choice for exile. King Haakon, however, refused to leave Norway while his countrymen were still fighting the enemy. Instead, they decided to move north, assessing the situation as it unfolded.

When the British belatedly realised Norway's peril, they came to assist. British and French troops were landed in order to help stem the German advance. At sea, the British were superior and sank many German warships. Germany, however, kept pouring troops and equipment into Norway. The Norwegians resisted and – with the help from Allied forces – stemmed the tide for a while. But gradually they were forced further north. Norwegian towns were extensively bombed. The King had to keep moving north with his cabinet, always one step ahead of the Germans. A British Navy ship brought them to Tromsø, which became the Government's temporary headquarters.

The fiercest battle took place at Narvik. The Germans had taken it with very little resistance on the 9th April. Now the British Navy attacked from the sea, while the Norwegians, with the help of French and British troops, attacked from the surrounding mountains. Germany needed the iron ore from Sweden (which was shipped out at Narvik) and the British were equally determined to stop the ore going to Germany. The Germans were pushed towards the Swedish border on the brink of defeat, as Narvik was recaptured.

On the 1st June, the news of withdrawal by the British and French troops came as a great shock to the Norwegian forces. With Germany's invasion of Holland, Belgium and France in progress, the Allied forces became overstretched and had to be moved into Europe. Norway, unfortunately, had to be sacrificed.

Many German and British ships had been sunk in the battle of Narvik, and many lives were lost. (*Eidsvoll* and *Norge*, Norway's only warships had been sunk there on the first day of the invasion).

On the 7th June 1940, HMS *Devonshire* left Tromsø with King Haakon, Crown Prince Olav and members of the cabinet on board, bound for England. They could not risk being captured. Having fought back longer than France, Holland and Belgium, Norway finally capitulated. In spite of having no defences to speak of, and in spite of the surprise attack, it had taken two months to defeat Norway.

HMS Devonshire in Kirkenes Harbour April 1940.
Photo: Private collection.

King Haakon and Crown Prince Olav worked tirelessly for a free Norway, supporting those who came to Britain to fight against a common enemy. The King's speeches from the BBC to the Norwegian people gave them moral support in their struggles at home and abroad. He became a focal point for a free Norway and was much loved, and respected, for the stand that he took in April 1940.

Vidkun Quisling had betrayed Norway from within. During the

years of occupation, his power and influence grew. Reviled and feared by the Norwegian people his name became synonymous with treason. A new word entered our vocabulary, 'quisling', meaning traitor.

In the wake of defeat, however, a resistance movement was slowly emerging. It would have many shapes and forms, and would be further strengthened by the many atrocities to take place in the years ahead.

Much that was new and strange was about to enter our lives, following the invasion. How much it would change was beyond our wildest dreams. With its strategic position so close to Russia, my hometown Kirkenes, in north eastern Norway, was already earmarked as a gateway to the Soviet Union. And so, twenty five days after the invasion in the south, we woke up to the fact that Kirkenes was under attack.

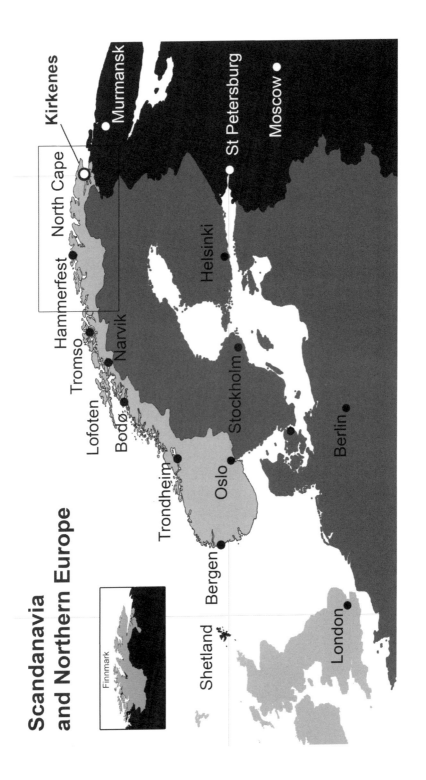

Scandanavia and Northern Europe

Kirkenes
Murmansk
North Cape
St Petersburg
Moscow
Hammerfest
Helsinki
Tromso
Narvik
Lofoten
Bodø
Stockholm
Berlin
Trondheim
Oslo
Bergen
Shetland
London
Finnmark

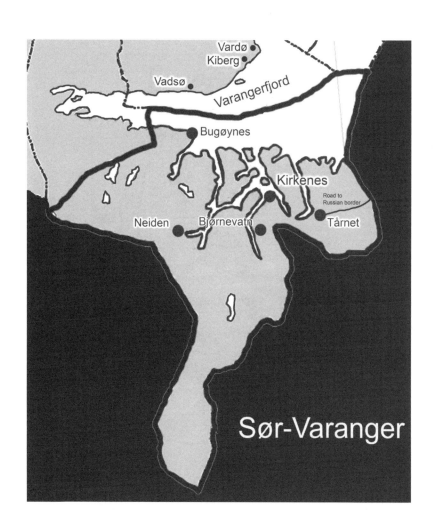

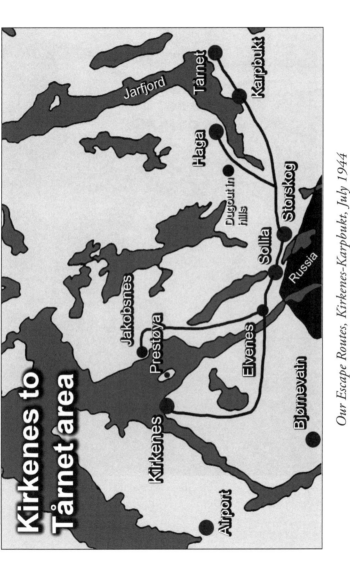

*Our Escape Routes, Kirkenes-Karpbukt, July 1944
and from Karpbukt to the dig out in hills, October 1944*

1

Rude Awakening

A deep and persistent noise was penetrating the fog of blissful oblivion as I was sleeping in our upstairs bedroom, shared with my sister Sonja. Turning around, pulling the downy over my head to get rid of the noise, didn't help, as the rumbling, thunderous noise grew in intensity until it filled the room.

Suddenly wide awake I jumped out of bed and ran to the window in time to see a 'big black thing' roaring past very low over the houses, obviously the source of all the noise. Sonja was already standing by the window craning her neck looking out, and as we stood there straining to see if this 'thing' was coming back, our mother came rushing in, propelling us at full speed down the stairs.

"Mamma, what was that big thing floating in the air?"

"Ssh child, be quiet! "hissed my mother. "We have to get your clothes on."

So coats went on over our nighties, hats were planted on our heads and as shoe laces were tied, with Mother fending off our mystified questions – a tremendous explosion, quickly followed by another, kept us rooted to the spot. As we stood there, Mother holding on to us so tightly that it was painful, we could feel the house shaking from the shock wave.

This was too much for Sonja and me. Nothing made sense any more, and, very frightened, we started to cry. Accompanied by the smattering of machine gun fire from Norwegian defences in Kirkenes, we were taken out of the house and rushed down the slope to the basement which was our first (and none too safe) shelter.

The date was 4th May 1940. The time was 4.45am. My sister was eight years old and I was five. The war had come to Kirkenes.

The night shift at the iron ore mining company A/S Sydvaranger finished at 6 am and my father returned home as soon as possible. The first bombs had fallen on A/S Sydvaranger's power station. On its second round, the German plane bombed another part of the iron ore plant and then dropped more bombs over the town. One of the bombs penetrated the roof of a house, passed out through the wall and landed in the street without exploding. To finish off the job, the plane flew over the town again, strafing it with machine gun fire. Amazingly, no one was hurt.

Due to the on-going battle in the south of Norway, several defence posts had been set up in and around Kirkenes. These had quickly been manned and were shooting back at the attacking plane. It was eventually discovered that a German plane had crash landed in northern Sweden that day, with one of the crew members dead. The Swedes also found a roll of film taken over Kirkenes. The bullet holes in the plane indicated that one of the defence posts in Kirkenes had found its mark.

Later that morning – when it was considered safe – we all went back to the kitchen where Sonja and I got properly washed, dressed and comforted. Breakfast arrived on the table as Mother and Father discussed the morning's events. We were told that the 'floating thing in the air' was an aeroplane; we were now at war but not to worry, they would look after us. To me this was all a mystery. What was war, and what was an aeroplane? I had never seen an aeroplane before. But this was only the first of countless air attacks in store for us during the coming years.

After breakfast, Father decided to look at the damage caused by the bombs.

"I want to come, I want to come," I chanted.

"It is too dangerous," Mother said. Sonja joined in.

"We want to come too, Pappa!"

"Oh, let them come," said my father. "The plane will not be returning today. The Germans have made their point."

Aase, our elder sister, stayed at home to help Mother with the dishes; so in due course the three of us set off through the town to A/S Sydvaranger's power station – where the first bombs had fallen. Soon we found ourselves among small groups of people moving in the same direction, all discussing the day's events. Sonja and I, unable to make sense of this new development in our lives, held on to Father's hands for dear life. The power station had been badly damaged, but not completely destroyed. Smoke and flames were still belching out of the building. People stood around in groups, men with hands in their pockets, others linking arms with their wives or holding a child's hand.

"Have you heard?" or "Did you see that?" "The people in that house were so lucky" "When do you think?" etc. were snippets of the conversations going on around us. Standing there holding hands with my father, this was all beyond my comprehension. But the memory of that day, and the destruction we were looking at, still remains.

Back home again, Sonja and I were not allowed to go out to play. Normally, the only times we had to stay indoors were when we were ill or if the weather was bad.

"You needn't go on about it," said my mother, "It is not safe."

Life as we knew it was changing fast. Father was going to a 'crisis' meeting we were told and no further explanations were given. Sonja and I sat down on the floor and started playing with our toys. Aase breezed in and Mother brightened up.

"Where have you been?" she asked.

"I had a look at the power station with some friends. Terrible."

"Everybody is talking about the war," she continued, "and wondering whether the Norwegian soldiers are able to hold back the Germans."

"Who knows," said Mother. "It doesn't sound very good on the radio. Parts of Norway in the south are already occupied – and our soldiers are being forced to retreat further north."

"What are we going to do if they come here as well," said Aase gloomily. "Where can we go?"

"There's nothing we can do, I am afraid. Today they have shown us what they are capable of – besides, we have nowhere else to go."

Mother was sitting at the table mending socks. When she wasn't cooking or cleaning, she was often busy mending our socks.

"Switch on the radio, Aase. I want to listen to the broadcast from Stockholm," she said. "We can't believe what is coming from the Norwegian radio at the moment."

The news from Stockholm meant nothing to Sonja and me. But as soon as Father came home from work, I would sit on his knee, helpfully telling him to set på Stockon (switch on Stockholm) which he was about to do anyway.

"Why don't you play with your sisters while I make dinner, Aase? They are very unsettled after the frightening events of this morning."

Aase, who was now seventeen years old, was very good and often played with us. She sat down beside us and started singing funny songs, followed by word games and other games. Soon we forgot about the troubles earlier that day and had a great time together.

Father returned when dinner was ready.

"Let's have dinner first," he said, "and then we'll talk." So we sat down to the table and folded our hands while Father asked the Lord to bless our dinner. I don't know what we were eating, but I am sure it was good as Mother was a good cook; that's what Father said so it had to be true!

After dinner, the adults gathered around the table to talk. Sonja and I were told to be quiet and play with our toys.

"The Company says that their workers, and others who are worried about the German attacks, can take shelter in the tunnel under their works in Kirkenes," Father said, "at least for the time being till we see what happens. We have to bring warm clothing and bed clothes and also food. What do you think?" Mother was frowning.

"I don't like it," she said slowly, "but we have to think of the safety of the children. The German planes may return again while we are sleeping. The twenty-four hour daylight up here is to their advantage, I am afraid."

When we were told that we were going to sleep in a tunnel the next few nights I thought at first that it would be a great adventure. Voicing this thought with great delight made Aase laugh and Sonja look at me with scorn. Mother and Father refrained from commenting and started packing food, blankets and other essentials.

"Many people will go to the shelter tonight," Father said. "We have to leave early in order to find a place to sleep before it gets too crowded. But first we shall pray to the Lord that he will look after us and all the Norwegian people in our hour of need."

So we knelt and prayed to God that all would be well with us and all the people in Norway. Closing the door behind us, we walked away from our house to the safe shelter of the tunnel under the iron ore works.

What we didn't know was how frequent these trips would become, when we would be running, not walking, to the shelters.

The tunnel turned out to be large, dark and damp. Already it was filling up, as people made their way there. Father found a place for us, trying to make us as comfortable as possible. I soon found out that this was not really such an adventure after all and was very disappointed. There must have been boxes and benches to sit on, because Father set me on his knee and, trying to comfort me, was murmuring,

"Don't worry, Baby; we'll soon be home again."

I didn't much like to be called baby, but my parents unfortunately seemed to like calling me that. Paraffin lamps and candles were lighting up the place – and the murmur of hundreds of voices kept the place alive. Slowly the noise died down, however, as people prepared to get a few hours' sleep.

The next few days we went home in the morning and returned at night. After a while we stopped going to the tunnel. There were, however, a few more attacks by German planes. The large sawmill at Jakobsnes (near Kirkenes) had a substantial store of timber, bought by the British, who had been trying to find a way of getting it out. Neither the British nor the Germans were destined to get the timber.

Surprisingly, German bombers attacked and destroyed it. The resulting fire continued for days.

An attempt to destroy a large army building at the outskirts of the town didn't quite go as planned either, with most of the bombs falling short.

After Norway's capitulation on 7th June, the attacks by German planes ceased. But the new rulers of Norway were soon to make their presence felt.

2

Life in the Arctic

Finnmark is by far Norway's largest county. Covering an area greater than Denmark, it lies well beyond the Arctic Circle, and stretches across the top of Scandinavia.

The flat plains of the tundra are dotted with lochs, feeding the salmon rivers on their journey to the sea. Long and deep fjords cut into the country from the north. Moving east around the Varanger peninsula, the last of the great fjords, Varangerfjord, cuts into Finnmark in a westerly direction from the Barents Sea. From its southern coastline Bøkfjord, a smaller fjord, leads to Kirkenes in the district of Sørvaranger.

In 1905, at the time of Norway's independence from Sweden, Finnmark was sparsely populated. The nomadic Sami people with their reindeer flocks dominated the tundra; here and there small fishing villages clung to the barren coast as whalers and seal hunters roamed the Arctic seas.

A land of contrasts, the summer temperature may peak at 30 degrees Celsius, followed by winter temperatures inland falling to minus 40 degrees C. or even lower. In late November – when the sun retreats below the horizon for two months – white glittering snow and sparkling stars lend a ghostly light to the landscape. The moon's monthly visit across the sky is a welcome addition to the polar light. And then, adding a touch of magic to a clear winter night, the magnificent northern lights appear, dancing across the skies in ever changing shapes and colours.

With the arrival of spring, snow and ice must give way to new life, as the midnight sun returns, moving around the sky in silent splendour – never setting for two months. The migrating birds are back; the brown bear comes out of its den – and with the short growing season lasting only three months in the Arctic, there is a flurry of activities and excitement in the air.

At the dawn of the 20th century, Kirkenes (church on the ness) was a small hamlet on a tongue of land pointing northeast, dividing Bøkfjord into two channels. To the south and west, a barrier of rocky hills defines the peninsula.

Only a church and a few houses had found foothold there. Iron ore had recently been discovered at Bjørnevatn about 10km south of Kirkenes. The mining company AS Sydvaranger moved in – and from 1906 to 1912 built processing plants in Kirkenes, a crushing plant in Bjørnevatn and a rail link connecting the two. The rail link was in regular use, transporting the roughly crushed ore to Kirkenes to be refined and shipped out as pellets.

The deep water in Bøkfjord was ideal for shipping. New piers were built to accommodate the ships that would load the iron ore for transport south. People from other parts of the country flocked in to work at the new company – especially from the Lofoten Islands.

The third of a family of seven, my father, Bjarne Wian, grew up on a small croft in Lofoten. Two cows and some sheep were all their land could sustain. The family turned to cod fishing in the winter to supplement their livelihood. As the boys grew, they all, in turn, followed their father to the fishing grounds.

When rumours of good pay in the new iron ore company in Kirkenes reached him, my father made up his mind to try his luck there. He travelled to Kirkenes in 1925 and got a job in the pellets factory at first. Later, on request, he worked on maintenance of the railway line for the next 40 years.

The iron ore company continued to develop. Houses for the workers and their families were soon under construction. Business-minded people arrived to set up shops, build roads and more houses. New piers made trade much easier, opening up the area to the outside world.

The extreme Arctic temperatures led to a thick layer of ice forming on the smaller fjords. The problem of sea ice in Bøkfjord was overcome, when the new iron ore company brought in an ice breaker to keep the channel open. When the first coastal steamers made their appearance in 1914 and became regular visitors, the infrastructure for the area was complete. By 1940 Kirkenes was a bustling town of about 4,500 people and Bjørnevatn's population had grown to between 1,200 and 2,000. There was plenty of work; people had food on their tables and nobody locked their doors.

Kirkenes's pre-war architecture was surprisingly varied. One or two of the fine buildings in the 'business area' of the peninsula were adorned with Russian-inspired onion-like domes. Our beautiful new school had been built overlooking the sea to the north east, and a pretty white-painted church nestled nearby. Some of the streets were lined with Finnish-inspired, log-cabin type houses while other streets had more traditional one and a half or two storey wooden houses. Set into the hill looking west, the imposing presence of the iron ore company's buildings and factories was spread across the hill towards the harbour. Here the ore was refined and transported on belts directly into the holds of waiting ships.

My mother, Borghild Borthen, was born and brought up in Vardø (north east of Kirkenes). Her ancestors had moved north to Finnmark in the 1830s and 1840s from Trøndelag and Stavanger. As the border dispute with Russia had been settled by then, people from the south were encouraged to move north to the largest and least populated county of Norway. My mother's paternal grandparents set up shop and ran a small shipping business in Vardø where, among other things, they traded with the Russians. Her grandfather was also appointed French consul. My mother's maternal ancestors had settled in Jarfjord about 24km southeast of Kirkenes, where they bought land and worked as crofters, fishermen and teachers. Their settlement was called Haga, after Mother's great grandfather.

Mother was a widow when she met my father. After they were married, her daughter Aase came to live with them on Haugen, where my father had been allocated a house for his family.

The new iron ore company in Kirkenes looked after its workers well – providing cheap housing, electricity and fuel. The locals always referred to it as The Company.

The square of Haugen where we lived was on an elevated hill of solid rock, surrounded by eight semid-etached houses. Three roads lined with houses spread away from Haugen, two of them in the general direction of the town centre.

The houses on Haugen didn't have a mains water supply. Water was fetched from a stand pipe in the square, where a low wall enclosed an area of about five to seven square metres. A drain in the middle completed the facility. Here the housewives came to fetch water, or to rinse clothes and gossip (unless it was too cold). In periods of severe frost the water frequently froze, covering the washing area with ice.

Washing clothes was hard work. Mother used to fetch water; warm it on the iron stove, kept going with wood and coal; pour the water into a tub placed on two stools and there – using a scrubbing board – she washed and scrubbed the clothes. Next, she squeezed out the soapy water by hand, transferred the clothes to another tub and carried it out to the washing area at the stand pipe for rinsing. When we were old enough, we helped her hang out the clothes on the line. In winter the clothes froze solid, almost as soon as they hit the line. But after two or three days they softened up and could be taken in to air. Our fingers soon lost their feeling in the process and cost us a lot of pain as they thawed out. Mother eventually got a hand wringer, which was screwed onto a wooden tub. This was a great improvement, making things much easier for her.

All the houses had electricity, but used paraffin or carbide lamps as standby. The outside toilets were placed discreetly behind the houses in small buildings, each serving two houses. Next to them were large wooden boxes with hinged lids for coal storage and smaller ones for discarding ash. The Company bought coal in bulk from Spitsbergen providing cheap coal for their workers. Firewood was stored in our basement where Father kept a chopping block and axe. The basement was also our first air raid shelter.

We had little money, but managed well enough on Father's earnings at the Company. In those days women didn't go out to work, but stayed at home to look after the family. When Father was at home he chopped up fire wood, fetched water and coal – always helping Mother as much as possible.

In the spring of 1940 Father was 34 years old and very fit. He had been an amateur boxer in his younger days and liked weight training and athletics. He would, for example, put one hand on the seat of a kitchen chair and the other on the back of the chair in a handstand and then walk the chair across the floor, to the delight of Sonja and me – with Mother somewhat nervously looking on. When he had time there were other acrobatics to follow, where Sonja and I tried to copy his antics, without much success but with much fun and laughter. These were happy times for us all.

On Saturdays we went to the Seventh Day Adventist meetings. On Sundays – when the weather was fine – we dressed up and went out to the 'Promenade', a stretch of road near the sea where people walked, met friends and socialised.

Each Christmas our grandparents in the Lofoten Islands sent us a parcel. In it was rolled lamb seasoned with herbs and spices; then cured in salt brine. Father soaked the meat for a while before boiling it. When the meat was still hot, it was pressed between two boards with a heavy stone on top. The lamb was sliced and eaten with other food at Christmas. Sonja and I got boot-like footwear made of thick knitted stockings, with quilted felt soles and layers of knitted wool stitched in place on top of the foot and around the ankles. Tremendously light to run around in, they were surprisingly warm – and used over thick socks outside in severe frost, nothing else was needed.

At Christmas we always had a real tree. The base for the tree was made of metal, with four large metal Santa Clauses sitting on a flat ring, which was connected to a pipe-like insert for the tree and its water supply. It was beautifully painted; the Santas' jackets were red with black buttons and white collars, their knee-length trousers were black over white stockings and black shoes, and on their heads, red Santa hats.

To Sonja and me, the highlight of Christmas, after fetching the Santas, was getting out the decorations to help Mother decorate the tree. She decorated it with lovely coloured balls, and Aase helped us make paper hearts in various colours to hang on the branches. A pretty star was put on the top, with strings of small Norwegian flags cascading down from it.

For lights we used small candles in holders with clips, which were secured carefully to the branches. All these pretty things were kept in boxes in one of the upstairs bedrooms. In the war years – when life was grim and there was nothing to enjoy – Sonja and I would sometimes sneak upstairs and quietly take out the pretty Christmas decorations to look at and play with. Mother discovered this but let us play with them, as long as we were careful.

Our nearest relatives in the town were Aunt Reidun and Uncle Edvard. They lived at Saga with their two children in a fine two-storey house – which Uncle Edvard had built. He was an excellent joiner and worked at a sawmill nearby

Aunt Reidun, Mother's sister, was plump, jolly and laughed a lot. Their son Odd, about Sonja's age, liked to tease us when he had nothing better to do. His sister Ruth was a little younger than me, with big blue eyes and fair hair, almost as white as snow. She was one of my best friends. Our families got on well and often visited each other.

Saga was at the outskirt of Kirkenes and Aase occasionally brought Sonja and me for a visit. Ruth often came back with us – but although Ruth and I were good friends, we didn't always agree. Father had a lot of fun with her. He would lift her up, throw her in the air, then set her down and tease her. At times he would spin her around like a top. Ruth didn't like this very much and before she would come home with me, started to ask,

"Is your father home?"

"No, no, he is working," I would say, which was not always true. Then she was very cross after yet another session of acrobatics with Father.

"I shall never come home with you again," she said, and was very angry. But it was soon forgotten and we were friends again.

In those days few motor vehicles were to be seen around town. Wood, coal and other deliveries and collections were done by horse and cart, with the result that horse dung regularly messed up the roads.

Sitting at the kitchen table one morning, looking out on the square, I noticed the round deposits from a horse and cart just gone by. I enjoyed sitting there watching the comings and goings on the square. As I sat there with nothing better to do, two small children appeared, presumably sent out to play. They started to collect the round deposits from the horses, carrying them to the side of the road which was all right. But then to my horror first the boy, then the girl started to smell the dung and put their tongues on it.

"Mamma," I shouted, "They are eating the horse's dung!"

Mother came running, took one look out the window, ran out and grabbed them, marching them into their house.

"They won't do that again," she said when she returned, and, looking sternly at me, continued:

"I hope that you won't do anything as stupid as that."

"Me!" I was thunderstruck at the very thought of it.

My best friends and playmates at that time, apart from Ruth, were Astrid and Gunhild. Gunhild, who lived nearby, came around regularly, standing outside shouting my name over and over again.

"Oh, you better go out and see what she wants," Mother said, which was of course for me to come out to play. Sometimes Gunhild and I would visit her Aunt Camilla, who lived just across the road from them. She was always pleased when we visited, and would usher us into her sitting room which was a clutter of beautiful furniture, pretty velvet cushions and lovely ornaments. We always admired her beautiful things while she made room for us to sit down.

During our visits in the early days, Aunt Camilla brought in a tray with juice and cake or biscuits, while she had the most fascinating conversations with Jesus. She was strange, but very kind, and not like anyone else I knew.

The first time I saw Gunhild's Aunt Camilla was at the Co-operative, when I was shopping with my mother – just before the war started. I was standing between Camilla and Mother waiting our turn, while she did her shopping.

Camilla: "Jesus says that I need half a kilo of sugar."

Shop assistant looking at Mother and back at Camilla:

"What did you say?"

Camilla: "No, I didn't say anything. Jesus said that I need half a kilo of sugar." Camilla gets her sugar.

"Anything else?"

Camilla: "Jesus also says that I need one kilo of flour and half a kilo of butter." Camilla got her flour and butter and everything else Jesus had told her to buy.

I was very impressed – and when we got outside I asked my mother:

"Mamma, does Jesus tell you too what to buy?"

"Don't talk nonsense child," she said, which was not very helpful. But Aunt Camilla became a favourite person to visit with my friend Gunhild.

3

Arrival of the Germans

"Why can't we go out and play, Mamma?" Outside the sun was shining on this nice summer day and I couldn't understand why we were not allowed outside.

"Because I said so," said my mother. But her voice lacked conviction and Sonja decided to try her luck.

"We want to go out and play with the other children," she pleaded, as she looked first at Mother before switching her attention to Father. My father had not gone to work that day, which was unusual – and now he and my mother looked anxiously at each other.

"You are not allowed out today because German soldiers have arrived and we are at war," he explained.

"But the other children"… I started.

"Come here both of you," he cut in, pointing out the window. "Do you see any children playing?"

Strangely, there were no children out playing at Haugen.

"Where are they?" I exclaimed, very surprised.

"At home with their parents the same as you," he explained patiently.

"It's dangerous for you to go out just now but we are here to look after you," my mother added seriously.

To me this was very mysterious as I pondered what to ask next.

"And no more questions," Father said firmly, before we could find out any more about this new and unexpected situation.

"I don't see any soldiers," I complained to Sonja. "What do they look like?"

"Like men in uniforms, silly. But they will be here. Pappa told me that they came off a ship and marched through the town."

"Do they look like the Salvation Army people?" I had observed them in their uniforms singing and preaching on a street corner in the town.

Overhearing this, Aase burst out laughing and suddenly they were all laughing.

"Can you imagine them marching down the street, singing hymns, with guns slung over their shoulders," she spluttered.

"That's enough, Aase," Mother said, attempting to put on a serious face but not really succeeding.

"Come here and I shall tell you something." Father put me on his knee and put an arm around Sonja.

"The Salvation Army people are good religious people. They help to feed the poor people who are hungry and to give them clothes to keep warm. That's good isn't it?"

I nodded seriously. "Why don't they come to our meetings then?"

"Because they have their own meetings," Father said and put me down.

"Now go and play with your sister."

Still disgruntled, we settled down to play with our toys, looking longingly at the sunrays which fanned through the window, lighting up the floor where we were playing.

The arrival of the first Germans in early July 1940 had a huge impact on the local population, as the foreign soldiers flooded ashore in their hundreds.

As more and more of them arrived, people watched and kept their distance. The soldiers, marching smartly through the streets with their guns slung over the shoulders, were oozing power and confidence – their war songs echoing around the town, to the dismay of the reluctant spectators.

At first the German occupiers meant very little to us children, except that we were kept indoors for a while. Life had to go on, however, and slowly our confinement was relaxed until we were out playing again, but under close supervision of our mothers, who quickly came looking if they lost track of us.

Kirkenes in 1940 was a widespread sprawling town with many open spaces. This suited the German invaders to perfection. Barracks for the soldiers soon sprang up close to private houses. Buildings for storage, garages and fuel depots followed in quick succession. Requisition of rooms in private houses for officers and their attendants was not good news, but went ahead regardless of any objections. Luckily, this didn't happen on Haugen, perhaps because the houses there belonged to the iron ore company and had limited space.

Official buildings, or parts of them, were taken over. Even the school didn't escape. Children returning to school after their summer holidays in 1940 found their fine school occupied by Germans. But they needed education, and rooms for school classes had to be found elsewhere. And they were found – in the sitting rooms of private houses, in rooms above shops – in fact, any building with a vacant space would do.

The infiltration continued. The iron ore produced by A/S Sydvaranger had to go to Germany from now on, with the result that all workers (about 1600 in 1940) found themselves indirectly working for the Germans. All local administration, including police, telegraph and post office became answerable to German rule and censorship, and had to follow new directives and regulations.

Strangely enough, the first German soldiers arriving in Kirkenes had no idea that they would be attacking Russia the following year. They believed that they were protecting Norway from an invasion of British and Allied troops. Treating the Norwegians well and making friends with them was encouraged as far as possible.

To the right of our house, and the first in a line of semi-detached houses, was the Wara family's house. It was light blue in colour, whereas the other houses on Haugen were dark brown or black. Theirs was built into the hill of Haugen, with its basement partly buried in the hill and the basement of their neighbour's house fully exposed.

From the square of Haugen a steep slope, passing the Wara's house, led down to our unofficial playground – an open area which extended around the basements of the two houses. Here we played all sorts of games. One favourite game was called 'dead ball'. You could be excused for thinking that this was a children's version of cricket. A line was drawn and two of us would stand at one side of the line, one with a wooden bat and the other with a ball. On the other side a number of circles were drawn at various distances, one for each player. The object of the game was to bat the ball towards the other players who would try to catch the ball and move among the rings. If you were outside the ring, failing to catch the ball, you were 'dead' and out of the game.

Another game, very popular with the girls, was lining up to play ball by knocking it onto the much favoured stone wall at the play area for as long as possible using head, knees, feet and hands to keep it going. When you lost the ball, it was the next one's turn.

In the winter time, the older children poured water on the slope to the playground, which immediately froze, giving us an excellent icy slide. There we whizzed down at full speed, one after the other, sitting on our mothers' little metal dust pans and holding on to the short handles in front, having great fun.

Sometimes we managed to find a large cardboard box, which we opened up. Five or six of us piled on top of the cardboard and with one or two pushing, we jumped on as it began to slide – sailing down the slope at full speed – spilling out in all directions at the bottom, having great fun.

Some of us owned a 'spark', which may best be described as a 'push sledge'. The 'spark' is very useful in the Arctic. It has runners, and a seat, on an upright construction with handlebars. It is great to hold on to, especially in slippery conditions. Widely used as a push chair for children in the wintertime and for transporting boxes of groceries, they come in several sizes – but basically a large size for adults and a smaller size for children.

When we had five or six of them slotted together like a train, we set off down the slopes with each child on the seat of their own 'spark' holding on to the handle bars of the next one. With two of us pushing, then jumping onto the runners as 'the train' gathered speed, we went weaving down the slope, trying to steer with our feet or the handlebars, invariably ending up in a ditch or tipping over, falling off our 'train'. But we all enjoyed the experience and kept repeating the performance till we thought of something else to do.

Snowball fights sometimes ended in tears, especially if it was boys versus girls. The boys were better than the girls at finding their targets, namely us. A snowball in the face or eye could be very painful.

My sister Sonja – who was nearly three years older than me – went to school every day. Sometimes she was allowed to bring her little sister. I loved going with her and would sit very still with my pencil and little notebook. This started in the winter of 1939 – 40. Normally children only went to school when they were seven years old – but because of my trips to school with Sonja and no doubt Mother's encouragement, I quickly learned to read and write.

Reading became a lifelong passion. In the early days there were Sonja's school books to read and stories from the bible. Illustrated bible stories for children were provided at the Adventist meetings to look at and borrow. A new and fascinating world of books was opening up for me.

As I was so fond of reading, I was given my first book as a present from my friend Arne, a neighbour's son from across the square. Arne was a bit older than me and had two older brothers. Our families were good friends and often visited each other. In the winter time, Arne sometimes brought me on his sledge to meet our fathers at the factory gates, when their shift was over. The Company worked three shifts – the end of each shift marked by a siren which was heard all over town, signalling that our fathers were coming home. I loved these outings with Arne and was always pleased when he came.

I was totally delighted with his wonderful gift, which was a pretty blue-covered book of fairy tales with coloured pictures. How I treasured that book! What I did not realise, however, was that my mother and father were less than pleased. It did not fit in with their religious beliefs. Strict rules guided their religion at the time – and many surprising and unsuspected things turned out to be 'Sin'. Our parents were good and kind to us, but very strict in their religious beliefs.

Unfortunately, I hadn't managed to enjoy my lovely new book for very long when one evening the book was confiscated, after I was found looking at it in bed. I was told that God did not want me to have this book, because it was a sin to read it. I cried hysterically, wanting them to give me the book back. But my protests didn't help at all. I was marched into the kitchen, where Mother took the lids off the stove and Father stood by, while I had to put the book into the fire myself.

"In time you will understand that it is for the best," Mother said while Father put me on his lap trying to explain the unexplainable. But I never understood, and for me it was the worst thing that had ever happened. That night I cried myself to sleep.

The coastal steamers, so vital for transport and communication, had ceased their sailings after the invasion in April 1940. Sadly, tragedy struck when the sailings were resumed in the late summer. The first casualty was D/S *Prinsesse Ragnhild*. On her way across Westfjorden to the Lofoten Islands in October 1940, D/S *Prinsesse Ragnhild* had just left Bodø behind when a massive explosion shook the vessel.

Aunt Carly, my father's oldest sister, was on board returning home after an eye operation at the hospital in Bodø. Two of her brothers, Trygve and Mareno, who were working in Bodø at the time, had seen her safely settled on board. As the ship started to sink, Aunt Carly managed to get herself on deck, desperately holding on to the ships railing. A German soldier grabbed her and, with her in his arms, jumped over the side into a descending lifeboat. His quick action no doubt saved both their lives.

Her brothers, having heard the explosion, watched in horror as the ship sank within minutes. Between 220 and 280 lives were lost. More than half were German soldiers – the rest were passengers and crew.

The most likely explanation for the tragedy was that the ship had struck a mine. The British had mined the fjord in the early days of the war.

After three more fatal incidents where the coastal steamers had been torpedoed by the Allies – and with a combined loss of hundreds of lives it was decided that the ships would stop at Tromsø, letting smaller vessels take over the onward transport along the coast as far as Kirkenes. Small freighters were considered to be less likely targets for torpedoes. However, this was not the end of the attacks on the coastal steamers.

4

'Festung Kirkenes'

"The answer is to leave Kirkenes!" My father's statement put a stop to our board game.

Startled, we turned to look at him. It was Sunday and we had come for a visit to my mother's sister Reidun and her family.

"But what about work, and where would we go?" Uncle Edvard asked.

"You and I can come back again, at least for a while. But Borghild, Reidun and the children would be safer away from here."

They had been discussing the war while Odd, Ruth, Sonja and I were playing Ludo. But leaving Kirkenes? All our friends were here! We looked at each other, no longer interested in the board game.

Our parents were very worried about the huge build-up of German troops and what was in store for us if we remained in Kirkenes.

"We could try Lofoten," suggested Father, "but none of my family has much space."

"Or perhaps Vesterålen," added Mother. "What do you think, Reidun?"

"I think our aunt in Vesterålen is our best bet," Aunt Reidun replied. "They should have room enough for both families."

Mother and Reidun's aunt and uncle lived in Vesterålen, close to the Lofoten Islands. Retired business people, they owned some property as well as a large and comfortable private residence.

It was decided that Mother and Aunt Reidun should approach their aunt by telegram asking permission for the two families to stay with them until the war was over. In anticipation, they even started to pack.

When the reply came several days later, it was addressed to Mother. The telegram was short and to the point:

"Sorry, we have no room for you."

It has to be said, however, that the Germans in due course requisitioned most of their house and property – to the delight of us all when we eventually heard about it.

The question of leaving Kirkenes to travel south never came up again.

During the winter of 1940 – 41 the German activities gained momentum. The harbour had never been so busy as ship after ship arrived, unloading weapons, tanks, lorries, fuel, building materials, food, liquor, and other stores needed for an army. More soldiers arrived too, as additional barracks were built to house them. Horses and mules in their thousands trotted ashore to be used for transport, and with them huge bales of straw and hay. Gradually every available space in Kirkenes was taken up by the needs of the ever increasing number of soldiers.

Between Kirkenes and Bjørnevatn – and at other selected sites in Sørvaranger – large ammunition stores sprang up. Those closest to us were built near two lochs just outside the town.

The building of an airport at Høibuktmoen (a few kilometres from Kirkenes) went ahead. Over 800 skilled and highly paid workers had been brought in to build the airport as quickly as possible.

Elsewhere, the Germans were busy constructing gun-emplacements in the rocky hills surrounding Kirkenes, heavy foundations for anti-aircraft artillery along the waterfront, and around the outskirts of the town machine gun nests were constructed, camouflaged and well hidden among the rocks.

The island of Prestøia to the east of Kirkenes was also targeted for development. Organisation Todt, which specialised in construction work, built a causeway across the short, shallow sound to the island. This road was later maintained and upgraded by Russian prisoners of war after the invasion of Russia. With feverish haste, heavy foundations for cannon positions, anti-aircraft guns and searchlights were constructed on the island. Living quarters for officer and soldiers followed, and finally, a graveyard for their fallen soldiers was laid out there too, increasing in size as the war intensified.

The German build-up was operating in top gear until June 1941. By then, stores for everything a large army required were strategically spread out in Sørvaranger. In total the stores in place were designed to keep 100,000 men supplied for one year. In sheer logistics, this had been a massive operation. People watched from the side-lines, wondering what was behind this enormous build up. It was hardly likely that the Allies fighting in Europe would venture up here, as the Germans would have them believe!

By June 1941 Kirkenes resembled an army camp. The estimated size of the German garrison residing in the district of Sørvaranger during the war is from about 30,000 in the early stages increasing to 70.000. But the numbers would have been considerably higher at times of transit to and from the front. As the flow of soldiers of the 'Wehrmacht' peaked, the locals were outnumbered by at least ten to one.

'Festung Kirkenes' had emerged, the name bestowed on it by the Germans. And a fortress it certainly became. With 1012 air raid alarms and 328 direct bomb attacks, the number of raids on Kirkenes came second only to those on Malta during World War II.

The Germans needed extra workers, and in September 1940 put up notices to that effect. The promise of good pay lured some people to apply. The pending threat of forced labour influenced others to volunteer. Kalle Wara from Neiden was one such young man. Along with some of his friends, he volunteered for work. They were given passes and put to work, building army barracks.

Soon they discovered that they might as well have been prisoners. The German guards watched them all the time and if they stopped working, they were told in no uncertain terms to get on with the work or else…

In the spring of 1941 the young Norwegians involved in building barracks were ordered to pack their gear and report to the commandant at Høibuktmoen airport.

"You will go immediately, otherwise you will be listed as saboteurs; you know what that means don't you?" said the German manager.

Kalle and his workmates knew what that meant. At the airport Kalle was set to work making metal shields for aeroplanes on the ground, to protect them from shrapnel in the event of air attacks. This was to be his workplace for the next three years, where he saw, and experienced, more than he would have thought possible of human atrocity.

Near the outer end of Bøkfjord a U-boat base was blasted out of the rock face and made ready for future operations. It was well hidden and an important part of the German operations in the Arctic. Further in through the fjord the island of Kjelmøya was turned into a large and well equipped defence post, controlling all traffic in and out of Kirkenes.

A disturbing picture was emerging as the people of Finnmark watched the continuing build-up of strategic positions around their coastline. Being so far to the east and close to Russia, both sides of Varangerfjord were heavily fortified with gun positions, controlling all inlets, almost as far as the Russian border.

The most easterly fishing village in Finnmark – situated on the shore of the Varanger peninsula – Kiberg looks out on the Barents Sea and the entrance to Varangerfjord. Due to its strategic position, the Germans put up some of their heaviest batteries at the point of Kiberg. Shells of up to 28cm (11inches) diameter could be fired by their largest long range guns, and were used with devastating effect against the Murmansk convoys, if they came within range.

My mother's youngest sister Anna lived in Kiberg with her husband Ludvik and their six children. Life in the village revolved around fishing, which was the life blood of their community. The men brought back fish from the rich fishing grounds, the women and older children baited the lines, coiling them into half barrels in preparation for the next fishing trip. In the winter the unsalted fish, mainly cod, was hung up outside to dry on wooden constructions.

Aunt Anna stayed in *'London'* with her family. The house was two storeys high, dark in colour and quite long. Why the house was named *'London'* has been lost in the mist of time, but it may have been so called because of the size of it and the number of people sharing the house. My aunt and uncle had started out in one room which gradually extended to two and then three rooms. Still not much for a family of eight, but they managed.

The children of the village played together, and sometimes fell out; the women dropped in on each other to gossip, and occasionally quarrelled over the rights and wrongs of their children – but on the whole it was a happy and lively community.

When Mother brought us there to visit her sister, we normally stayed with the family for two or three days. It was quite an experience – so different from Kirkenes. But we enjoyed the change and the company of our cousins, climbing the rocky hills and roaming the sea shore looking for shells, starfish and pretty stones. When Uncle Ludvik was not fishing he sat contentedly in the kitchen smoking his pipe, listening to the women talking. He was very nice and never scolded us for anything.

One day when it was raining, we were all gathered in the kitchen. Mother and Aunt Anna were talking about the old days in Vardø, and then went on to talk about some strange people they had known.

"Do you remember the 'Whale'?" asked my mother.

"Yes," said Aunt Anna, "her with the fishy eyes?"

"Exactly," said Mother. "I wonder what happened to her."

"I think she married the 'Snake'. You remember him with the hat and the big ears?"

"Of course," exclaimed my mother and they both laughed till the tears ran down their faces. It was not the first time we heard about the names that Vardø people gave each other – it was also said that they were a good-humoured and jolly lot.

"Did the Vardø people give you names like that?" Sonja asked innocently.

The thought of that really set them going.

"If they did we never heard of it," they spluttered, almost as one.

Recovering some composure, Aunt Anna pointed at the door.

"Go upstairs and play till the dinner is ready," she ordered, trying to sound stern, but not quite succeeding.

"We don't need you lot to listen to everything we say," added Mother, trying to keep a straight face.

Reluctantly we obeyed, but it was much more fun listening to our mothers and their stories from Vardø, where they grew up.

The first ghost stories I can remember hearing were in *'London'*. At night – when we were all in bed in the same room – Einar started telling us ghost stories, one more hair-raising than the other. He was a few years older than us and had quite a repertoire. He had us so terrified that we didn't even dare to go to the outside toilet on our own. Our mothers were not amused when they found out about it.

"I have a good mind to let you sleep in the shed from now on, Einar," said Aunt Anna crossly.

His sister Kirsten was full of fun and mischief too, laughing and joking all the time, while the two younger ones, Reidun and Sverre, followed us around copying whatever we did. Inevitably we managed to get into a few scrapes while staying there. Aunt Anna would do the scolding; Uncle Ludvik who was smoking his pipe, trying not to smile just said,

"They are only children you know, let them be."

"Oh you," said my aunt. "You are always defending them!" But she had to smile too. It was all good-natured and soon peace was restored again.

As the war progressed, the visits to our family in *'London'* ceased. It became too dangerous to travel and we would not see each other again till the summer of 1946. By then all our lives had changed forever.

Germans unloading stores in Kirkenes, September 1940.
Photo by Rudy Toppmair – Sørvaranger Museum.

German tanks passing through Kirkenes in 1941.
– Sørvaranger Museum.

German troops in training, 21-3, 1941.
– Sørvaranger Museum.

Kirkenes 1942. Top left AS Sydvaranger iron ore works. The two tall
pipes to the right marks the company's power station. German barracks in
the foreground.
Photo: Edvardsen – Sørvaranger Museum.

5

An arrest in the family

Our foreign 'neighbours' had settled in to their new life in the Arctic. People resented the intrusion, but were powerless to do anything about it.

The abiding question on their lips was: "Why are the Germans here and why in such numbers?" There was plenty of speculation, but as yet, no answers.

A vital lesson in survival was soon to be learned.

Mrs Olsen, a friend of our family, often came to visit. She was plump, with dark, almost black hair, and was a widow with no family of her own. Sonja and I used to look forward to these visits because of the presents she often brought. The last presents she gave us that I can remember were two small teddy bears, one for each of us. We were delighted because we didn't have many toys; they were something you might get at Christmas or on your birthday. The women usually settled down to talk over a cup of coffee whilst Sonja and I played with our new toys.

One night after we had been put to bed, we were disturbed by a great commotion in the kitchen. Voices were raised and we could hear German being spoken. We listened for a while and then heard Mother shouting:

"No, you are not taking her away!" Then Father's voice to Mother: "You have to calm down Borghild."

"I haven't done anything wrong," Aase chipped in, sounding frightened.

Then German voices were followed by a Norwegian voice saying: "It looks like you both have to come along."

Having listened to this with growing fear, Sonja and I burst into the kitchen, seeing two Germans there with their guns at the ready about to take Aase and Mother away with them. Frantic with fear, we clung to our mother, crying hysterically, and wouldn't let go. Mother tried to soothe us and calm us down, but without success. Then one of the Germans barked something in a loud voice and the Norwegian policeman who accompanied them turned to Father and said:

"Get those children out of here, now!"

Poor Father, seething with rage, would have liked nothing better than to order them out of our house. Instead he had to tear us away from our mother, march us into the bedroom and try to calm us down, saying that Mother and Aase would soon be home again. Then, when the door slammed shut after them, there was renewed crying and fear as we could not understand what was happening, thinking that we would never see Mother and Aase again.

When news of the arrests became known, concerned neighbours began to call, offering help and support and to look after Sonja and me when Father was at work. However, our next door neighbours, the Nordhus family, had heard the commotion through the wall and it was decided that we should stay with them while Father was working. Their youngest daughter Rigmor was about a year older than me, and as we were friendly with the family, this arrangement worked well until Mother and Aase were released.

What had led to the arrest of Mother and Aase was bizarre, to say the least. Our family friend, Mrs Olsen, had been observed several times fraternising with the Germans. Aase was still very anti-German at this time, and had stopped Mrs Olsen in the street one day, telling her in no uncertain terms that what she was doing was wrong. Didn't she know that the Germans were the enemy who had occupied our country? Mrs Olsen was not going to take that from an eighteen year old girl, and promptly reported her to the German head office in Kirkenes.

The Germans, who resented being referred to as the enemy, decided to make an example of Aase – but when Mother refused to let them take Aase away, she too was arrested. They were both sent to a German headquarter in another town, where they were put in separate cells and questioned at length. After about a week they were released and sent home, with a warning to behave and to watch their tongues.

This experience rattled us all, and taught us how dangerous it was to say or do anything against the Germans. Needless to say the friendship with Mrs Olsen came to an abrupt end. But I wonder if even she had realised what her action would lead to.

Following the release of my mother and sister I often heard my parents saying, "Not a word" or "Say nothing."

Worse was yet to come. A new enemy was emerging. A Norwegian version of the Nazi party 'Nasjonal Samling' or N.S. for short, was formed and, regrettably, many misguided Norwegians joined. Records show, however, that the party was weak in Finnmark with a relative low membership.

Some didn't do any particular harm to their fellow Norwegians; others thought nothing of betraying their countrymen, causing untold misery and harm, and at times even death. They were named 'Quislings' after the biggest traitor of all, Vidkun Quisling, who had hopes of becoming 'Prime Minister' of Norway under the new regime.

Any person known to have joined the N. S. Party was shunned by ordinary people. But there were also Nazi sympathisers to watch out for; those who didn't necessarily join the party. For all these reasons, gradually and painfully, the great majority of true Norwegians had to learn to watch very carefully what they were saying and doing, and to whom they were talking.

When Mother and Aase returned, we clung to our mother and didn't want to let her out of sight. The resilience of children carried us through, however, as we gradually got over our fear and began to play with our friends again.

The Germans were very visible around town, as they quickly outnumbered the locals. Their troops marched regularly through the streets with guns slung over their shoulders, singing their war songs. One of the songs in the early days was "Wir fahren, wir fahren, wir fahren gegen Engeland!" Another song sounded like an endless repeat of "High lee High loo, Hah, Hah, Hah, Hah High lee High loo." The children formed small groups with sticks of wood for guns, marching in goose steps a bit behind the soldiers trying to sing the same songs. But the Germans didn't suffer this for very long and usually sent one of the marchers after us shouting, "Raus kinder, raus!" (Get lost), which we did laughing, thinking that we had made fun of 'Them'.

One day, while I was playing with my friend Astrid in their garden, we decided to show the Germans that we didn't like them. After all, they had arrested Mother and Aase and sent them away, and who knows what they might do to Astrid's mother and sisters! We filled our pockets with as many stones as we could cram into them, clutching a couple in each hand as well. Nearby was a large barrack which the Germans used as a store. Sneaking up quietly to the nearest opening, we looked cautiously round the corner and, lucky for us, could see only one German in there, wearing heavy boots and a large belted overcoat.

"Now," I whispered to Astrid. We rounded the corner and attacked the unfortunate German with a hail of stones.

It should be said that we were pretty good at stone throwing, having practised it often enough for fun. A string of German words erupted (presumably swear words) as he tried to protect himself from the stones. The only words we understood were 'ferdamte kinder', but then, as we ran out of stones, he turned and came after us. That clinched it. We ran. The unfortunate German had no chance of catching us, and we escaped into Astrid's garden, into her house and, quiet as mice, tiptoed up the stairs to their attic, where we sat for a long time. Our parents never found out about this attack on the Germans, or we would have got into bigger trouble.

Aase, who had many friends, didn't go out much for a while after her scary experience. Instead she spent more time with us, or helped Mother with the daily chores. She also took us for walks to visit Aunt Reidun and her family.

Mother's oldest sister Margit was now living in Aunt Reidun's house where she had a room to herself. Her home was in Narvik, but she had fled to Kirkenes when the battle of Narvik started. Her oldest son, Erling, was away on a Norwegian merchant ship and her younger son Kåre had travelled with her to Kirkenes. After the capitulation Kåre returned to Narvik, where he became involved in resistance work.

Aunt Margit soon got work at the hospital in Kirkenes as a cook. She was quite a character; short with bushy dark hair, she had a great sense of humour and many stories to tell. Because of her parents' connections, she had been able to live and work in Russia before the revolution. With an ear for languages, she soon learned to speak Russian, and in time Finnish. Being an adventurous young woman she moved to Finland, where she found work in hospitals, and where she met and married her future husband. In time they settled in Narvik but before the invasion of Norway took place, she was already a widow.

Aunt Reidun's kitchen was the gathering place when we came to visit. There, Aunt Margit had centre stage with her stories. She was great fun and when she, Aunt Reidun and Mother got together they laughed so much at each other's stories that their bodies were shaking, tears were rolling down their faces and we laughed just watching them. But as the war rumbled on, these happy occasions turned into serious discussions about shortages and what they would do if we survived the war.

Aunt Margit's knowledge of the Russian language would prove very useful when she found herself in a difficult and dangerous situation a few years later.

6

The German invasion of Russia

June is the lightest month of the year in Finnmark – with the sun circling the sky high above the horizon – encouraging people to get up early and stay up late. The buds on the silver birches have burst open to reveal the trees in all their green glory. An abundance of buttercups and other hardy flowers in pink and purple decorate the landscape, and along the roads dandelions cling to the edges, nodding their yellow heads in a gentle breeze.

By June 1941 the Germans were finally ready to invade Russia in the north, and the true purpose of the huge build-up in the Arctic was finally revealed. They were not here in order to 'protect' us from the western Allies but for an altogether more sinister reason – the simultaneous attack on the Soviet Union from both north and south.

The airport at Høibuktmoen was finished, with two runways, hangars, buildings and other constructions. German bombers and fighter planes had arrived and – with the Luftwaffe in place – preparations for an attack on the Soviet Union in the Arctic were complete.

At 5.15 on the 22nd June 1941 the calm of the morning was broken by the droning noise of bombers and fighter planes – approaching and passing over Kirkenes – on the way to attack an unsuspecting Murmansk. The early-birds among the locals watched and knew that history was being made. Father was one of the observers. Someone said as they observed the aeroplanes heading east:

"Now we know the real purpose of their massive build-up. They are on their way to attack Russia!"

At the Norwegian / Finnish border the build-up of land troops, tanks, guns and other equipment had steadily increased; ready to advance across the border when the order was given. The attack on Russia in the Arctic had been planned to coincide with a major German offensive taking place along Russia's southern borders. The agreement between Hitler and Stalin not to attack each other's countries had been disregarded by Germany. The German invasion of Russia – with all its consequences – had begun.

It is unclear at which point the German soldiers had been told that their real target was the Soviet Union. But when they left for the offensive against Russia, they were laughing and in high spirits saying:

"In six days we'll be in Murmansk and in three weeks, Leningrad!"

A German war hero from the battle of Narvik, General Eduard Dietl, led the invasion into Russia through a narrow tract of land east of Kirkenes. This corridor was at the time Finish territory. It had been acquired from Russia in a political agreement in 1920, separating east Finnmark from the old border with Russia. It stretched from Finland to the Barents Sea. As Finland and Germany were now allies, allowing the German Army to cross Finnish territory was not a problem. Finland's winter war with Russia in 1939 may have been behind their ill-fated liaison with Germany.

To their cost, the Germans had greatly underestimated both the Russians and the Arctic. In summer their tanks, guns and vehicles got bogged down in the soggy marshes of the tundra, which hosted millions of mosquitoes and other insects ready to make life almost unbearable. The exasperated soldiers dubbed the biting mosquitoes 'Little Russians'!

Winter was a more dangerous enemy, though, with snow, severe frost and winter storms, often enabling Russian troops on skis to slip past the German lines and attack from behind.

This, then, became Germany's most northerly front against Russia.

Kirkenes had been chosen as the stepping stone to achieve their goal in the north – by turning it into a supply base and a fortress.

After 3 months Dietl's Arctic army had reached the Litza River, about 60 kilometres (36 miles) from Murmansk, and 120 kilometres (72 miles) from Kirkenes. It was as far as they would be able to penetrate into Russian territory in the north. The German soldiers had fought hard against tough and resisting Russian soldiers to get this far. But the battle had cost them at least 10,000 men – dead, wounded or missing. The number of casualties among the Russian troops are difficult to ascertain – but one must assume that they had heavy losses too.

With falling temperatures and winter fast approaching, the Germans dug in at Litza – which became known as the Litza Front, and their battle ground in the north for the next 3 years.

The German lifeline for the conflict in the Arctic was the ships that brought in soldiers and their war materials to Kirkenes, for onward transport to the front. The harbour therefore became a prime target for Russian planes. It has been said that the Russians, on their bombing raids, tried to avoid civilian houses. If it had not been so, Kirkenes would have been in ruins long before the end of 1944.

We did not have long to wait for the Russian response to the German invasion. Two days later the alarms went off, but it was a false alarm. The following weeks saw a number of air raids, where bombs dropped at the harbour were aimed at German ships lying at the pier or at anchor.

At the beginning of the war, certain basements had been selected as shelters. The one nearest to us was the basement of the Wara family's home which was set into the rocky hill of Haugen. An added bonus was that it was at our play area and close by.

The children were instructed in what to do if they were caught out when the air raid alarms started up. If we were nearby, run home; if not, get to the nearest shelter; if that was not possible, shelter behind or under something, but lie flat and cover your head.

It didn't take long for that lesson to sink in. A group of men were appointed to go out and look for children when the alarms started up. They wore tin helmets and white armbands for identification. We were not allowed to go far from our house but I tended to stray and was often caught by one of the guards that I could not outrun – then carried kicking and screaming to the nearest shelter. But that would change. Nothing spurs one on more than fast approaching planes and the smattering of gun fire. After the war was over and we were back at school, the only sport I got a gold medal for was running. The war had indeed been a good training ground!

On a sunny day in the early autumn of 1941 we were out at our playground – perhaps twelve to fifteen of us – when we heard the distinct singing tone of an aeroplane above. We all froze as one, and just stood there, the games forgotten, looking up into the sky trying to spot the plane.

Suddenly, the whistling sound of a falling bomb reached us. That spurred us into action. The children disappeared in all directions. Unn and I ran to a house close by where we could hide under the steps to the main entrance. She got there first, and I crawled in behind her. We were so terrified that we didn't even cry, but held onto each other hardly able to breathe. Then all hell broke loose. A tremendous explosion shook the house where we had taken shelter, mixed with the sound of shattering glass from the windows – and as the noise began to die down, the wailing of the air raid sirens took over.

Numb with fear and shock, we just sat there until all was quiet, then cautiously crawled out from under the stairs and darted across the playground to the shelter at the Wara house. As we knocked on the door, it was immediately opened and we were pulled in, hugged and patted by the women in the shelter, who were frantic with worry about their children. My mother was there too and cried with relief to see that I was safe. She had been standing with one foot in the kitchen and one in the sitting room, rooted to the spot, when she heard the bomb coming. Then she threw herself flat on the floor with her arms covering her head. The other children – having hidden behind houses or in a ditch – were all safe and turned up at the shelter one by one.

The house where Unn and I were hiding was the first in a row of houses on each side of a road leading from the playground down to the town centre. The bomb had fallen in the middle of the road between the next two houses, in a direct line from our play area, and less than fifty metres away from us. We were all shaken by this experience, and for me this was the beginning of a habit of sticking fingers in my ears to try to escape the noise of shooting and bombing. Later that day my father dug a large piece of shrapnel out of the wall of our house – a souvenir from that bomb.

The Pedersen family, who lived in the next house down the road, had just sat down to dinner of fresh fish, livers and potatoes, when they heard the whistling of a bomb coming closer and closer. With just enough time to get down on the floor, the bomb exploded in the street outside. The shattering of glass as their windows blew in put paid to their dinner. It was riddled with broken glass, as was the whole kitchen. The family was shaken but unharmed though they had to pick broken glass off their clothes and hair. Their three younger daughters, Margot, Lilleba and Gulle often played with us at the play area, but on this particular day they had gone home early for dinner. The only casualty from this incident was a cat from a nearby house. It was killed by shrapnel.

That autumn saw the beginning of the Arctic convoys. Stalin had appealed to the Western Allies for help with food, weapons and other equipment, as the Soviet Union was attacked by Germany on two fronts.

The Allies responded, and the first convoy of seven ships left Liverpool on 12th August 1941, arriving at Archangel 31st August without any losses. But this promising start was only the beginning of a relentless and bloody struggle to get the convoys through, lasting until the end of the war.

7

A hard lesson

The sound of air raid sirens became uncannily familiar. Because of my tendency to stray, I was frequently picked up and brought to the nearest shelter. My friend Gunhild and I were once picked up together and carried, under much protest, to the shelter at the local cinema. The man must have been big and strong as he was able to carry us, one under each arm, right into the shelter.

Mother was in distress over what to do with me. She couldn't very well lock me in either. Other mothers had the same problems, and lived in fear of what could happen to their children. Sonja, at three years older, fared better and was able most of the time to get home or to the shelters by herself.

We saw less of Father now. He had become a volunteer fire fighter in addition to his job at the Company. In 1940 the fire brigade in Kirkenes was run and managed by the iron ore company A/S Sydvaranger. It consisted of 30 men who all worked for the Company, doing the fire fighting as an extra job with extra pay.

Because of the huge increase in population, and with German barracks everywhere, the call out of the fire brigade became much more frequent. The fires often started in German barracks due to carelessness. It soon became clear that more fire fighters were needed and a call went out for volunteers. They had to be trained, and Father regularly went out on training exercises with them. One day he arrived home with a steel helmet and a gas mask. This looked very serious and we all tried them on in turn, even Mother, who looked very strange in a gas mask.

In spite of it all, Father found time to help in the house. He fetched water, cut fire-wood and fetched coal. One day after cutting up wood in the basement he came into the kitchen and sat down on the nearest chair. Leaning forward with elbows on his knees, supporting his head in his hands, he was very pale.

"What's wrong?" My mother was concerned.

"I have just put the axe into my leg," he replied. "It slipped when I tried to cut an icy log."

That was enough. Mother fainted. Father just managed to get to her to cushion the fall and then he had to sit down again.

"May I see it?" Aase asked with great interest.

Father obliged by pulling apart the cut trouser leg. Aase bent forward to look and her face took on a sick look. Her eyes seemed to roll back as she too fainted. Turning to me who had watched it all with awe, he said,

"Pop in to Mrs Nordhus and ask her to come right away. I can't deal with those two just now."

So I ran in to Mrs Nordhus, afraid that Father too might faint. It wasn't the first time we had called on her in an emergency and she was always there, ready to help. Luckily Mrs Nordhus was not the type to faint at the sight of blood or even at the thought of it, like Mother.

At Father's request, she set about trying to revive the two women first. Then she turned to Father.

"I want to look at your leg now. They will come around soon enough."

"This has to be bandaged to stop the bleeding," she said after examining Father's leg, looking around the kitchen for something to use.

"You will find dish-towels in that drawer," Father said, "just use them."

Mrs Nordhus went to work making a bandage using the dish-towels.

"Better get yourself to the doctor as soon as you can," she said. "This needs to be cleaned up properly and stitched."

Mother and Aase were coming around.

"Go now," urged Mrs Nordhus. "I will look after them."

Afraid that Father would faint on the road, I put on my jacket ready to go with him and, with my hand firmly in his, we left. After a long wait in the doctor's waiting room Father was taken care of. His leg was stitched and bandaged, and we could walk home again.

In spite of the increasing number of German soldiers in Kirkenes, not many were seen on the square of Haugen as yet. Sitting at my favourite place by the window one day, watching the comings and goings on the square, I spotted 'Søttenåringen' approaching the square. 'Søttenåringen' (the Teenager) was a woman past middle age who liked to dress up and put on plenty of makeup. With greying hair, pretty clothes, red lips, rosy red cheeks and black eyebrows, she was very colourful and certainly noticeable. For these reasons she was dubbed 'Søttenåringen'. I thought she looked very pretty.

"Mamma, Søttenåringen is outside," I shouted.

"Stop calling her that," Mother scolded me.

"But everybody calls her that," I protested, not quite understanding why I could not. But this time Søttenåringen was just passing by, and as she spotted me in the window I waved and she waved back.

Watching the variety of people crossing the square was of constant interest to me. Another character was 'Bror' (Brother). I didn't know if he was anybody's brother or how he got this nickname, but he was very tall with dark shabby clothes and always carried a large dark hessian-type bag on his back. All the younger children were afraid of him because we were told that 'Bror' would come and take us away in his bag if we misbehaved. 'Bror' was strange and different, but unknown to us, completely harmless.

Two sirens signalled oncoming air raids. One was close to us and had a fast urgent beat to it. The other siren had a rising and falling, drawn out wailing sound. Together they made enough noise to wake the dead – at least that's what Father said. The frequent alarms and trips to the shelter that autumn were only a taste of what was to come.

One forenoon in October 1941, with many people out shopping, aeroplanes came in over the town at great height. Since no alarm was sounded nobody took much notice. But, when the whistling sound of bombs finally stirred people into action, it was too late. The explosions left three dead and nine wounded; all were civilians. A lot of damage was done to the surrounding buildings but none to any military installations.

However, when the firemen recovered the tail of a bomb marked with the German Eagle holding the swastika, rumours began to circulate that this was deliberately done by the Germans, using their own planes to set people against the Russians. Whatever the truth was, it only served to make people resent the Germans even more.

Father was fuming when he came home:

"If they can do this to people in the country they have occupied, what will they do next?"

There was no answer to this question as yet, and we settled down to a reading from the Bible and prayers, before our evening meal. We were still going to the meetings in the Adventist church, but it was getting more difficult because of the air raids and the fact that Father might be called out.

The air raids continued – and we ran to the bomb shelter. Sometimes the alarms sounded as the bombs came whistling down. At such times we lay face down on the floor, and instead of covering my head, I put my fingers in my ears to keep out the noise. The Russians were attacking the ships in the harbour and military installations but when dog fights developed, bombs could fall anywhere.

A new and better shelter was prepared, called 'Bertakanalen' (Berta's tunnel), not far from us. It was not big, but much safer than the basements of private houses. Already, plans for another and much larger bomb shelter were on the table. It would consist of three tunnels – designed to meet under the square of Haugen. Work on the first of the three tunnels was already going ahead under the leadership of Anders Elvebakk, a man whose name would always be linked to 'Andersgrotta'. The tunnels would provide shelter for about 800 people.

Needless to say we became regular visitors to 'Bertakanalen'. Equally regularly – when the alarms went off and we arrived there – a young woman was brought in with spasms racking her body. Her eyes were rolling unfocused, and she was foaming at the mouth. The first time I observed this I got quite a fright, but Mother explained that the lady had epilepsy and the alarms brought on her attacks.

She was a short dark haired woman, with short straight hair and round thick glasses. She always wore a dark navy double-breasted coat with a belt. Her husband was also dark haired and not very tall, wearing dark trousers, a thick knitted jumper and a seaman's cap. Invariably, when we arrived, they were either there being attended to or she was being carried in whilst having a fit. In spite of my mother's explanations, I didn't understand what epilepsy was and wondered why no one else got fits when the alarms sounded.

New orders to the population were pasted on walls and telegraph poles at intervals; one was regarding blackout. Any householder breaching the blackout restrictions could expect harsh punishment. Radios were not allowed and had long since been delivered at collection points. Anyone refusing, or hiding their radios, would be treated as saboteurs. Rationing of food and other essentials had been in force for a while and was now beginning to take effect.

One evening Sonja and I were sitting at the kitchen table. She was doing her homework from school, and I was looking at a book of Bible stories. Father was out with the fire fighters and mother was knitting. Aase came charging in leaving the door open behind her.

"Close the door immediately," Mother said sharply. "We can't show any light or we will be in trouble. You should know that by now." Aase hurriedly closed the door.

"Where have you been?" continued Mother. Aase, who had been running, was trying hard to get her breath back.

"I went to the spiritualist meeting," she said, "and it was terrible. Mamma, do you know, the table began to move. How can that be possible? It was so frightening that I left. I could not stay there a minute longer!"

Mother, having put away the knitting, was looking at Aase now.

"I told you not to go to these meetings; they will do you no good at all."

Aase, still looking frightened, was persisting: "How could a table move all by itself?"

"It was probably a trick by the people you were visiting," Mother said drily.

"Absolutely not." said Aase. "The table moved without anybody touching it. There must be another explanation."

"Then it's better you don't find that out. Let this be a lesson for you to keep away from them and pray to God for help and understanding. We shall say no more about this." Mother had closed the subject and I knew better than to ask questions about moving tables at that particular time.

My best friends in those days, apart from Ruth, were undoubtedly Astrid and Gunhild. Astrid and I played regularly together, either in my house or hers, or in her dolls house in the summertime. Her dolls house was a great attraction, and sometimes four or five of us gathered in Astrid's garden to play. I was always welcome there, and as she lived nearby we met frequently. Astrid had nice clothes and shoes, and she had several pairs of knitted gloves in pretty colours. I admired her gloves, and couldn't understand why Mother wouldn't get a pair for me.

In our house, a stairway led from the hall to the upstairs bedrooms. A small storage area under the stairs provided space for boots, thick socks, scarves and mitts. Whilst playing with Astrid in their house one day, temptation got the better of me, and I put a pair of her fancy gloves in my pocket when nobody was looking. Mother and Father were always telling us about 'Sin', and that lying and stealing was 'Sin'. But I told myself I wasn't stealing; I was just borrowing her gloves!

Back home again, I hid Astrid's gloves under the stairs, and later on pretended to find a pair of gloves there.

"Mamma, look what I found under the stairs," I said showing her the gloves. "Aren't they pretty?"

Mother, smelling a rat, looked at me. "Where did you get them from?"

"I found them under the stairs," I said again.

"We have never had gloves like that," said Mother sternly. "I am asking you again, where did they come from?"

"But I found them under the stairs," I tried once more, beginning to feel very worried.

Mother wasn't going to be taken in by this and set me down in the kitchen before fetching Father.

"Now tell us the truth," said Mother. "You know God is watching us and knows when we are lying, don't you?"

"Yes," I whispered miserably.

"Those gloves look like the ones Astrid has, and you have been playing with her today," continued Mother. They were both studying me now.

"Did you take these gloves from Astrid's house?" asked Father and continued: "And I want the truth."

"Yes," I whispered, too frightened to deny it any longer.

"I am ashamed of you," said Father. "God is very unhappy because you have done this, and you have to be punished. Come here."

So I had to stand in front of him, pull down my pants and was then put across his knees to be severely smacked on my bottom.

When the crying stopped and the tears had dried, I was told that I had committed a great 'Sin', and that I had to pray to God for forgiveness. So prayers were offered for forgiveness, and after that came what was even worse.

"We shall now come with you to Mrs Fjeld, where you have to give back the gloves and apologise for what you have done," said my mother. I was mortified, but there was no way out.

They were holding my hands as we set off for Astrid's house. Mrs Fjeld answered the door and looked surprised to see us together.

"Come in," she said, holding the door open for us.

"We won't stay long," said Father. "My daughter has something to tell you."

So I had to confess to Astrid's mother and give her the gloves back.

"Don't forget to apologise," he chided, which I managed to do between sobs.

Astrid's mother looked very strange, saying some soothing words to me, but it wasn't until years later that I realised she had been on the verge of tears herself.

That day I learned a hard but valuable lesson, a lesson I never forgot, but it would have been just as effective without the smacking.

Astrid came to look for me a couple of days later, no doubt sent by her mother who felt sorry for me. We resumed playing together again – that awful experience fading into the background but never forgotten.

8

New Year in the bomb shelter

Prisoner-of-war camps began to appear at various locations around Sørvaranger. One camp was built quite near us; only a few minutes walk from our house. It consisted of several army barracks, a cook house and a compound which was soon full of Russian prisoners.

Watching from a distance while out playing, what caught my eye in particular was the guard house at the entrance to the camp which looked to me like a distorted dolls' house, only large enough to hold one soldier. I had been studying it from Astrid's house which was nearer the camp. The guard house had a pointed roof and no door, just an opening large enough for the guard to step in, turn and stand with a gun slung over his shoulder.

"Mamma, that soldier at the camp must get very cold standing in his little house all day. Why is there not a door on it?"

"The guard has to see around him and check that nobody comes near the camp or the prisoners."

"But we will not be bad to the prisoners," I said, already knowing that the prisoners required our sympathy.

"Of course not," replied my mother patiently, "but I want you to stay away from the camp. We don't want trouble with the Germans."

"Will they arrest children too?" The arrest of Mother and Aase was still etched in my memory.

"No, but if the children cause trouble the Germans may arrest their parents instead. Remember that!"

My mother's words were proved all too true at a later date, when two children were caught smuggling their food parcels under the fence to the Russian prisoners. Their mothers were promptly arrested and put in jail for a month.

During the final months of 1941, wounded soldiers had been returning from the front. Rumours of heavy casualties, as a result of the invasion of Russia, soon spread. The walking wounded were the lucky ones – or perhaps not so lucky – as they would be sent back to the front again when they recovered. Others, with more serious injuries, were filling up the German field hospitals and barracks, waiting for passage back to Germany. Thousands more died at the front. The locals commented on the madness of it all – and where would it all end?

It had turned very cold outside, with a recent heavy snowfall covering the ground. People-watching through the kitchen window was as ever my favourite pastime, when I had nothing better to do. Looking out at the square as usual, a gang of boys were engaged in a snowball fight. Sonja and her friends turned up and got involved. It got quite heated and in the end the girls ran away defeated, leaving the boys laughing and in high spirits.

One of the boys was nicknamed 'Graut' because his mother regularly came out shouting his name, followed by "kom hjem å få koka graut!" ("Come home for your boiled porridge!") I never found out what he thought of his nickname, but the name stuck and 'Graut' took over from his real name.

Another one was Arne, a boy from the square who became 'Gulrota' (the carrot) because of his red hair. Of the girls, 'Grinungen' (the cry-baby) comes to mind, as it took very little to get her tears flowing, something the boys in particular took advantage of. Then there was 'Lille Per', so called because he was small for his age – but he could still hit us hard with a snowball.

Sonja came in, complaining about the boys and my mother – who rarely sided with us when playing with the other children – just said,

"What else did you expect?"

Father often came home exhausted. The fire fighters were expected to be at their posts as soon as air attacks started. The shortage of men and proper equipment meant that the firemen had to work very hard to contain the fires.

Many incidents occurred. In early November 1941, a fire had started in a building used as a repair garage. Half of the building was occupied by Germans and the other half by Norwegians. The fire had started in the German part of the building. After reassurances that all oxygen and gas bottles had been removed, the firemen set to work. Emphasis was put on stopping the fire spreading to nearby buildings.

Just as the fire was getting under control, a violent explosion engulfed six firemen in flames. They were quickly taken to hospital, where all but two could go home after treatment. Luckily Father was not hurt, but he was angry and shaken when he came home to tell Mother about the incident.

"The explosion happened in the German part of the building and one of the Germans was killed. We had been assured that no gas bottles remained in the building," he continued and added: "You just can't trust them."

My mother was deeply concerned. "I am afraid for you. Please be careful."

Sonja and I were listening and knew we were not supposed to interrupt. Nevertheless, we went to Father and put our arms around him, and he hugged us calling us his little angels!

Christmas that year was very subdued. Father came home with a tree; Sonja and I brought down the stand with the Santas from the attic along with the decorations. For once we could all be together and enjoyed decorating the Christmas tree – while at the same time we listened anxiously for the sirens. Aase was helping Mother, setting the table.

"I hope the sirens stay quiet this Christmas," said Mother and sighed.

"Let's pray together before supper." Praying together and going to the meetings had become less frequent. Visiting friends was also curbed by the need to be near a shelter. We could not be sure whether we would spend Christmas Eve at home or in the bomb shelter. I can't remember what we ate, but food shortages were not yet bad enough to cause a real problem. After the meal we sang Christmas carols before going to bed. It would be the last peaceful Christmas that the five of us enjoyed together.

On Christmas Day we visited Aunt Reidun and had an enjoyable day with her and the family. Sonja and I played 'Ludo' with Ruth and Odd, while the adults chatted. Odd won most of the games and when we accused him of cheating he laughingly denied it. He loved winding us up.

I think it was about this time that the expression 'If we survive the war' started. Suddenly it was there – I hadn't noticed it before.

"If we survive the war," one of them was saying, and I am not sure who said it first.

In the early days it didn't mean much to me, but when it began to crop up time and again in conversation, I started to wonder what it really meant. Sonja informed me that it meant that we could be killed in an air raid. I didn't like this explanation at all and asked my mother what it meant.

"Don't worry about it," was all she said. "God will look after us. You know that don't you?"

However, this ominous expression 'If we survive the war' became a standard talking point whenever people met.

New Year's Eve 1941 started quietly enough. A thick blanket of snow covered the ground; the temperature had plummeted to minus 24 degrees centigrade. This was the darkest time of the year, with just a couple of hours of pale daylight, and the sun never above the horizon. But with snow on the ground, a clear sky and moonlight – it was 'bombing weather'. People knew to be on the alert and ready to run at the sound of the sirens.

By early afternoon the alarms went off, and we trotted off to the bomb shelter 'Bertakanalen'. No sooner had the all clear sounded and we were back at the house, than the sirens went off again – so it was back to the shelter once more. The woman with the epileptic fits had been carried in as usual. Somebody was always attending to them, especially members of the Red Cross. One of them, Arnold Johnsen, lived with his parents in the house next to us. Arnold and members of the Red Cross were always ready to help, giving first aid and treatment where necessary.

New Year's Eve continued with air raids and heavy bombing, mostly at the harbour. During one of the attacks the German headquarters in Kirkenes was hit and 11 Germans lost their lives. Because of the low temperature fire fighting was more difficult. Water quickly turned to ice, and the firemen had a cold and tough New Year's Eve.

We took in 1942 in 'Bertakanalen' but instead of fireworks, as was usual at New Year, we had a concert of exploding bombs accompanied by anti-aircraft artillery. This went on for some time, and we finally got home, cold and tired, about three o'clock in the morning on New Year's Day. I can't remember if anybody wished each other 'Happy New Year' in the shelter that night. There was not much to be happy about as everybody had someone they worried about. Our concerns were for Father who, along with the other fire-fighters, was not allowed to be in the shelter.

Playing outside was getting more dangerous that winter as the air attacks continued with clockwork regularity. Nevertheless, we played in the snow, making snow tunnels, snow houses and snow men. We still sailed down the icy slope to the playground on our dustpans or cardboard boxes and had snowball fights with the boys. We no longer strayed too far from the house, though, for fear of being caught out in an air raid.

As soon as the sirens started, our mothers were out looking for us. It must have been a nightmare keeping track of their children.

On occasions when the planes came unannounced, we tried to get home or to 'Bertakanalen'. If that was not possible we hid behind houses or under outside staircases. And there was always the shelter under the Wara house.

Our friends, the Nylund family on the square, had moved away from Kirkenes. I missed my old friend Arne who had given me the ill-fated book, and who used to bring me to meet our fathers from work. That seemed a long time ago now. Other people had moved into their house, but the new tenants didn't have any children. I often sat at the window watching people passing by when I had nothing better to do. 'Søttenåringen' (the Teenager) as colourful as ever, walked by regularly. On occasions when she popped in for a chat with Mother, she cheered us all up with her funny ways and her optimism.

"The war will soon be over and the Germans sent packing," she would say.

"You don't know that." My mother was sceptical.

"Oh, I'm sure of it," she said loftily. "Somebody will get rid of Hitler and that will put an end to the war."

"Huh, huh," Mother was unconvinced.

'Søttenåringen' spotted my mother's curling tongs on the kitchen stove.

"I didn't know that you used curling tongs. These are nice. You'll get two waves with it," she declared with great enthusiasm.

"Aase uses them, but I seldom bother."

"Oh but you should. Your thick hair is perfect for it. It would make you look very attractive." Mother just laughed. It was impossible to be annoyed with Søttenåringen, she said.

Another regular on Haugen was 'Bror', as always carrying a large sack slung over his shoulder – but we were no longer afraid of him and he usually ignored us. 'Soot-Hans' was worth watching too. When he arrived with his brushes, a ladder and other equipment, I always wondered which chimney he would sweep this time – holding my breath as I watched him balancing across a roof. With coal used in practically every house, he had an awful lot of chimneys to sweep.

The winter continued with snow, hard frost, and regular bombing raids. A German medical depot took a direct hit, and the flames shot 100 metres into the air. It burned down in spite of the efforts of the firemen, who were forced to stay out during a second attack. The chief of the fire brigade wrote to the police department in Oslo asking for permission for the firemen to seek shelter during air raids. No answer was received. When he approached the German authority in Kirkenes, the answer was:

"Befehl der Wermacht." (By order of the German Army): "Be there and do your duty or be arrested for sabotage!"

To be arrested for sabotage could carry a death sentence. That left the firemen with no option other than to be out during the air raids. Better to die by a Russian bomb than a German bullet, they said.

Our parents had started to discuss evacuation out of Kirkenes. Many people had already moved to family or friends in the countryside to get away from the continuing air attacks.

"You know I have family on both sides of the fjord in Jarfjord," my mother said.

"Yes I know, but which of them will you ask?"

"Reidun wants to try the ones at Haga, and I think I shall ask my cousin Aslaug in Karpbukt. Her brother Trygve runs the shop and farm there. If we could hold on till spring, Sonja would be able to attend school as much as possible."

"Even that is getting more and more dangerous," my father said frowning.

They decided to contact Aslaug in Karpbukt, but to hold on for a while to see what happened.

Bombing weather meant clear nights with moonlight, and the arrival of Aunt Reidun, Uncle Edvard, Ruth and Odd. As there was no proper bomb shelter near them they slept on the floor in our house with all their clothes on, ready to run when the alarms started up.

When the alarms and the attacks coincided, we sheltered on the floor, listening to the familiar whistling of the bombs. The deeper the whistling tones, the closer they would fall. I am sure that we all as one held our breath until the explosions came and we knew that we were all still alive.

Each time this happened, it was equally terrifying. My mouth went dry, I couldn't breathe, my heart was pounding, my stomach in a tight knot – and I knew with a sickening certainty that I was powerless to do anything about it. I couldn't even outrun it! "If we survive the war" was taking on a whole new meaning, in spite of Mother's assurances.

As soon as the explosions died down and we were able to breathe again, we were out the door and away to 'Bertakanalen', taking care to put out the light before opening the door. Showing even a glimmer of light was an offence, and could lead to arrests.

Evacuation was decided on for Aunt Reidun and her family, when, during an air raid, a bomb fell nearby and blew in the wall of their house, while the family were sheltering in the basement. They moved to Haga in Jarfjord to stay with family. Uncle Edvard came back alone. After repairing their house he continued going to his work at the saw mill. Aunt Margit moved back in again and continued her work at the hospital.

The Company handed over the responsibility for the fire brigade to Sørvaranger County. Nordhus, our neighbour, and a man called Paulsen were promoted to fire chiefs of the fire brigade, which had now grown to 84 men. More and better equipment arrived and, with better training, their capacity to deal with the ever increasing demands was greatly improved.

When my father wasn't working at the Company, he was out with the firemen, training or fire fighting. There weren't many acrobatics on the kitchen floor that winter; he was too exhausted.

During April 1942 there were so many air raid alarms that Mother and Father decided that we must get out as soon as possible. The records show that there were 52 alarms that month, and school for Sonja was basically non-existent.

At the Litza front the fighting was on-going. The Russians were determined to keep the Germans from advancing any further but the Germans had their eyes on Murmansk, aiming at stopping the easy movement of Russian troops on the railways and intercepting the supplies from the Allied convoys.

Warmer weather announced the arrival of spring. German and Russian soldiers replaced their winter uniforms with lighter ones, suited for spring and summer. The Germans had prepared for a major assault on the Russian lines at the Litza front, and equally, the Russians were building up their defences. No sooner had the assault started, than the weather suddenly changed. The temperature dropped, and a snowstorm was brewing. Both sides probably thought they could use the weather to their advantage. Instead the wind force reached 100m/second (about 200 miles/hour), and the snowstorm raged for three days. The piercing cold penetrated their thin clothes; soldiers from both sides got lost in the snow storm and froze to death. Both sides suffered heavy losses of life in a battle nobody could win under such atrocious conditions.

After the battle, when the weather settled down again, German and Russian soldiers were found huddled together in death in the same trenches. The Germans still didn't get to Murmansk, and the Russians were content with keeping them at Litza for the time being.

9

Falling for the enemy

Father was shouting. That in itself was unusual. Sonja and I were in bed, but couldn't help overhearing the exchange between our parents.

"What in heaven's name does she think she is doing? Not long ago she got herself and you arrested for anti-German behaviour, and look at her now, working for the Germans! Is she mad?"

"Calm down, will you. You will wake the children. We don't want them to hear what we are saying." That was Mother.

"Can't you talk some sense into her, and get her to back out before it is too late?" There was urgency in Father's voice now.

"I wish I could," sobbed my mother. "But she will not listen to me either. She can be very stubborn, you know." They lowered their voices and we couldn't hear the rest.

Sonja and I were wide awake now.

"Why are they shouting and what's wrong with Aase?" I demanded, very worried.

"They are angry that Aase is going to work for the Germans who are our enemies," Sonja informed me. She too was worried at this unexpected development.

As it was quiet in the kitchen now, and I had no idea how to respond to this new information, I soon fell asleep.

What prompted this exchange between our parents in the early winter of 1942 was that my beautiful sister Aase had made a decision that would affect us all. She began working for the Germans. A vacancy in one of their laundries had come up, and two of her friends, already working there, persuaded her to apply. At first she wouldn't hear of it, but the temptation of a good meal and good pay helped overcome her reservations. She had just turned 19 years old a few weeks earlier.

When she applied, she was offered a job in their laundry. After all, there were few work opportunities in Kirkenes, except in establishments and offices run by the Germans, directly or indirectly. Father, appalled, tried to talk her out of it. Mother was caught in the middle, and suggested she should look for something else. Aase, however, stubbornly decided to take the job.

As she took her first step into unknown and dangerous territory, the harmony in our home was shaken. Flattered by the attention she got from the young and often handsome German soldiers, she began to bring her German friends home to our house. Their policy was to befriend the civilians wherever possible, and after the episode when Mother and Aase had been arrested, it was not wise to show them the door. So Father fumed, Mother tried to soothe him, and Sonja and I kept out of the way as much as possible. Other families had similar experiences, where a daughter working for the Germans brought them home, sometimes falling in love with a German soldier or officer.

The Germans had requisitioned rooms for officers and their servants in private houses, and had, in some cases, taken over the whole house, forcing the unfortunate family to find other accommodation. Those who lived in requisitioned accommodation were in most cases considerate to their reluctant host family and treated them well. One family not far from us had been forced to let out two rooms to an officer and his valet. The officer was very kind and sometimes played with the family's two small boys, Jan and Idar, making farm animals, fences and buildings, using paper, cardboard and glue. The boys, of course, were delighted with their toy farm.

Infiltration by the Germans into every part of people's lives was taking place, and people had to learn to live with it. Some women started to wash clothes for the Germans, who paid well enough, but after a while there was very little to get for the money, so they bartered instead. A little food or real coffee, and sometimes tobacco, helped to make ends meet.

Three of Aase's new 'friends' were stationed on Prestøya, the island now connected to Kirkenes by a causeway built by the German 'Todt' regiment and Russian prisoners of war. The island had been fortified with heavy artillery and gun positions. Powerful searchlights were installed there too, and fingers of light crisscrossed the sky during air raids at night.

Getz was the name of one of her friends. He missed his home back in Germany and liked to show us photos of his wife and family. Wolf was another friend. He was quite short, very jolly and a bit of a comedian, always telling stories, joking and laughing. Then there was Herman Lang, tall, dark, and slim, always wearing a long, dark grey overcoat. Aase had warned us about him. He was a Nazi and liked talking about 'Der Fuhrer' and 'Das Vaterland' and how they soon would defeat the Russians. He often clicked his heels, raised his arm, and said 'Heil Hitler' before he left. But he could smile as well, and sombody who would give us a sweetie couldn't be all bad, could he? Luckily we didn't see too much of him, or Father may not have been able to contain himself.

Others who came to our house were young soldiers from Austria. They carried pressed edelweiss flowers in their wallets along with photos of their families. Edelweiss is a white European mountain flower and was a symbol of 'Wehrmacht' and 'Waffen-SS Gebirgsjager', the mountain infantry. Many of them gave the impression of not wanting to be in the war at all. So they came and went. Some of them we never saw again, as they were killed or wounded at the Litza front.

One day there was a knock at the door, and when Mother went to investigate, Wolf was standing there looking really bad. His head was covered in a blood-stained bandage. His left shoulder and arm were also bandaged, with his arm in a sling. He had come from the front, and told us about a battle he had been part of – where many Germans had been killed and many wounded. Wolf had been shot in the arm and shoulder, and also hit at the side of his head. As he was now going to be sent back to Germany, he had come to say goodbye and wish us well. No other German ever approached us quite in that way and even Father couldn't find it in himself to wish this German soldier any ill.

The sight of wounded German soldiers in Kirkenes became increasingly familiar. Many of them, returning from the front, were severely wounded. They were very noticeable as they moved around on crutches, some with bandages around the head, arms or legs.

That winter another shock was in store for us. Aase had fallen deeply in love with a German officer or NCO, whose name was Peter Haupt. He often wore a long, black leather coat with a leather belt holding a gun. She began to bring him home regularly, and as things went from bad to worse, my mother had her hands full trying to calm my father down; at the same time she was trying to get Aase to see sense, but to no avail. Peter was a handsome man, and when he smiled I noticed a gleaming gold tooth, which I thought looked really nice.

As the romance between Aase and Peter deepened and developed, it was also stormy. They sometimes quarrelled and shouted at each other until Peter stormed out and stayed away for a day or two. When he returned he always brought her something and called her 'liebling'. So they were happy again for a while. Peter was very talented. On his nights off he often brought his accordion, singing and playing his German songs. Sometimes he step danced around the floor to the delight of Sonja and me, who forgot that he was also 'The Enemy'. But Father didn't forget and kept his distance.

Aase was out much of the time during this period. Aunt Reidun often came to visit and brought Ruth. Odd seldom came, as he was not very interested in being with us girls. The discussion often turned to Aase, if she was out.

"What got into her?" Aunt Reidun said one day. "She is normally a very sensible girl."

"She has fallen in love," Mother said defensively.

"And with the enemy," Father added. "How could she do this to us?"

"To think that it is not very long ago since she got herself and you arrested, Borghild," Aunt Reidun continued, "I would have thought she had learned something from that experience."

"The whole thing started with her working for the Germans, which she shouldn't have done," Father said, "but she wouldn't listen, and now we see the result!"

Mother had not said much during this conversation. Aase was her eldest daughter from her first marriage and Mother was very fond of her, as we all were.

"I only hope she does not get herself pregnant," she said wistfully. "She is so young."

"And pretty too," Aunt Reidun chipped in. "With so many handsome soldiers around, is it any wonder that the girls fall for them?"

Father was frowning. "This war is going to be a lot worse before it gets better," he said. "If we survive the war, there is sure to be a day of reckoning for those who have betrayed our country."

"Aase has not betrayed the country, she has just fallen in love," said Mother sharply. "Let us leave it at that!"

Sonja, Ruth and I had heard most of this conversation, but didn't dare to butt in with any questions. What did 'pregnant' mean and what would it do to Aase? We had no answers as yet. But it made us worry about Aase. She might be grown up, but she was still our big sister and we loved her very much.

"How can the war be worse," I wondered quietly to Sonja, "when we have to run to Bertakanalen in the air raids all the time?"

"I don't know, but the house could be bombed and we could all be killed," she whispered back.

That was a terrifying thought. I did not like that idea at all and decided that our house would not be bombed and I did not want to speak about it anymore.

"I don't want to be bombed and killed," Ruth said looking at us with her big round eyes and a frightened quiver in her voice.

"Don't talk nonsense Ruth; nobody is going to harm us. Get your jacket and shoes, we are going home." Aunt Reidun was ready to leave.

"To think that we could sit in peace with no air raids," she sighed.

"That was great. We'll see you soon," she said as they left.

Aase, however, continued working at the laundry. Her affair with Peter had not 'run its course', as Mother had hoped. Instead, they spent as much time as possible together. Aase's relationship with Father was at low ebb. He hated what she was doing and she – besotted as she was with Peter – often turned on Father. Mother was caught in the middle, trying to keep the peace. But it was an uneasy peace; a peace that was often shattered and had to be repaired time after time by my mother. So, as the war around us continued and the conflict at home escalated, there was not much harmony in our family.

10

The Teachers' rebellion

Something was very wrong. We could tell. Of course, the war and the air raids were *all* wrong, but we had got used to that. This was different. The worried looks on their faces, as our parents, and neighbours dropping in, anxiously discussed 'the teachers and their plight', said it all.

They were clearly very worried about a new situation to do with the teachers and closing of schools. Words like 'mass arrests' and 'teachers in prison' were repeated over and over again. It was blamed on 'that traitor Quisling' and the Germans, we heard. Often someone would say, "What next?" Sonja picked up on it one day.

"What next, what, Pappa? Will the Germans arrest all of us?"

Father laughingly replied,

"Well, if they do that, they will have no time to fight the war!" Then he added sternly: "You know not to repeat anything you hear in this house, don't you?"

We nodded solemnly, already aware of the dangers, after the terrifying experience when Mother and Aase were arrested.

D/S *Skjerstad*, one of the coastal steamers, was due to arrive in Kirkenes.

"There are hundreds of teachers on board," said Father darkly. "I wonder what they have in mind for them."

Along the coast, people had shown their solidarity by bringing food parcels to the ship. Sometimes warm soup or milk was brought by the

Red Cross, but they were not always allowed on board. When the teachers were marched ashore in Kirkenes the day after the ship arrived, people watched in silence, trying to show their support.

We were out too, and as the teachers were herded on by their German guards, I lifted my hand and waved. One or two noticed me and smiled, but Mother quickly grabbed my hand and pulled it down.

"Don't do that," she whispered. "The Germans won't like it."

I knew of course that we were not allowed to wave to the Russian prisoners, but why not the teachers? By this time I was seven and-a-half years old, with many more questions than answers.

My father was fuming when we arrived home, as he and my mother discussed this latest development.

"Quisling and his German friends have a lot to answer for," he thundered. "Are the children to go without education till the war is over? Or is the alternative really to see them marching in the Hitler Youth uniforms under the Nazi flags shouting: Heil Hitler!?"

"Calm down, will you," said my mother soothingly. "It is great that the teachers are holding out – and they have our full support. Let's see what happens and find out how we can help. There is trouble in the churches as well, you know, where the Bishops have resigned."

"The situation is very bad indeed and getting worse." said Father gloomily. "But what can we do?"

"Nothing at the moment," Mother said slowly. "We have to find out where they have taken the teachers first. Then we'll see how we can help. They will need food and clothes, and we must find ways of getting it to them."

Father was deeply troubled. "The whole town is behind the teachers of course, and people will help, as they are trying to help the Russian prisoners," he said. "But it is very difficult to get near the foreign prisoners. Let's hope it will be easier to get close to the teachers."

"The trouble is that food and clothing are getting scarcer now, but we must help them as much as we can," concluded my mother.

Vidkun Quisling had waited in the shadows until the German invasion was well under way. He had then gained access to NRK (the main Norwegian Radio station in Oslo), where he, in a broadcast to the Norwegian people, appointed himself the country's new Prime Minister. Neither influential Norwegians nor the Germans wanted such a development at that time, and soon Quisling was forced to stand down.

Talks between German leaders, Norwegian politicians, and others, to find common ground for an independent assembly to govern Norway, failed. The Germans had hoped to keep the King and his government in place. But as they had refused to capitulate or agree to a later request for abdication, the King and his government in exile were disregarded by the Germans.

Josef Terboven was appointed 'Reich Commissar' and was Hitler's top man in Norway. But not until the 1st February 1942 was Quisling finally appointed leader of an administrative government with specially selected people. The party was given wide-ranging powers and Quisling got the title of 'Minister-President'.

Quisling had finally got what he wanted. He and other leaders in the NS Party (National Socialists) were quick to decide that all levels of Norwegian Society would conform to the Nazi Doctrine, starting with the children. Two new laws were designed to achieve this.

The first law concerned all children aged 10 years old and over, who would become members of a NS Youth Organisation, to be educated in the 'New Order' until they were 18 years old, similar to Hitler Jugend in Germany. This provoked a huge outcry and protest from the Norwegian people. Parents got involved, and the church, along with many other organisations, protested. The Germans could not arrest two to three hundred thousand protesting parents who refused to send their children to the so called 'Youth Service.' After a prolonged power struggle, the first law failed.

The second law concerned the teachers, who would be compelled to co-operate with the Nazi authority in teaching the children what was decreed. Membership of a new 'Teacher Organisation' was compulsory, and all teachers were expected to sign the agreement. But the teachers rebelled. There was no way they would participate in such a scheme.

Their rebellion resulted in arrests of teachers throughout Norway. About 1,100 were arrested in the first round up. Women teachers were excluded (initially). Imprisonment, however harsh, did not break their determination. Parents stood by the teachers, and faced with such opposition, other means had to be found to break them. And the Nazis found a solution, one they had already put into practice in Europe: deport the teachers and use them as slave labour. 'Fortress Kirkenes' was chosen as their destination.

It was a sad day indeed when the first 500 teachers arrived in Kirkenes on 29th April 1942 on board the D/S *Skjerstad*. The ship was carrying twice its normal number of passengers. The journey from Trondheim had taken 16 days, with poor facilities and very little food. Most of the teachers were put in the hold of the ship; others had to share public rooms, as few of the cabins were available to them.

Unknown to us, the teachers were being marched to Elvenes, about 8-10 km. away, where Stalag 322 was located – one of the four main prisoner-of-war camps in Norway. Speculation as to what the Germans had in mind for the teachers had been rife. The cramped accommodation was dirty and very basic, with thin walls, no insulation, and providing only the minimum of facilities. They faced twelve hours hard labour every day. Poor clothes and very little food added to their misery. This was the punishment for their defiance of the 'New Order'.

On 11th May another 150 teachers arrived, and were dispatched to the camps at Elvenes. Most of them were set to work to build a better road from Elvenes to Jakobsnes (east of Kirkenes). This road became known as 'Lærerveien' (the Teachers' Road). Some teachers were based in Kirkenes for a time and others were at Sandnes south of Kirkenes.

Local teachers didn't fare better than their brothers from the south. Some of them ended up as forced labour at Høibuktmoen airport. Kalle Wara, to his surprise, one day found himself working alongside his former teacher.

Father took the plight of the teachers as a personal insult. He was always on the outlook for extra clothing, a pair of socks or mitts and, of course, food to make up a parcel with Mother's help. The parcels could not be too large – that would draw attention to those who tried to help. It was easier to get close to the teachers from the camp in Kirkenes. The locals would find a reason for walking or cycling past, when the teachers were working on the roads. In passing, they conveniently 'lost' a parcel when the guard wasn't looking. Some 'good' guards would turn their backs, whilst others watched like hawks. However, people were always looking for new ways to help the teachers.

Following our evacuation to Jarfjord, Father cycled up every weekend and, at the same time, bringing parcels to the teachers at Elvenes. A bridge spanned the wide Pasvik River at Elvenes, where Stalag 322 was already home to Russian prisoners and German deserters – now also joined by Norwegian teachers. If he couldn't get near them, someone else would take charge of the parcel, and smuggle it to the teachers.

German deserters were treated worse than Russian prisoners, and got even less food. Just outside Kirkenes, near the 'First Loch', Camp no. 28 was situated, nicknamed 'Death camp 28' by the Germans themselves. As far as is known, only German deserters were kept there. The deserters were mainly young Germans who found it hard or impossible to carry on their duties as soldiers. Many committed suicide; others ended up in camp 28 or at Elvenes. Of those who did survive during the German retreat, incidents were told of Russian prisoners trying to help German deserters with a bit of food.

Unnecessary brutality by many guards was meted out to all prisoners. If they didn't move fast enough, they were kicked and pushed, or hit with a rifle butt. Over the weeks and months, hard work, lack of food and warm clothing, along with the brutal treatment they received, began to take its toll. If the prisoners didn't die of sickness, disease or starvation, they were often helped on their way by their guards.

One day, as they were marching back to the camp, a Russian

prisoner stepped out of his line, picking up a cigarette butt he spotted on the road. The furious guard lifted his rifle, swinging it down over the poor man's head with such force that his skull was cracked. This brutal attack was followed by a bullet in the prisoners head and, unbelievably, all this for a cigarette butt! It would seem that a prisoner's life had no value beyond the work he was doing, and that many guards needed very little excuse to unleash their sadistic tendencies.

Helping the foreign prisoners was risky, but a risk many people were prepared to take – using both ingenuity and imagination. A widespread practice was putting food parcels in rubbish bins, if prisoners were working nearby. The prisoners soon got wise to this, and another way to help was born. Apart from the German guards there were ones from Austria, Lithuania, and Ukraine. Those from Lithuania and Ukraine were volunteers. A few of these guards would let parcels for the teachers through, possibly putting the teachers in a different category of prisoners.

Nenne Isaksen, telephonist at the local telegraph station, became an expert at sending coded messages from the teachers to their families in the south, right under the noses of the Germans. When the teachers were able to get their messages out, Nenne got them sent. She used a variety of code names for messages to and from the teachers. Her assistance continued for as long as the teachers remained in Kirkenes. She worked at the station throughout the war, in spite of the danger she was in, until she and the others working there had to close down and evacuate.

As the teachers showed no sign of backing down, Quisling sent one of his ministers (Sverre Riisnæs) to Kirkenes. But neither promises nor threats had any effect. After his departure, however, the teachers in Sørvaranger took a serious look at their perilous situation. The debate that followed, for or against signing, may have been influenced by coded messages from the south. When the teachers finally agreed to sign the paper, they had decided that signing under duress would have no legal standing. They had taken a stand and made their point. A major consideration was that they had little chance of surviving the Arctic winter that lay ahead, with its unrelenting hard labour, meagre food rations, inadequate shelter, and lack of warm clothing.

After six to seven months, the teachers were sent home; the older ones first in October; the rest during November. There had been casualties, and many left with lasting health problems – but all of them left with their spirits unbroken. In the meantime, the new 'Teacher Organisation' had been declared non-political. The 'second law' became nothing but a paper exercise. The teachers had won their point, and when back at their schools they carried on teaching as they had done before the war.

After the war was over and Kirkenes had been burned to the ground, the teachers who had been in Kirkenes raised money for a new library, in gratitude for the help they received from local people in 1942.

The plaque outside the door reads:

> 'Reist av norske lærere som takk for all hjelp
> folket i Sørvaranger gav 636 lærere i tysk
> fangenskap 28-04 til 04-11,1942'.

> (Raised by Norwegian teachers in gratitude for
> all the help given by the people of Sørvaranger
> to 636 teachers in German captivity from
> 28-04 to 04-11, 1942).

Today the 'teachers' library' is an arts exhibition centre, and a new and larger library in the centre of the town has taken its place.

After a long dispute in which the clergy also refused to conform to new teachings in the church, and stood against the proposed new laws, some were banished to an island in Norway's largest loch, Mjøsa. Others were exiled; some were arrested. Quislings Nazification plans for Norwegian institutions had failed.

The attempts to Nazify Norwegian society were, of course, much more complex, and only the main points are covered here. The teachers sent to Kirkenes as slave labour touched us directly and therefore have a place in this story.

11

Evacuation and new experiences

The marked increase in bombing raids throughout the winter and spring of 1942 saw many people leaving Kirkenes to stay with relatives or friends in the countryside, or elsewhere in Finnmark. Others had already travelled south on the coastal steamers to get away. Sadly, some never reached their destinations, as several of the ships were torpedoed, and whole families lost their lives. We knew one such family whose little girl was about my age.

As Mother had relations in Jarfjord, we were offered a room in Karpbukt, at her cousin Aslaug's house. Karpbukt is about 24 kilometres to the south east of Kirkenes and, at the time, was well away from the horrors of constant bomb attacks. Aunt Aslaug – as we called her – was small, a bit plump and very nice. Uncle Ragnvald had a nice smiling face, and their daughter Torgunn – a few years older than us – was very friendly and often brought us along to visit her uncle's family in Tårnet, a couple of kilometres away. Her uncle was manager of the power station there. Two of their boys were about our age.

Aunt Aslaug's family had a small croft with two cows, a calf and a horse called 'Elsa'. This was my first encounter with farm animals. I became a regular visitor to the byre, watching Aunt Aslaug milking the cows. It was warm in there, smelling of cows, hay, and dung – but it was a pleasant smell, and an entirely new experience, seeing how milk was squeezed out of the cows. The milk was very good. We hadn't had milk for a long time, since all we got in Kirkenes, after queuing for hours, was a little dried milk.

The cows – which were kept in the byre all winter – were called Dagros and Fagros. One of them was the mother of Litago, a lovely little calf. Dagros was reddish brown and white, while Fagros was black and white and so was Litago, but she was more white than black.

"Which of them is Litago's mother?" I asked one day, sitting on a stool in the byre watching the milking.

"She is like her mother," was the answer, and she continued, "Who do you think is her mother then?"

"She looks awfully like Fagros," I offered.

"You are quite right, Fagros is her mother," Aunt Aslaug said with a smile.

"Where is Elsa today?" I asked, having noticed that the horse was missing.

"Uncle Ragnvald went away with her early this morning to fetch wood," she answered patiently, moving out of the byre before I could ask any more questions.

Following her into the kitchen, I watched her straining the milk before pouring most of it into two large bowls. A small cup of milk was set aside for me.

"Drink it, it is good for you," she said.

"The milk is warm," I said, surprised.

"Of course," said Aunt Aslaug, "It came right from the cow."

She proceeded to remove the mat on the kitchen floor, covering a hatch, with a ring set into the wood. Opening the hatch revealed a steep ladder descending into the basement. She set one of the bowls of milk on the floor beside the hatch, moving gingerly downwards, facing the steps and holding on to them as she descended. When she was level with the milk, she grabbed the bowl and, very carefully, moved down the last few steps – putting the milk on a shelf at the back wall. Watching this perilous journey down the steps, I held my breath. What if she fell and lost this precious milk? After repeating the trip down the steps successfully with the second bowl of milk, she came up again, closing the hatch and covering it with the mat.

Later on, I discovered why the milk was stored in the basement. It was cool there, helping the cream to form on the top. She skimmed the cream off the milk and made butter with it, using a strange-looking wooden contraption which needed vigorous action. When she was finished, she divided the butter between two or three plates, formed them into dome shapes, and made them nice and smooth with a butter knife.

Staying with them was like a voyage of discovery for me. Sonja had stayed with our grandparents in the Lofoten Islands before the war started, and knew about crofts and animals. But this was a first for me, and I loved this new and strange life in Jarfjord. However, there were also some hard lessons in store during our stay there.

One morning, not long after our arrival, I went outside looking for a sledge. There was still snow on the ground and very cold. I didn't find a sledge, but I spotted a 'spark' (push-sledge) standing behind the house. Lacking something better to do, I decided to borrow the 'spark' to see how fast it would go down the short slope below the house.

However, it wouldn't move when I tried to push it. Turning it upside down, I discovered that the metal runners were clogged up with ice. I looked around, but saw nothing useful for scraping off the ice. The idea popped into my head that I might be able to melt the ice with my tongue. I knelt down and put my tongue on the runner. But instead of melting the ice, my tongue stuck to the runner. I couldn't get it off, and I couldn't shout. So there I was, with my tongue firmly stuck to the runner of the sledge, trying to make loud noises to attract attention.

Unfortunately no one heard or saw me. Eventually I managed to tear my tongue away, but a piece of it was left on the runner. Crying I ran in to Mother, who didn't quite know what to do. Aunt Aslaug was consulted, but she was not sure what to do either, and suggested lukewarm water to rinse out my mouth.

"What you don't get up to," said my mother, shaking her head. "That was very foolish,"

"Oh dear, it must be very uncomfortable and sore," said Aunt Aslaug sympathetically

I continued hanging around their kitchen like a little dog. Uncle Ragnvald did many interesting things too. When he took Elsa out with the sledge in the winter to collect timber from the woods, he prepared himself well for the cold weather.

A bench seat stood in a small recess in the kitchen, where Uncle Ragnvald sat down with a pair of 'skaller', which were short boots made of reindeer skins, coming to a point at the toes and rolling in over the top of the boot in a curl. This type of footwear was used by the Sami people in the winter time, and widely used by the locals for its lightness and warmth.

Uncle Ragnvald kept a basket of special grass called senna grass in the recess. He lined the soles and insides of the boots with liberal amounts of the grass; then put his bare feet in the 'boots', packing more grass on top of his feet.

It was with utter astonishment that I watched this procedure. The next stage was to fasten a wide band or ribbon at the ankle, then wind it around the ankle and up over the trouser leg, to be fastened around his knee.

"You forgot to put your socks on," I said accusingly, the first time I watched him getting ready.

"No, I didn't forget," he informed me with a smile.

"But you will be cold," I persisted, "It is very cold today."

"The grass keeps my feet warm and dry, and that is all I need," said Uncle Ragnvald, "Someday you'll understand."

At the time I certainly didn't understand how anybody could go out in the snow and frost with only grass on their feet and be comfortable.

After putting on his reindeer skin top, which reached down to his knees, he left with Elsa and the sledge – and with a wave of the hand he was off.

"Can't you make him put his socks on," I said, turning to Aunt Aslaug, still on the subject of socks.

"Your daughter is full of questions," she laughingly said to my mother who had come in to the kitchen.

"I know," said Mother." If she bothers you too much just tell her to go."

73

"No, no," said Aunt Aslaug, "I couldn't do that; she is very amusing."

None of this was very helpful to me, as I pondered over boots with grass and bare feet in them. Years later, I discovered that the special grass used in the boots grows in certain fresh water lochs.

Aunt Aslaug's kitchen was quite large. A half-moon-shaped sink was mounted on one wall where waste water was disposed of. Above it, a hand operated pump with a long handle was used to pump in water from the river nearby. I watched this procedure with fascination, thinking that this was far better than fetching water in a bucket from the stand pipe on Haugen!

Summer was approaching, and with it a fascinating display by the animals when they were let out of the byre for the first time. Sonja and I were told to stay out of the way, and sat on the steps outside the house watching. When the cows came charging out of the byre into the sunshine, they seemed disorientated at first. Their heads went down, their backs curved, as they jumped up in the air with all feet leaving the ground – galloping around in circles and at times head butting each other. Litago was even funnier. She jumped up in the air, took several jumps sideways and then circled around herself before running off with her tail in the air.

When questioned about this extraordinary behaviour, Aunt Aslaug said that they did this every spring because they were happy to get out of the byre. To me this sounded about right. Who wouldn't be happy to get out after spending a whole winter inside?

The best time during the war was the year we spent in Jarford 1942 – 1943. Although German vehicles passed through Jarfjord regularly, as they were building a road from Tårnet to the Russian border, there were no direct attacks on Jarfjord during that period.

In June we followed the family a couple of miles through the countryside to Karp valley, where they were setting potatoes and sowing vegetables. Everyone had to help. The children were shown how to put potatoes in the rows. The men prepared the ground for vegetables and the women sowed the seeds. When Sonja and I – along with the other children – had done our chores, we explored the area looking for wild berries (they were not ripe yet), and enjoyed ourselves wading barefoot in the river. Later in the day, a small fire was started where our parents brewed 'coffee'. Occasionally someone was lucky enough to acquire real coffee by bartering. This lightened the mood and was an excuse for a party. After a few hours' work, we all gathered around the fire for sandwiches with milk for the children and coffee for the adults. It was peaceful and pleasant; the adults discussed the war, food shortages and what they would do if they survived the war – while the children were running about without worries about the next air raid.

On warm sunny days Torgunn brought us to Karpbukt to meet up with our cousins, and we would all go down to the beach and splash around in the sea, having great fun.

Throughout the summer Father cycled from Kirkenes every Friday after work, and we, of course, were always on the lookout for him. Sometimes he was late due to the air raids, or if he had to be out with the fire fighters after a bomb attack. But he always came.

One Friday he arrived with a surprise present. It was a small dog, sleek, with short hair. She was white with some black spots, and she had black ears with a black patch around one eye. After it was cleared with Aunt Aslaug that we could keep her, we named her Lappi. Lappi was blind on one eye. Father had been approached by a friend to look after the dog, which had been rescued from its German owner who no longer wanted her.

At first she was very timid. If we lifted an arm or a foot, or made sudden movements, she would cower on the floor, her ears back as if she expected to be hit or kicked. But we loved her and petted her, and she soon began to respond. She was particularly protective of Mother, snarling if any stranger came near her. She learned to understand when Father was expected. When we said "Lappi, Pappa kommer," she made for the door and took up position on the steps outside, looking expectantly down the road, with her head to one side so that she could see better with her good eye. When he appeared, and she realised that it was Father, she was off, jumping all over him, licking his face, and wagging her tail furiously. She followed Father everywhere when he was home, and played with us or looked after Mother while he was away.

Later that summer, the men gathered to cut hay with their scythes. The scythes were strange contraptions, with long sharp, slightly curved blades, and had to be held in a special way when used. The men lined up and started cutting, with a swinging movement that laid down the grass in flat rows.

Unfortunately, there were many rats around at that time – large ones called water rats. They were hiding in the grass. Now and then they got hit by the scythes, which made them squeal and try to run away. Lappi used to chase them – but didn't quite know what to do if she caught one. The Germans were blamed for the huge increase in vermin. Their shipments of large bales of straw and hay were said to conceal the rats.

After the hay was cut, the women and children gathered to rake and shape the hay into small manageable lots. These in turn were hung onto a three-wire fence to dry. Those of us who had never done this before were shown what to do. The children were given smaller rakes and a lesson in farm work. It was all very enjoyable, and when we tired, there was always the river to attract us.

From its tributaries south east of Jarfjord, in the Russian border area, the large Karpelv (Karp River) winds its way for many miles through the fertile Karpdal (Karp Valley), before spilling into the fjord at Karpbukt (Karp Bay). The river was always noisy, especially where it turned into waterfalls.

A shop and a small farm, owned and managed by Aunt Aslaug's brother Trygve, were at the centre of the village of Karpbukt. Trygve lived above the shop with his wife Dagrun and their two children, Henrik and Turid. A low building set apart from the shop served as a school, but also contained a flat, where Trygve's brother Solmund lived with his wife Guri and their two sons. Stables for their horses, and a large byre for cows and calves, completed the settlement. A sprinkling of houses and a few crofts, spaced well away from each other, made up the Karpbukt area.

The reasons for our numerous relations in Jarfjord were that my mother's ancestors, both maternal and paternal, had travelled north about 100 years earlier, settling in Vardø and also on both sides of Jarfjord.

When the cloudberries began to ripen in July, women and children gathered together to go berry picking. The cloudberries grow in marshy places, mainly in the Arctic. Full of vitamin C, large and yellow, they are considered the best of the wild berries in the north. Our two families, and the relations from Karpbukt with their children, made up the group. We were given small buckets or tins with handles, whereas the adults carried large buckets for the berry picking.

On a fine sunny morning, we started off in high spirits on the well-known path to Karp Valley. The weather was nice and warm, and we were looking forward to what we thought would be another great outing. After a short stop at the Valley, we carried on through the heaths and marshy landscape of the upper valley and beyond. Eventually we arrived at a large marshy area covered with yellow berries, almost like a carpet.

"Oh," said Aunt Aslaug, "At last."

"I didn't realise that it was such a long walk," Mother commented.

"Let's have something to eat before we start."

To general relief, we all sat down to rest and eat.

"It's a shame that there is so little sugar to get now," said Mother.

"That is so," said Aunt Aslaug, "But the berries will keep all right without sugar, if you boil them and keep them cold. We usually keep them in a wooden barrel, and they are fine all winter. I think Ragnvald has one you can use; if not, Trygve may be able to find one for you."

"Splendid," said Mother, looking pleased. "It will help to eke out the rations."

"I brought some mosquito oil," said Aunt Aslaug. "Rub it on your arms and faces. The mosquitoes will get worse when we start picking berries."

Mother gave us head squares to cover our heads and, after rubbing on some oil, we were ready to start.

The cloudberries are quite large, producing one berry to each plant.

When they are plentiful, as they were here, they are quite easy to pick. So we spread out and started gathering berries. Soon the mosquitoes were buzzing around, biting us in spite of the oil. The mosquitoes in the Arctic are large and bloodthirsty, and at times the use of mosquito nets is essential. However, we persisted picking the berries. Each time my little bucket was full, I emptied it into Mother's bucket.

After a while we moved on to another area, and kept moving until everybody had enough. The children were sent off to gather juniper branches, whilst the women were getting a fire going. Juniper gives out a lot of smoke, which keeps the mosquitoes at bay – and we could sit down for a well-earned rest and some food.

Suddenly there was a shout. Mother jumped up waving her arms and holding on to her head.

"Something bit my eye," she cried leaping around.

"Stand still and let me have a look," said Aunt Aslaug. "It looks like you were bitten on the side of your eye by a klegg." (A klegg or gadfly looks like a fly but is much larger.)

"Their bite is very painful and it may swell up," she continued. "I will put some mosquito oil on it. That is all I have."

"Thank you," said Mother who didn't look very happy.

"It is time to pack up and make sure the fire is out," declared Aunt Aslaug.

Most of the day was gone when we started back. After a while Dagrun said anxiously:

"I don't think this is the right direction."

So we stopped and looked around us. Wherever we turned, everything looked the same. With the sun getting lower on the horizon, the light had taken on a slightly different colour, and the landscape around us suddenly looked different. A debate developed as to which direction to go, with each of the women having different ideas.

"I thought you all knew the area," said Mother crossly, "After all you live here."

"That is true enough," said Aunt Aslaug, "But I have never been so far before without Ragnvald. Your eye is swelling up, is it sore?"

"It feels as if I have a lump there," said my mother, holding a hand over her eye. The women decided on a direction, and we walked on. I was very tired and wanted to sit down. The other children were also tired, and getting fretful. We had a short rest and carried on again, this time in another direction. Nobody was cheerful anymore, and very worried, because we were completely lost. After several more rests and changes of direction someone exclaimed:

"The river, can you hear the river?" And sure enough, a faint noise was bearing our way.

"Good, let's follow the sound and find the river," Aunt Aslaug said, with relief. "Then we'll follow it to Karpbukt."

They all agreed, and soon we could hear the thunderous noise from one of the waterfalls.

With renewed energy, we approached the river, and followed it down the valley. After a rest and some water from the river, we set off for the last leg of our journey. It was midnight by the time we arrived home. Mother's eye had swollen so much that it was completely closed – but although exhausted, we were all happy to be home again.

Several more berry picking expeditions were organized, but we never went as far again. In due course we had a quarter barrel full of lightly cooked cloud berries, enough for the whole winter of 1942-1943.

12

Falling through the ice

The warm weather we had enjoyed suddenly turned colder, signalling the arrival of autumn. The growing season was over. After three months in the ground, the potatoes and vegetables were ready to be harvested before the snow came. During the short summer season – enhanced by two months of midnight sun – the crops grew and ripened very quickly.

Another expedition to Karp Valley was called for. On a bright morning in September we were all ready to go. Uncle Ragnvald, with Elsa pulling a cart full of boxes and barrels for the crop, led the way. It was quite a long walk, but Torgunn, Sonja and I were skipping away ahead of the others, arriving at the valley well before the rest. On the way we picked and ate wild berries, which were still plentiful, like blue berries, heather berries and cranberries. At the Valley the crops were harvested and packed in boxes. My father was there too, so it must have been at a weekend. With all hands helping, Elsa had a heavy load to bring home in the evening.

Now and then – when he was in Jarfjord at weekends – Father had a chance to go fishing with Uncle Ragnvald. They would sit outside to talk and bait lines; then they rowed towards the entrance of the fjord setting their lines. The next day they went out again, and came home with cod, saithe and 'uer'. 'Uer' (Norway Haddock), is a deep-water fish with orange/red coloured skin.

"Pappa, why are the eyes sticking out on that red fish?" I asked curiously, as the eyes on the other fish were different.

"That fish," replied my father "is called Uer and lives in deep water. When it is pulled up to shallower water, the pressure changes and the eyes are pushed out. Do you understand?"

"Uhm," I responded, not really understanding why it should be so. But I had got my answer.

Father loved fishing, and was very good at gutting, cleaning and filleting fish; at least that's what Uncle Ragnvald said, so it had to be true. The next few days we had fresh fish and livers or fried fish, and when he left for Kirkenes on Sunday afternoon, Father took some fish back with him.

School started in early September 1942 in Karpbukt, and Mother brought us there to enrol. It wasn't a proper school, but a large room in a private house which belonged to my mother's cousins. The local children got their education there. However, due to lack of space the children attended school only two weeks per month, alternating in two age groups.

I would soon be eight years old, but had not yet attended school because of the war. At least I could read and write. Our teacher was very strict. If we didn't pay attention, teased someone, or were guilty of some other misdemeanour, we were sent to the 'shame corner'. There we had to stand with our backs to the class being ashamed of ourselves – until it suited the teacher to call us back.

One day I was sitting at my desk, completely forgetting to listen to the teacher. Working my pencil round and round on a dip in the desk, I was rudely brought back to the present by the teacher standing over me. She grabbed a handful of my hair and violently shook my head back and forth.

"I will teach you to pay attention," she said angrily. "In to the corner with you, and stand there till I tell you to come back."

There was silence in the class as I made my way to the 'shame corner', and covered my face while the tears started to flow. After that I was too afraid of her not to pay attention. Other pupils suffered similar fates in the course of the term.

That year I discovered Love. I had recently had my 8th birthday, and one of the boys in the class – whose name was Johan – was very nice. I liked him a lot, and kept looking at him and wanted to play with him. Soon the other children discovered this and started to tease.

"She is in love with Johan, she is in love with Johan," they chanted.

I, of course, hotly denied this, and kept away from him the rest of the winter. Instead, I admired him at a distance. What he thought of me and the whole thing, I never found out.

My best friend at school that year was Anny Johnsen. I often followed her home to Tårnet – about a kilometre away – where the Germans were busy constructing a road to the Russian border. On our way to her house one day, we had just rounded a corner on the road, when a fast-moving German motorcycle with a sidecar caught up with us. It failed to take the corner, left the road and crashed through trees and undergrowth. We heard angry shouts from the two Germans, and ran away, too scared to stop.

The weather turned very cold, with long periods of hard frost. Ice formed on the fjord, and the Karp River froze over. The snow kept coming, and soon the ice was covered with a heavy layer of snow.

Uncle Ragnvald was continually clearing away snow from the doors and down the path. For my father, coming to see us was no longer easy. The bicycle wasn't much use in the snow, and he had to use skis instead. The main road was kept open by snowploughs, as more and more German vehicles passed by, on their way to the Russian border where fighting was intensifying at the Litza front. The locals used horse and sledge to get about, and to cross the fjord with as soon as the ice was thick enough.

Sonja and I often went down to Karpbukt to play with our cousins. I played outside with Henrik, who was a couple of years younger than me, and Sonja looked after Henrik's two year-old sister Turid.

Madvig, a Sami, worked for them on the farm in the summer and cut timber in the winter. He had a long nose and moustache. In periods of hard frost, he wore a long tunic made of reindeer skins, decorated with colourful ribbons around the cuffs, neck and front. A large Sami hat, decorated with ribbons, was pulled over his ears. His 'skaller' (foot-wear), made of reindeer skins and decorated with ribbons around the ankle, completed the outfit. He cut a large and colourful figure, speaking in a strange, almost whispering voice.

Henrik and I were outside playing in the snow one day. The snow had been thawing and then freezing again, making it hard and crisp on the surface. We were happily cutting out squares of the icy snow to throw at each other. While we were playing, Madvig came marching around the corner and made for the hatch to the basement. Ignoring us, he grabbed the large hatch, swinging it back till it was leaning against the house wall and descended the steps to the basement.

"Quick," whispered Henrik, "Let us throw some big ice sheets after him."

"But what if he catches us?" I whispered back.

"We will just run in to Mamma," whispered Henrik confidently. And so we had two large ice sheets ready when we heard him coming up. Henrik threw his snow down the hatch first, and ran for it as I sent mine down the hatch, hitting Madvig squarely on his head. A string of angry words flowed upwards from the hatch, in a mixture of Norwegian and Sami languages. Madvig appeared so quickly that my retreat was cut off. The only way open to me was out the gate and homewards. I ran for dear life, but Madvig caught up with me on the bridge over the river. Before I knew it, he grabbed me, put me over his knees and gave me a right spanking saying tersely with each smack:

"I.. will.. teach.. you.. not.. to.. make.. fun.. of.. Madvig!" When he had finished he set me on my feet saying:

"If you try anything like that again, I will tell your mother and let her deal with you as well. Now, get going!"

So I ran homewards with my bottom smarting and tears streaming down my face. Mother, of course, was never told, or there would have been more trouble in store.

During the long, cold, winter months we missed having Father around. He came as often as possible, but had a long trek of twenty four kilometres on skis to Jarfjord. One day Aunt Reidun and our cousin

Ruth came to visit. They were staying at Haga on the west side of the fjord, and had been offered a lift across the ice with horse and sledge. Their hosts came over to Karpbukt on regular shopping trips.

Sonja and I met Ruth in Karpbukt. Pleased to see each other again, we stayed behind to talk and to introduce Ruth to her cousins. Aunt Reidun had already left to visit Mother, after telling us not to be long.

Shortly afterwards the three of us started off down the road to the track on the river. The track was a well-used short-cut to our house. Stepping on to the track I looked down-river and noticed a large shiny area, like glass, whereas the rest of the ice was covered with a blanket of snow. I got curious.

"Look," I said, "let us go down there to see if we can see the bottom of the river."

"No, absolutely not," said Sonja. "We can't go there; we were told not to leave the track."

"Well, I want to see what is under the ice," I said, and left them. Sonja was alarmed now.

"It could be dangerous," she shouted. "Come back here!"

But curiosity got the better of me. I just had to find out why the ice was shiny there and nowhere else. Craning my neck and leaning forward as I got to the edge of the shiny area, the ice suddenly gave way and I plunged into the river. Shocked by the ice-cold water, I splashed around wildly till I got my head above water, gulping for air.

"Help," I wailed in panic. "Sonja, Ruth, help me!" I managed to grab the edge of the ice and tried to climb up, but it broke, and I went under again. Next time I surfaced and got my hands on the edge of the ice, I saw Sonja and Ruth holding on to each other, crying. Shouting for help as I tried to get onto the ice, it broke again, and I went under for the third time.

Surfacing again – very cold and very frightened – I grabbed the ice with both hands and tried to put my weight on it. This time the ice was stronger. In sheer desperation, I somehow managed to haul myself up onto the ice and crawl away from the danger area. Luckily, Sonja and

Ruth had been too frightened to come to my rescue. If they had, the three of us probably would have ended up in the river – perhaps with fatal consequences.

Later, we heard that the reason for the shiny area on the river was a small whirlpool underneath. It was a miracle that I was not carried out to sea under the ice, never to be seen again. Shaking with cold and teeth clattering, I was escorted up-river and home by Sonja and Ruth.

To say that Mother was angry is putting it mildly. She was shocked at what might have happened, and when anger took over, I was severely scolded for having been so stupid and disobedient. As if that wasn't enough, I was sent to bed. Nobody cared about me, I thought unhappily. It would have served them right if I had drowned, then they might have been sorry!

In early spring 1943, not long before we returned to Kirkenes, something terrible happened. Sonja had gone to a neighbouring farm to get some milk, and had taken Lappi with her. It must have been on a Friday, because Father was expected, and was bringing a lead for the dog, to keep her under better control when out walking.

After a while, Sonja arrived home, crying hysterically, without the dog and with no milk. When Mother got her calmed down, Sonja between sobs told us that as she approached the farm, a lorry full of German soldiers drove past. As it was about to pass, Lappi ran out in front of the lorry, and was hit so hard that she was thrown into the ditch. The German soldiers at the back of the lorry were standing up laughing as they drove on without stopping. Sonja had tried to speak to Lappi, but there was no response at all.

"She must be dead," cried Sonja utterly heartbroken. We all gathered around her, unable to believe that our beloved little dog might be dead. Mother was trying to comfort Sonja, but with tears rolling down her own face kept saying:

"Oh no, not Lappi, and your father is coming home today too. What will he say?"

"It is not true," I wailed, "She can't be dead. It is not true, it is not true!"

Aunt Aslaug put her arms around me, "Ssh child," she crooned over and over.

"There, there, we shall get Lappi home," but she too had tears in her eyes. The whole family had loved our cute little dog.

The first thing Father said when he arrived was:

"Where is Lappi? She always meets me when I come home." Then seeing our miserable faces he knew something was very wrong.

"Tell me what's wrong and where is Lappi?"

When Mother related the story to him, he looked thunderstruck.

"Our Lappi," he said miserably, "and I brought her a proper lead today to keep her safe." He sighed deeply. "Well we cannot leave her in a ditch; we have to get her home. Sonja, will you come with me and show me where she is?"

Sonja nodded unhappily, and followed him outside. He strapped a wooden box behind the seat of his bicycle before they left. When they came back he said to my mother:

"With the blow she got when the vehicle hit her, she would have died instantly – that's something at least."

What that something meant I was at a loss to understand. She was dead, wasn't she? She would never lick our faces or wag her tail again, would she? The thought of it all brought on even more tears and misery.

"I'll make a coffin for her so that we can bury her properly. We want to give her a proper funeral so she can rest in peace, don't we?"

We all nodded in agreement, and when the coffin was ready, and my father had consulted with Uncle Ragnvald on where to bury her, it was carried uphill to a secluded spot, shaded by birch trees. The funeral was very simple and attended by all of us. Father said a few words from the Bible; we threw some earth on the coffin, and then the grave was filled in.

"Is Lappi in heaven now?" I asked my father tearfully.

"Yes," he said and tried to smile. "But she might miss us for a little while, as we will miss her." Lappi, however, was missed for a very long time and never forgotten.

The family in 1940: Father, Aase, Mother, Bjarnhild and Sonja.
Photo: Private collection.

Section of Kirkenes in the 1930s showing Haugen and the house where
we lived.
– Sørvaranger Museum.

About six years old and best friends. Bjarnhild and Astrid Fjeld .
Photo: Private collection.

Our first evacuation to Jarfjord . A fine summer day in 1942 in
Karpbukt with relations. Front left: Bjarnhild, Sonja, and Henrik sitting
on the sea shore, surrounded by Henrik's parents, little sister Turid and
Torgunn with the two little boys Terje and Arnulf; all three whom had a
narrow escape in 1944.
Photo: Private collection.

December 1943. Aase, and Petter (Karlhans) Haupt with their baby
Heide Marie.
Photo: Private collection.

Aase with baby Heide and our mother, Borghild. December 1943.
Photo: Private collection.

*Ragnvald and Aslaug
Rasmussen, our friends
and providers in Jarfjord.
Photo: Private collection.*

*Summer 1944. 'Aunt
Aslaug', Sonja and
Torgunn with Bjarnhild
in front.
Photo: Private collection.*

Bjarne Wian

My father trained regularly with the fire brigade and civil defence during the war.
– Sørvaranger Museum

Bjarne Wian, my father, circa 1947.
Photo: Private collection.

13

Returning home

I don't know at what point my mother learned that Aase was pregnant. But as spring approached, Mother became increasingly worried and distressed. She already knew from one of Father's earlier visits that Peter had moved in with Aase, taking over our upstairs bedroom. That Father was powerless to do anything about it increased the stress and pressure he was under. However, he still came to see us as often as possible at weekends, weather permitting.

The constant worry about Aase prompted Mother to cut short our stay in the country, and to bring us home much sooner than she otherwise would have done.

After school finished in early June 1943, we were ready for the long walk home. I know Mother didn't take this decision lightly. The huge increase in German transport from Kirkenes, through Jarfjord to the battle zone, meant that the roads were no longer safe to walk on.

Sonja and I were very sad to leave Aunt Aslaug and her family, and all our newfound friends in Jarfjord. Before we left I had to go to the byre to say goodbye to the animals. Litago was nearly as big as her mother now, and really cute. I wondered sadly if I would ever see them again.

After having said our goodbyes to the family, we were on our way. We walked and walked. The distance to Kirkenes seemed to increase rather than getting shorter. The German traffic didn't bother us too much, but as the day wore on our stops became more frequent.

At Storskog, about half way to Kirkenes we had a proper break, and visited relations who offered us food and let us rest. Sonja and I played in the garden with their daughter Aase, while Mother talked to her parents. All too soon we had to be on our way again, much to the chagrin of us children who would have liked to stay.

With blisters on our feet, after many hours of walking, we arrived home, tired and exhausted. Father, who was not expecting us, exploded.

"Have you taken leave of your senses?" he shouted. "You know how dangerous it is on the roads now, and the situation here in the town is getting worse, not better!"

"I had to get back to see how Aase is getting on and you too," Mother defended herself.

"Well I am fine and Aase can look after herself," continued my father, not easily mollified. "You were putting our children at risk, and I am not happy about that."

So Mother cried, and Father melted, having to comfort her first, and then we got the hugs we had wanted all along. It was all very unsettling, as this was the first time I can remember Father being angry with my mother.

Presently we sat down to a small meal at the kitchen table. It was lovely to see our father again, but we were very tired, and went to bed in our parents' bedroom while they settled down to talk. After such an exhausting day, we were soon fast asleep.

Aase had not been at home when we arrived, and it was not until the next day that we saw her and her German boyfriend, Peter. Aase was well rounded now, and seemed very happy. She smiled and gave us both a great hug.

"I have missed you," she said, studying us. "You certainly are getting taller, both of you."

Curiously we looked at her stomach which was quite big and heard the word 'pregnant' again, referring to Aase.

"Why do you think her stomach has grown so big?" I whispered to Sonja.

"It's because she is pregnant." Sonja knew more about many things than I did.

"What does 'pregnant' mean?" I persisted.

"It has something to do with her stomach," Sonja replied knowingly in a very low voice. "Perhaps it's because of all the food she gets from the Germans."

Her explanations sounded plausible to me. What else could it be? In those days children were not told about sex or how babies were made and brought into the world; so we were very ignorant. The story was that the stork brought the babies to their mothers, and that was that.

I couldn't wait to see my friends again and my first visit was to Astrid. Her mother was surprised and very pleased to see me when she opened the door.

"Oh, how you have grown!" Her smile was warm and welcoming.

"Astrid has missed you. Come in and tell us about Jarfjord. Did you like it there?"

So I had to tell them about Aunt Aslaug and her cows, and about Elsa the horse, about school, and many other things that we had done in Jarfjord. Astrid listened with great interest, and when I finished she turned to her mother.

"Mamma, I would like to go there too and see all the animals."

"Someday we will," promised her mother fondly. But what we didn't know then, was that Astrid would never have that opportunity.

Astrid had also grown taller as we were still equal in height. Happy to see me again, she showed me toys she had received from the Russian prisoners. There was a pretty little box with a hinged lid, decorated with beautiful carvings, an unusual wooden doll, and a fascinating toy with a bird on a perch. It had two wheels and a long wooden handle. When pushed along the bird bobbed up and down as the wheels made a tapping noise. I have often wondered how the Russian prisoners managed to produce these ingenious and artistic toys, in their often appalling conditions. Perhaps it helped to keep them sane, and gave them a measure of joy to make toys for the children – in exchange for their food parcels.

Astrid told me how she and another girl had a special place at the fence around the camp, where they could not easily be discovered and where they put their little food parcels under the fence.

"Next time we go you can come too," she offered generously. "I am sure your mother will give you some bread for the prisoners." I agreed with great enthusiasm.

My next visit was to Gunhild. We had been away a long time, nearly a year. Her mother opened the door when I knocked.

"Oh, it's you!" She smiled. "Come in, come in. Gunhild is playing with Bjørnar. Let's see if he recognises you."

Bjørnar had learned to walk before we went to Jarfjord – but as a year is a long time in a small child's life, he was shy, hiding behind his mother. Gunhild was happy to see me back again too and we had much to talk about. I had to tell them about Jarfjord and school there, and they talked about the new bomb shelter, Andersgrotta, which was very close to them and, luckily, close to us too. During the coming year we would meet nearly as much in the new tunnel underground as we did above ground. Aunt Camilla was fine they said, and we decided to visit her soon.

Shortage of essential food was now taking its toll, as typhoid, diphtheria, dysentery, and scurvy swept through the population. It was so bad that the Germans put in their own doctors to help. People had to be treated at home, because the hospital and other buildings used as temporary hospitals were full to capacity.

When Mother contracted dysentery, two weeks passed before any doctor came to see her. During that period she lay in bed, very sick with severe stomach pains, only able to drink boiled water. By the time a doctor appeared she was already getting better, apparently due in part to the boiled water. Sonja and I were fine, and so was Aase. But unfortunately, because of the stress he was living under, Father had developed a stomach ulcer. For this reason he was able to get a few eggs or egg powder and a little milk for a short while.

Mass inoculations provided by the Germans to stop the spread of disease came too late for some. Due to vitamin deficiencies, the general resistance to illness was very low. We got repeated injections against diphtheria and typhoid, and were already given vitamin C and B tablets.

Many died in the epidemics. Our next door neighbour tragically lost both his wife and oldest daughter. Their two younger children – who were our friends – were devastated by the loss of their mother and older sister.

During that summer and autumn, the sound of church bells was a constant reminder of yet another funeral about to take place.

The epidemics wreaked havoc in the camps too, where the Russian prisoners suffered terribly, and many of them died. The hard work and absence of care for their welfare were without doubt contributory causes.

In due course Aase's baby arrived – brought by a stork we were told. The stork must have come during the night, because we never saw it.

The baby was a girl, and was given the name Heide Marie, which is a German name – but we just called her Heide. She was lovely, and we all fell for her and loved her. Even Father adored her. Mother was at hand to help Aase and show her how to care for the baby. So life in our house continued changing, with the new baby to care for and look after. When the sirens sounded, my mother grabbed Heide and ran with her and us to the new bomb shelter, Andersgrotta. Aase refused to come. She was not afraid, she said.

The path from Haugen to the new bomb shelter became a lifeline. The large new shelter had three entrances. To get to the nearest one we only had to get out of our house and run down the hill. Gunhild's family used the same tunnel as us, often arriving there at the same time. Astrid's family used one of the other tunnels closer to them.

The tunnels came from three different directions – to benefit as many people as possible – meeting under the square of Haugen. Where they met a large room had been blasted out, in order to set up first aid facilities for people wounded in the air raids. There were toilet facilities too, but considering that Andersgrotta could hold up to 800 people, they were inadequate, to say the least.

As the air raids increased, more and more time was spent there. One day Aase arrived, white faced and in shock. The bombs had fallen so close that she had crawled under the bed when she heard them coming. The explosion had shaken our house and blown out some windows. After that experience, she no longer needed persuasion to come with us to the bomb shelter.

We regularly watched as people were brought in to Andersgrotta, wounded in various ways during the attacks. Many were carried in; some were led in. One day, I observed two Red Cross people coming in through the tunnel with a wounded woman. She looked a mess with one of her eyes bulging out of her head, but she was still able to walk with their help. She lived near us and had, to her cost, chosen to stay home instead of seeking shelter.

While we were sitting out the air raids in the safety of Andersgrotta, we constantly worried about Father. The fire fighters, unfortunately, were not allowed to use the shelters. Mostly they were lucky, but had many close encounters with death. When people were trapped in the basement of a collapsed house or where fires threatened, the firemen were there to help. In close collaboration with the Red Cross and other volunteers they, brought out the wounded and helped to get them to the hospital.

One day, firemen and volunteers had rescued wounded people out of a building. The ambulance was coasting along towards the hospital with the wounded inside, and the volunteers standing outside the speeding vehicle holding on, two on each side. Suddenly, a shell came out of nowhere and exploded 20 to 30 meters behind them. The resulting blast blew the roof off the vehicle and the four helpers off the ambulance. Amazingly, no one was killed or seriously injured, and the ambulance carried on to the hospital undaunted. It was all in a day's work.

The firemen were the unsung heroes of the war. In danger of their own lives they fought the fires, rescued trapped people and saved many lives.

They all deserved medals for their services to the community.

14

The loss of a friend

School started in early September 1943, and my class was assigned to a room above a shop. We were instructed to bring spoons for the daily dose of cod-liver oil. I hated the stuff, and on the first day quietly poured it out under my desk. I was not alone in disposing of the oil in this way. It was, of course, discovered, and after a lecture on the benefits of the oil, we now had to swallow it in front of the teacher. The oil made me feel sick, and the teacher told us to bring a bit of bread to chew after taking the oil.

"It helps," she said. Whether it did or not I am not sure, but for me the thought of getting a spoonful of cod liver oil each morning spoiled going to school.

At the start of the term we were all weighed in turn, and at the age of 8 years and 10 months I was skinny, weighing 21 kilos. The lightest one in the class was a boy a little younger than me who weighed only 18 kilos.

I had not seen Astrid for a few days. They had gone to their summer cabin on the other side of Bøkfjord for the weekend, and usually rowed across the fjord.

Shortly after they had gone, we heard that Astrid was very ill. She had begun to feel ill soon after they arrived at their cabin. When she gradually got worse, a doctor was persuaded to visit her. He diagnosed a stomach upset, gave her some medicine for it and left. But her condition worsened and she died the following day. When the news of her death broke, I wouldn't believe it. Only a couple of days earlier we had played together. My best friend had died? Impossible.

"Astrid can't be dead, Mamma. She wasn't ill when I played with her," I pleaded.

Mother, very serious, set me down in front of her. She had tears in her eyes and swallowed hard before she could speak.

"It is true that Astrid has died and gone to heaven, and you have to learn to accept that. There are so many things which we can't explain. Only God himself knows the answers."

"But I don't want her to be dead," I sobbed, "I want to play with her. She's my best friend!"

Mother's attempts to comfort me didn't help at all as I sobbed my heart out, unable to understand why God would want Astrid in heaven when we all wanted her here!

A member of their family approached us, and asked if I had been with Astrid before they rowed across the fjord. It had been discovered that she had eaten dried fish with rat poison on it, and if I had tasted the same fish I might also be affected. Luckily for me I hadn't been with Astrid for a few days, so I was fine. Nobody knew where she had found the fish.

Chewing dried fish was quite common when it was available. It was good, and an alternative to the sweeties missing from the shops. The unsalted fish was dried hard as a board and then softened with a hammer or the back of an axe. Pieces of fish were then torn off and eaten.

For Astrid's family it was a terrible blow. Her brother and two sisters were grown up, and they all doted on Astrid. But her mother took it worst of all.

On Astrid's funeral day, our family and other friends were asked to their house before the service in the church. Astrid was lying in a coffin, nicely dressed, with white silk or satin sheets draped around her – her hands folded and eyes closed. Her mother was kneeling in front of the coffin, stroking Astrid's hair, and crying her heart out. To me this was utterly unreal. My friend was dead and still; yet her hair moved when stroked by her mother!

I had never seen a dead person before and instinctively wanted to get away from there, but my mother held onto me as we filed passed the coffin, stopping for a few moments to say goodbye to Astrid.

After the service, when we were all gathered at the graveside, and the coffin was lowered into the grave, Astrid's mother could not take any more and broke down. Crying hysterically, she tried to leap into the grave after her daughter. Luckily, her son and husband managed to restrain her before she could jump in. By then everybody was crying and very upset.

Death had just been a word before, something that happened to other people, but now it had reached out and touched us all. Holding on to Father's hand for dear life, speechless and crying, Sonja and I just stood and watched, while Mother and some other women tried to comfort Astrid's mother.

This was the first time I had attended a funeral, and to date I have never attended one more emotional than that of my friend Astrid. For as long as I could remember, I had been playing with her – and I found it very difficult to accept that I would never see her again. Astrid was missed for a very long time, and never forgotten.

In the following years Astrid's mother always stopped when she saw me and wanted to talk – no doubt I reminded her of the daughter she lost so tragically. Many years later, she gave me a photo of Astrid and me standing by the fence outside their house during the war. She had it enlarged and framed, giving it pride of place on their sitting room wall.

Bad news had reached my father from Lofoten. Kurt Vian, a son of his oldest brother Peder, had been arrested almost a year earlier, and Father had only now heard about it. As a result of his activities, Kurt had first spent time at Grini in Oslo, a notorious prison where torture was routinely used to get prisoners to talk. There he had encountered two future prime ministers of Norway, Einar Gerhardsen and Trygve Bratteli, both imprisoned. They were all sent to concentration camps in Germany. We didn't know it at the time, but Kurt ended up in

Sachsenhausen concentration camp. Father didn't know any details, but I overheard his discussion with Mother.

"I wonder what happened. Was he betrayed or was he unlucky enough to be discovered?"

"Who knows? It could be any of those things. I do hope he hasn't been hurt." My mother was very concerned.

"Chances are that he has already been tortured, since he was sent on to Germany," said my father gloomily. "I wish it was possible to speak to Peder."

Unfortunately, he was unable to establish contact with his brother at that time. Communications were unsafe to use, and letters got lost. Sonja and I wondered what activities our cousin had been up to, and asked Father. His face took on the 'I am not happy with you' expression.

"You hear too much, things you shouldn't hear. I want you to promise me not to mention this again. It is too dangerous, and could land us all in big trouble. Understood?" We both nodded vigorously.

The loss of my long time childhood friend Astrid was difficult to get used to. During school term that autumn, however, I made two new friends, Kirsten and Berit, who were both in my class. Kirsten in particular took over where Astrid was missing. We got on very well, and spent as much time together as possible.

A young girl who had been Kirsten's friend had just died in the epidemic. She was to be buried in the graveyard at the outskirts of Kirkenes. The service would take place in the chapel at the graveyard. Kirsten talked me into going with her to the chapel the day before the funeral to see the body. The weather was pleasantly warm and sunny for the time of year.

"I want to see her before she is buried," Kirsten said, "and I don't want to go alone; besides, Berit refuses to come with me."

I was astounded. "Are we allowed to go there?"

"I don't know, but nobody needs to know. I know that the door to the basement where she is kept is open, and if there is no one around, we can slip in unnoticed."

I was not keen to see a dead body at all, especially with Astrid's death freshly in my mind, but did not want to show that I was afraid either. Reluctantly I agreed, quietly hoping that someone would stop us going in to the chapel.

Amazingly, the door to the basement was open, with nobody in sight. Cautiously, we moved through the door into the semi-darkness of the basement. Three or four bodies were lying on slabs, covered with light green sheets. I felt a chill down my spine and stopped. Kirsten, however, moved from body to body, lifting the sheets which covered their faces and putting them back again, till she found the girl she was looking for. She turned and beckoned me to come closer. The girl looked as if she was asleep. She was about our age or slightly older, with dark curly hair.

Standing there with Kirsten, surrounded by dead bodies, was utterly unreal. I felt nauseated and afraid and couldn't wait to get out.

"I am going," I whispered. "Are you coming?" She nodded, and after carefully putting the sheet back over the dead girl's face followed me out. This was one of the most bizarre things I had ever been involved in, but Kirsten had been able to see her friend for the last time, and had tears in her eyes when we left.

I missed Astrid terribly. However, as the days and weeks passed, I began to spend more time with Kirsten. Our friendship grew, and as Kirsten had lots of books, we often sat in her room reading about Nancy Drew – a young girl who solved crime mysteries. Knowing my parents attitudes to books, I didn't dare to bring any of them home.

On the way back from school one day, Kirsten wanted me to follow her home.

"We can read one of the Nancy Drew books this afternoon," she said, persuasively.

Of all her books, these were my favourites.

"Oh yes, I will come for a little while," I said giving in to the temptation of 'Nancy Drew', also knowing that I should go home first.

We went right up to Kirsten's room and, without thinking to let her mother know that we were there, pulled a blanket around us and lost ourselves in 'The Nancy Drew Mysteries' – forgetting all about time reading this exciting book.

In the meantime, our families became worried when we didn't return home after school. They went around to all our known friends first. Sonja was sent to Kirsten's house, but her mother said she had not seen us either. She too was worried at our absence. Anne Marie, Kirsten's older sister, was sent out to join in the search for us which was extended to cover most of the town. In desperation, Kirsten's mother thought she would look upstairs in her daughter's room just to make sure. She opened the door – and there we were – wrapped up in a blanket reading, completely unaware of the troubles we had caused.

I was marched home by my mother, who was relieved that we were found, but also angry at the worry we had caused them. However, Mother liked Kirsten and her family, and didn't stop me going back there in spite of having found out about 'Nancy Drew'. She must have realised that the books we read were harmless enough. Many afternoons after school (after reporting home first) were spent reading in Kirsten's room. My interest in mystery books and thrillers must have started right there, reading 'The Nancy Drew Mysteries'. In time I discovered Agatha Christie, who became one of my favourite authors.

One afternoon, after a relatively quiet period, the air raid sirens started up while we were sitting on Kirsten's bed reading. I jumped up, raced down the stairs and out the door while Kirsten's mother shouted after me:

"Bjarnhild, come back here this minute! You must come with us to the shelter!"

It fell on deaf ears. There was only one thought in my mind: Home! So I ran. By this time I was a very fast runner, no longer easy to catch. I heard more shouts as I ran down Storgata (the big street), rounded the corner of the next street which was 'Carl Lund's gate', ignoring shouts of "get to the shelter", and sped along, passing a large blue building on the corner of the Pasvik road, running towards the small hill that would take me to Haugen where we lived.

However, crossing the Pasvik road I heard planes approaching, many planes. I continued running. The noise from a bomb explosion reached me – probably at the harbour – amid more noise from anti-aircraft guns and planes. I dived into the nearest ditch, where I curled up with my fingers in my ears, sobbing with fear. When the noise grew more distant, I was on my feet again, running uphill. I could taste blood in my mouth, either from the running or from biting my lips. As I was nearing the last stretch for home, the noise from aeroplanes and shooting suddenly increased, becoming very loud and very close.

Uncertain what to do, I stopped and looked up. I froze. A battle between German and Russian planes was going on in the sky above me. I could see the bullets like little lights flying between the planes. By now I was petrified. I could not move, nor breathe. I was so terrified that I didn't even try to protect myself. And as I stood there, watching the battle in the sky, two planes directly above me were circling each other quite low, engaged in a dogfight, with lots of angry little bullets like fireworks flying between them. This continued until suddenly, one of the planes was hit across the wing and, as if in slow motion, it folded, broke in two and began to fall.

The broken plane was coming directly at me, or so I thought. That got me going. Filled with renewed terror I turned, running in the opposite direction, squinting up now and again to see how near the plane was to me. When I realised it was not going to hit me, I stopped again and watched as the plane spun round and round and disappeared from view.

As it was spiralling down, a parachute was slowly descending, also disappearing from view. An explosion and a column of smoke on the outskirt of the town was the inevitable end of the fighter plane.

I never knew whether it was a Russian or a German plane being shot down that day, or what became of the man in the parachute.

15

Mixed Blessings

Our dear little Heide was growing. We played with her, and loved holding her, while she responded with smiles and funny baby talk. Sonja often took her out in the pram for a walk around the square, where the other children soon gathered around to admire her.

Peter, Heide's father, liked to sing, dance and play the accordion. When he was in the house, he often entertained Heide with German songs as he step danced around the floor with her. Sonja and I were delighted, forgetting that he was supposed to be 'the enemy'.

One day Peter had come for a visit. He was very serious, and not his usual self. Aase was at work in the laundry. Little Heide was lying in her cot without a nappy, and wouldn't stop crying. Peter suddenly got up and grabbed her. Putting her over his knees, he started smacking her bottom. Sonja and I were shocked. The poor little girl was only a few months old!

But Peter hadn't counted on a grandmother's fury. Mother snatched the baby from him and put her back in her cot. Grabbing the fire poker, she attacked Peter with it, and chased him out of the house, telling him never to come back. Backing out of the door, as he was trying to avoid Mother's fire poker, Peter was pleading:

"Nein nein, mutti mutti, nein!" But my mother kept swiping the poker at him, till he turned and ran.

Sonja and I tried to comfort Heide, but without success, until Mother put away the fire poker and took over.

Sonja was very impressed.

"Did you see Mamma?" she said to me afterwards. "Attacking a German soldier is dangerous; she might get arrested."

"Yes, but he shouldn't have smacked Heide." That Mother might get arrested again was a frightening thought – but Peter should not have smacked a small baby. To our great relief no one came to arrest Mother, and we gradually began to relax.

What Aase said about it when she came home is long forgotten. On his return to our house after this incident, however, I do remember seeing a loaf of bread flying through the air, hitting Peter on his head. Observing this, I thought how very foolish she was, throwing around food that we needed to eat! Couldn't she have used a stone instead? My mother was not amused at seeing him back and kept a close eye on him. But he was Heide's father and as long as he didn't smack Heide again she tolerated him, and he, in turn, had learned to respect her.

During this period Aase and Peter had fallen out again. Peter was marching around the house waving his pistol and shouting. Aase ran upstairs to get away from him but he followed her. More shouting, then Aase came flying down the stairs.

"Mamma, take Heide and the other two and get out fast," she urged in a whisper. "He is threatening to shoot us all! Go now and try to get help. I will head him off."

She was on her way up the stairs again and as Mother grabbed Heide, Sonja and I were already running out the door and across to the neighbours.

Few private houses in Kirkenes had telephones at that time. Luckily, the Johnsons' next door had one. It was essential for their son Arnold's involvement with the Red Cross. One of them rang the police, who in turn contacted the German police. They sent two of their own military policemen to arrest Peter. He was relieved of his gun, put in jail for a few days and told to stay away from us – but after some time had gone by, he was back again.

Living in such close proximity with the Germans year after year had its inevitable consequences. People were forced to adapt and co-exist with the foreign soldiers as best as they could. The Germans attended local dances and functions and even used the local saunas.

Quite a few young women in Kirkenes fell for the soldiers, and some of them got pregnant. A friend of Aase had a German lover who was the father of her baby. This soldier was said to be very jealous and possessive. In a fit of jealous rage one night he drew his pistol and shot her dead, then turned the gun on himself and pulled the trigger – leaving the baby an orphan. Perhaps battle fatigue played a large part in this incident, as it may have done with Peter, when he smacked Heide and later threatened to shoot us all. This episode a deep impression on us, and perhaps especially on Aase.

Shortages became acute. When Sonja and I grew out of our shoes, rubber boots had to take over. By the time I inherited Sonja's shoes, they were quite worn. My father had turned shoemaker – repairing our footwear as best as he could – using an iron last shaped like a foot. Occasionally he got so frustrated that a shoe landed on the wall with a thump, accompanied by some unrepeatable swear words. Mother, Sonja and I were shocked. After all, this was not what we did in our family! We prayed to God for his help and guidance and for forgiveness, didn't we? But I didn't dare suggest prayers to solve our problems. Prayers were becoming a thing of the past, except at bedtime if we were at home rather than in Andersgrotta. Father, of course, was under unbearable strain, at home, at work, and as a fire fighter.

Luckily for us, Mother was a good seamstress. She was self-taught in the art of sewing and had a good hand-sewing machine. Electric sewing machines belonged to the future. She let out seams and let down hems to make our clothes last as long as possible. When they wore out, she bartered. As far as I can remember everybody bartered and borrowed. Coats and jackets for Sonja and me were made from old clothes, acquired through bartering. Old curtains and flour bags became dresses and skirts.

Mother constantly repaired and patched up Father's clothes too. The wool from old jumpers was unravelled and made into hats, scarves, and mitts, as well as socks. She was continuously fighting to keep our clothes in order and to keep us warm; while Father's department was our footwear, as well as keeping us fed. Our life was turning into a struggle for survival.

The uneasy relationship between Father and Aase continued. Poor Mother was caught in the middle, trying to protect her daughter, and at the same time, having to soothe my father and calm him down. Sonja and I felt the strain but were too young to have any input.

Towards the end of 1943 and into 1944, the alarms and bomb attacks increased. At times we lived more in Andersgrotta than at home. Down at the seafront below Haugen, the Germans had built a string of concrete foundations, where they had installed heavy cannons and artillery as part of their defence of "Festung Kirkenes". They had also set up a watch tower there, to detect approaching enemy planes. The tower had a mast with three lights above each other. From the landing at the entrance to our house, we had a clear view of the tower. When the lights were green it meant all clear, but when the lights turned red we made for the bomb shelter, as the alarm was sure to follow.

Snow and full moon meant 'bombing weather', and keeping an eye on the lights. Under these conditions we kept our clothes on, lying on top of our beds ready to run – and when the alarms sounded, or the lights turned red, we were off at full speed.

If the planes came in over the town unobserved and started bombing, we were at their mercy, lying on the floor listening to the whistling of bombs coming down, hoping and praying that they wouldn't hit us.

I would lie there with fingers in my ears, not daring to breathe, engulfed in a rising panic, threatening to choke me. Along with the explosions came the sound of the sirens, mixed with an enormous feeling of relief that the bombs had fallen elsewhere and not on us. Then, as the noise died down, we were up and out the door, running for the safety of the bomb shelter once more.

Heide was growing and getting bigger. Sonja and I enjoyed playing with her as often as possible. The schools were more often closed than open now, thanks to the constant attacks. We were told that if we were not out of the shelters and sleeping by 2am, it was not necessary to attend school the next day. This was a sensible decision, as we were often too tired and exhausted.

I have no idea to this day what we learned that winter of 1943 – 44. I am sure the teachers did their best in the face of impossible odds. We were often hungry because of food shortages. My mother did her best with her meagre rations. I would arrive home after playing with some of my friends, to the rancid smell of fried cod liver oil when I opened the outside door. This dreadful smell compelled me to back out very quietly, and to stay away for a long time until dinner was well and truly past.

Well, who could enjoy turnips fried in cod liver oil for dinner? Or herring soup or anything else my mother dreamed up. So I stayed away as long as I possibly could. I was skinny but not ill. The shortages didn't harm me at all.

However, when Mother made herring soup, I couldn't get out of eating it. It was made with salt herring and barley, or oats if barley was unavailable. If I didn't come home for dinner the 'Soup' was waiting for me, and this time I was in for it. The plate was put before me, and stayed there for however long it took to eat it. No pleading or tears helped. To say that every mouthful was a milestone is putting it mildly. Mother, however, was adamant.

"You have to have some nourishment if you are going to survive," she often said.

But I was thinking quietly to myself that if the bombs didn't kill me, Mother's 'Soup' might surely do it instead.

Real coffee was sorely missed. As there was none to be had, people made 'coffee' from grains or dried peas, which were roasted on the frying pan till they had the desired brown colour. They were then brewed with hot water and served as coffee. It couldn't have been very good, but was regularly consumed nevertheless. To ease the pain of little or no tobacco, men collected cigarette stumps from the streets (left by the Germans), opened them to take out what was left and were then able to roll a cigarette. Plain brown paper was often used as cigarette paper. Women did not smoke at that time, or at least I never saw them smoking.

Allowances on the rationing cards did not go very far. We had to queue for everything we needed, often for hours. By the time our turn came most things were sold out, especially if one was at the end of the queue. Sonja was often sent to stand in the queues, as I was considered too young and Mother didn't always have time herself. Sonja, understandably, didn't like having to do this, but had to do what she was told.

Soap was in short supply too, and the only kind we could get was called B-soap. It had a dirty greyish white colour and didn't foam. Nobody liked this soap, but it was all that was available, and was used for everything, including clothes washing. Many people started to make their own soap by boiling caustic soda and any fat they could get. The result was said to be better than the despised B-soap.

The acute shortage of flour also showed how resourceful people could be. Potatoes were scrubbed clean, but not peeled, and put in a basin of water. They were then grated into the water, where the starch sunk to the bottom and the skin floated to the top. When the water was poured off, potato starch was left in the bottom. This was put into a pillowcase or a large piece of cloth, the water squeezed out, and the potato starch spread out on a flat surface to dry. The quality of this flour was very good, and although it was not suitable for bread making, it had many other uses in cooking. With the consistency of corn flour, it was also widely used on babies' bottoms, as talcum powder was unavailable. When Heide's nappies were changed, this was what mother and Aase used.

Mother mixed bread dough in a wooden 'trough' which Father had made for her. It was carved from a tree trunk and resembled a dug out boat with a flat bottom. Unfortunately the flour available in the shops was heavy and had a greyish colour.

"I would like to know what this flour is made of," I often heard my mother say while mixing the dough. "It is hopeless to bake with."

She used sour dough, as I suppose yeast was not readily available. After mixing the dough, Mother covered it with a towel and put it aside until the next day. When it was baked in the oven and the bread rose, an empty space often developed under the crust on the top. The bread underneath was clammy and not particularly good.

Potato shortages were acute at times, and turnips had to take their place. There were turnips with salt fish, turnips with herring, fried turnips and boiled turnips. In wintertime the turnips froze, and when potatoes became available again they were often frozen as well.

AS Sydvaranger, the iron ore company did its best to look after their workers. When possible, the Company bought large quantities of dried fish for standby. At certain times I remember going there with my mother, queuing for black syrup and milk powder, which the Company had managed to secure for its workers.

The Company was like a father and mother of the work force. Its main concern till the end of the war was the protection and well-being of the workers and their families.

16

Father's helmet

The sound of air raid sirens was as inevitable as getting up in the morning. That is to say, if one hadn't already spent the whole night in the bomb shelter.

Without fail the firemen were out tackling the fires as best as they could. Father, like all volunteers, had both his job at the Company and the work as a fire fighter to attend to. If the water mains were damaged by exploding bombs, sea water had to be used instead, which was both time consuming and labour intensive.

The men suffered from lack of sleep, burns, shrapnel wounds, and at times shell shock. In winter, getting wet was a hazard, as their clothes froze solid. Many of the men were arrested. The Germans needed very little excuse to put them in jail for a few days or more, possibly as an example or a warning. That they survived was in no small measure due to their own ingenuity. Because they were banned from entering the shelters during attacks, they had dug themselves a trench near the fire station where they could shelter when an attack was in progress. Mother reckoned that they were saved by a divine power. When quizzed about it she simply said that God was looking after them.

Aunt Reidun had come back from Jarfjord with Ruth and Odd to visit Uncle Edvard. Seeing how badly our lives were interrupted by the air raids, they spent the nights in our house to be close to Andersgrotta. We were delighted to see our cousins again – and however busy Father was, he still found time to have fun with Ruth. They were all charmed by little Heide and admired her.

"I wish we had a baby to play with too," Ruth said longingly, holding on to Heide's little hand.

Aunt Reidun laughed. "But we have you," she exclaimed.

"I am not a baby," Ruth said indignantly, as Sonja and I got a fit of the giggles.

Aunt Reidun ignored us.

"We shall return to Jarfjord shortly. This is far worse than when we left. I don't know how Margit can stand it."

Mother was frowning. "Her work at the hospital is important, Reidun. That is why she doesn't want to leave."

We seldom saw Aunt Margit now as she worked long hours at the hospital.

One morning, after having spent the whole night in the bomb shelter, we arrived home, tired and hungry. As Mother opened the outside door, the rise and fall of many singing voices flowed from our kitchen. We looked at each other, wondering what was going on. Forbidden under German rule, it turned out to be the Norwegian national anthem greeting us that morning!

The most amazing sight met us as we filed through the door. About half a dozen fire fighters were standing around a zinc bath tub, (none too sober) as they were singing the national anthem. They had 'rescued' as many bottles of spirits as they could carry, from a German depot which had taken a hit from a bomb. Most of the bottles were damaged, and Mother's pillow cases were being used to strain the contents into the bath.

Aunt Reidun and Uncle Edvard burst out laughing and Mother, trying to keep a straight face, was saying:

"You should not be drinking this," and "you could be arrested for singing the anthem, you know."

Father was not having that, and poured out drams for my aunt and uncle. Mother, however, refused as she did not like alcohol. Sonja and I were speechless. Neither of us could remember seeing our father drinking alcohol before!

In the meantime, I was standing with my back to the wall, and started to fall asleep; the noise and banter in the kitchen fading away as I slid down the wall, and ended up sitting on my father's upturned helmet.

I was dreaming: I had finally got to the toilet needing to pee, and so I peed through my clothes into the helmet. This pleasant dream was suddenly shattered, as the air raid sirens started up again.

Before realising what was happening, I was unceremoniously hauled to my feet and pushed towards the door, while Father put on his helmet – and its content poured down his face.

Roaring with laughter, everybody made for the door again. Father was not amused, grabbing a towel and his gas mask before setting off after the other men. Since there was no time to change, I just had to follow the others, wet as I was, which was very unpleasant.

After that episode I was teased mercilessly, especially by Ruth, who thought this was great fun, and a way of getting her own back for all the times I had brought her home, knowing full well that my father would be there to tease and perform aerial acrobatics with her.

Father was called out regularly to the inevitable fires following the air attacks. This now took precedence over their normal work at the Company, and was understood and accepted. Danger was their constant companion.

One day, during an air raid, some of the firemen were ordered to a German installation which was in flames after having taken a direct hit. As they were driving along, the whine of a shell reached them, seconds before it exploded on the road ahead. Keeping their heads down and skirting around the hole in the road, they moved along as fast they could towards the burning buildings. The Germans were rattled, running around shouting out conflicting orders, whilst the firemen were trying to get on with their work.

With the air raid still in progress and the men busy with their hoses, a Russian plane appeared overhead, letting its bomb cargo go, obviously aiming at the buildings the men were working on. The firemen heard them coming, left their hoses and jumped into a nearby bomb crater for protection. The bombs missed the German installations and fell on very stony ground above and about 20 to 30 metres away from the men. Apart from being a bit deaf and battered by the shower of stones from the explosions, they were basically unhurt. Again, for the fire fighters, it was all in a day's work.

Aunt Margit was on her way to work at the hospital one morning in late winter or early spring, when she met my father going home after a busy night of fire fighting. He was carrying two or three bottles of spirit, no doubt 'liberated' from one of the fires. As they walked passed one of the houses near Haugen, a man we knew shouted from an upstairs bedroom:

"Bjarne, what is that you are carrying? Is it spirits?"

"Yes," shouted my father.

"Could you give me a bottle?" shouted the man again.

"Yes I will," was the reply. "Just come down here and I shall smash it over your head!"

The window banged shut and Aunt Margit laughed as she turned to Father.

"You shouldn't have said that. The man is a Nazi."

"I know and I couldn't care less. He and his friends have had their own way for far too long. The war will soon be over anyway and then they will all be dealt with."

Luckily for us, nothing more came out of this episode. Years later, the story was related to us by Aunt Margit, who couldn't help laughing at the absurdity of it all.

Before Aunt Reidun went back to Jarfjord with our cousins, the sisters had agreed to meet and make up food parcels once more for the Russian prisoners in the camp nearest to us. Aunt Margit would see what she could scrounge from the hospital, while Mother and Aunt Reidun would pack as much as they could possibly do without. My mother packed salt fish, potatoes and bread. I suggested helpfully that the Russians might like salt herring too. She looked at me and laughed.

"You would like that wouldn't you?" Smiling, she went to the larder for some salt herring to add to the parcel.

Sonja and I wanted to go with them but were told to stay home.

"We don't want to draw attention to ourselves more than necessary."

The plan was that Mother and Aunt Reidun would stroll past the camp, make eye contact with the guard and engage him in conversation. They would position themselves so that the guard had to turn his back to the camp in order to talk to them. Margit would approach the camp from another direction, and if it was safe, throw the three parcels over the fence to the prisoners and move away.

By living in such close proximity to the Wehrmacht for nearly four years, most people spoke some German. German soldiers, like most men, were not averse to female attention, resulting in a certain amount of exploitation as in this case. Mother and her sisters had often practised this approach. It was risky, but when it worked it was an effective way to get food to the prisoners. People used any means they could think of to help, in spite of the risk.

Following an air raid in late winter, Aunt Margit arrived home early one day. She was still living in Aunt Reidun's house. Uncle Edvard was not yet back from his work. She heard a noise and went to investigate. Cautiously moving down the stairs to their basement, she surprised a man trying to hide behind the stairs. She realised immediately that he was an escaping Russian prisoner. Furthermore, she herself was now in grave danger, if the Germans should come into the house looking for him.

Undaunted, my aunt reassured the Russian in his own language that she would help him. The Russian relaxed, and told her that he could no longer stand up to the harsh treatment, but wanted to take his chances by trying to escape. He had seen his chance during the last air raid and chose this house, thinking the people here were friendly. Why else would they leave food parcels in the rubbish bin?

Aunt Margit told him to stay where he was while she checked outside to see if there were German soldiers around. There was some activity, but not close by. The Germans were sure to make a house to house search as soon as they discovered that one prisoner was missing.

She told to the Russian to come up, gave him some of Uncle Edvard's clothes and a pair of boots and socks. Hurriedly she put as much food as she could find in a bag, while keeping an eye out the window to check on the German movements. She drew a map showing him where the border was and where he should go. The story would be that, if he got caught, he would say that he had broken into the house, stealing what he needed and slipping away. Aunt Margit would say that there must have been a break-in before she got home, but that she hadn't noticed anything as none of her clothes were missing. She told the Russian to memorise the map before she burned it, making sure that nothing could be traced back to her. She also told him in which direction to go, and where he might be able to hide. He was very grateful.

It was getting dark now and my aunt wanted him to be gone before the Germans discovered that one prisoner was missing. She went outside again to make sure that the coast was clear, waved to the Russian to come out and pointed him in the right direction. With a last 'spasibo' he was gone.

Uncle Edvard was the only one to be told about the incident at the time. Unfortunately, we never found out whether the Russian prisoner made it to his own lines or was captured.

Aunt Margit came to visit Mother one day in the spring of 1944. She was not her usual jolly self. Speaking in a low voice, she said she was concerned about her son Kåre.

"I have not heard anything from him for months. I am so afraid for him. He can be too trusting and often reckless."

"What will you do?" Mother asked, very concerned.

"I think I will travel back to Narvik to see if I can find him," Aunt Margit replied. "I can't just sit here and do nothing."

"I understand how you feel, but you know that the coastal steamers are not running. You might of course be able to go on the small local vessels, possibly even as far as Narvik. Come and see me before you go."

"Of course I will." Aunt Margit was ready to leave.

Little did we know that Kåre was already a wanted man, hiding from the Gestapo, and that his days of freedom were numbered.

17

Does Jesus love the Germans too?

Although my friendship with Kirsten was developing, I also spent time with my new friend Berit. The daylight hours were getting shorter, as winter approached. After the 20th November the sun would not be seen again for two months, giving us only about two hours of pale daylight each day in mid-winter.

One afternoon Berit and I were out with her push sledge making our way up Storgata (the Big Street), planning to visit Kirsten. The sky was dark and cloudy – definitely not bombing weather.

Halfway up the street we met a German officer carrying a large box. He pointed at his box and our sledge, asking if we would let him put his box on the sledge and bring it to his quarter. We knew enough of the German language to understand what he was asking. Not daring to refuse, we nodded and he put his box on our sledge, noticeably relieved at not having to have to carry it any further. The box was heavy, but not difficult for us to push along on the hard packed snow.

As we made our way to the barracks where he lived, he kept up a running commentary in German to which we either nodded or shook our heads. He was very friendly and said 'Danke schön' upon arrival at his quarters, took his box and asked us to wait. Puzzled we waited, hoping secretly that perhaps he might give us 'bonbon'. Presently he came out with a parcel for us to share as a thank you for helping him. We of course smiled, said 'Danke schön' and left.

Excited did not quite describe how we felt. We were ecstatic, and couldn't get back to Berit's house fast enough. Berit's mother, a tall, homely woman with her hair rolled up in a bun at the neck, was very pleased when she opened the parcel to reveal its contents. The sweeties that we had hoped for were missing. Instead, a large leg of ham was the German's gift to us. Real food!

"How wonderful!" Berit's mother was smiling at us, clearly delighted. "And I had been wondering what to cook for dinner today. It was very generous of the German to give you a whole leg of ham."

Berit and I felt very proud of ourselves that we had been able to contribute food for their dinner. After all food was very important, and a constant topic of conversation.

"Half of it is yours to take home," she said to me, as she started cutting the ham in two.

I was already wondering what Mother would say. We didn't eat pork at that time. The Adventist church considered eating pork a 'Sin'. I said nothing about this to Berit's mother as I accepted the parcel she made up for me.

"Perhaps you should go home with it now," she suggested. "Your mother may want to cook it today."

On my way home I was really hoping that Mother would cook it. It looked and smelt very nice, and would be such a lovely change from our ordinary diet. But my mother said very little when I arrived home with the ham. She took it and put it away, cutting short any discussion about the meat. I have no idea what became of the nice piece of ham, but it never reached our dinner table. Instead, it was boiled salt fish or herring soup as usual!

The war was not going well for the Germans. News reached us somehow, even without the radios. German officers lodging in local homes had radios. When they were out, those who dared would take a chance, pop in and switch on the radio while the wife or husband kept watch, in case the officer should return unexpectedly. Secret agents working for the Russians also passed on information so, one way or another, news of the war filtered through.

The siege of Leningrad was still going on. Russian workers, termed 'Ost arbeiter' by the Germans, had arrived at Høibuktmoen airport. Their homes had been burned and their animals slaughtered. Young and old, men, women and children had been taken by force from the districts around Leningrad. Buildings to house them had hastily been constructed at the airport.

The first consignment of about 700 people had arrived towards the end of 1943. Old people and children as young as seven had to help clearing away snow at the airport.

Kalle Wara and his Norwegian friends, still forced to work for the Germans, wondered how they might help these unfortunate families from the east. By keeping a close eye on the fishing boats which arrived with fish for the Germans, they got their chance. (If there was surplus fish, the Norwegian workers were often allowed to buy some). One day they were able to secure a whole box of fish. As the new arrivals were poorly guarded, the fish was duly smuggled into the Russian camp at night, to the surprise and delight of its new inhabitants.

The prisoners of war were a different matter. Captured in battle after the invasion of Russia started, they suffered unbearable misery at the airport, where the allocated mass grave was filling up. Helping them was almost impossible. However, in danger of losing their entire workforce, the Germans decided to increase the prisoners' rations, as well as allowing them a bath twice monthly. This led to a gradual improvement in their condition.

The Germans seemed to have a thing about arresting people. The men in the fire brigade never pleased them, and the firemen took turns at sitting in jail for some mischief, real or imagined. Our next door neighbour, the fire chief, was put in jail for a whole month, after protesting against the harsh treatment of the firemen. Father frequently came home exasperated, talking to Mother about it. Sonja and I couldn't help overhearing what they were saying, but were warned to keep our mouths shut.

"The bombs that fell at the German bomb shelter yesterday killed

75 German soldiers," Father said one day. "Unfortunately one of the firemen at the scene has been talking about it and was arrested today. It is not safe to say anything at all."

"What will happen to the fireman?" Mother asked.

"I am not sure, but chances are that he will be in jail for a while."

"I hope they will not arrest you too," she said worriedly. "Do be careful."

"I'll watch my step, but nobody is safe, as you well know."

The parents of one of my classmates had recently been arrested and sent south.

"My belief is that they will be sent to Germany," Father said, with a grim look on his face.

My mother was aghast. "Oh no, surely not," she whispered.

"Oh yes. They are accused of being communists and helping partisans. That carries a death sentence, if it can be proved. You know Borghild, that all the things we believed in are disintegrating, and suffering is everywhere – the treatment of prisoners is unbearable to watch, and we are unable to ease their pain and hunger."

Mother was very sad too. "I am afraid that we don't pray enough anymore. Let us pray for them and Kurt, and all the prisoners who are suffering."

I had noticed the lack of praying lately. That night, however, the four of us knelt down to ask God to look after the prisoners and all those who suffered, and to help us get through the war.

Gunhild came around looking for me again, standing outside shouting my name as usual.

"Oh, go and see what she wants." Mother was preparing the dinner.

"Can I go out to play with her?"

"You can, but go to the shelter if the alarm goes. I don't want you to be away too long, and come home for dinner."

"What's for dinner, Mamma?" I asked innocently.

"It has to be herring soup today." She looked at me suspiciously.

"Don't think that you are getting out of eating it," she said sternly.

I said nothing and started to get dressed. Mother insisted that I put on extra clothes, which I did under protest. As I left the house to play with Gunhild, I was hoping that the 'Soup' would be finished by the time I got back. Talking about it to Gunhild later, she said sympathetically that her mother might give me dinner.

We decided to visit Aunt Camilla, as I had not seen her since before we went to Jarfjord. Aunt Camilla was pleased to see us.

"It is a long time since I saw you," she said to me. "How you have grown! Come in, come in."

As usual she had to pick up things from her chairs so that we could sit down. Nothing had changed in her house. It was as I remembered it, comfortably cluttered, with velvet covered cushions on her sofa, and many pretty things to look at. To get around in her sitting room was as before, an obstacle course – one always had to move something out of the way.

"Jesus said that you would come," said Aunt Camilla. "I have kept a small piece of cake for you."

How Aunt Camilla managed to have even a small piece of cake when nobody else had cake was a mystery to us.

"Jesus must be helping her in some mysterious way," I whispered to Gunhild who nodded and whispered back:

"Well, she does speak to him all the time, doesn't she?"

Of course we were delighted to get even a very small piece of cake and a glass of water.

"Jesus tells me that the war will soon be over, and that we shall all survive the war," she announced, beaming at us.

"Are you sure that he knows all these things?" I asked, hoping she was right and that we would survive the war.

"Of course he does, and if you listen, he will speak to you too."

But no matter how hard I tried to listen, he did not speak to me.

"You must be special, since he talks so much to you," I said, as I was savouring the unexpected piece of cake. She was pleased.

"Do you really think so?" she said, and continued "You know Jesus loves us all and wants to look after us."

"Does Jesus love the Germans too?" I ventured.

"Of course he does," said Aunt Camilla, nodding so vigorously that her hair fell down over her face. She had beautiful wavy hair, kept in place on top of her head with a comb.

"But how can he love the Germans when they are so bad to the Russian prisoners?" I was not giving up. "And they arrest people too, all the time."

Aunt Camilla looked at us in silence for a while, trying to pin up her hair again. I began to wish I hadn't asked all those questions, when she started to speak.

"The Lord works in mysterious ways and it is not given to us to know everything. When you grow up you will understand this much better."

It would seem that I had an awful lot to learn and understand when I grew up. The trouble was that I would have liked to know these things now, not many years into the future!

Aunt Camilla had begun muttering to herself, and entered into yet another conversation with Jesus. We listened in silence whilst finishing our cake.

"Come again soon," she said when we departed.

"You shouldn't ask her so many questions," Gunhild said accusingly. "She gets confused."

Aunt Camilla didn't seem very confused to me, but she was special, and we were very fond of her.

Back at Gunhild's house, we played with Bjørnar for a while. He was now a lovely toddler, learning to speak, and we had a lot of fun with him.

"Bjarnhild's mother is making herring soup for dinner," Gunhild informed her mother, who also knew that I hated herring soup.

She smiled at me. "Today we are having some boiled salt fish for dinner, and there is enough for you too," she said looking at me.

"Oh yes, please," I responded with delight. Anything was better than Mother's 'Soup'. So I stayed for dinner, and had a fine time as usual in their house.

Peter came and went, visiting Aase and Heide. Not many Germans came to our house now. They were either killed or wounded at the front or too busy with the war to come to people's houses.

"The less we see of them the better," was Father's favourite saying.

Heide was growing, and a delight to have in our house. We all adored her. Sonja and I played with her as much as we could, and she just beamed at us and laughed happily when we made faces at her.

We didn't go to the Adventists' meetings anymore. Our parents were too stressed to go, or so they said. I missed the meetings with the Bible stories, prayer sessions, and friendly atmosphere, which had been the only constant activity as far back as I could remember. But our old way of life had gone, replaced by a sinister and dangerous existence that was equally hard for adults and children.

At the Company, the iron ore production had stopped sometime in 1942, perhaps because of the many bomb attacks, but the word was that it would soon start up again. Work, however, carried on as usual, except for the 'faults' that developed to slow down any work in progress. This kind of sabotage had to be cleverly done to avoid suspicion. A general 'go slow' was also practised but never spoken about.

To brighten up our lives, the older children occasionally put on concerts in their parent's sheds. On Haugen, it was the older girls who dressed up, 'performing' their songs, and wiggling around trying to look grown-up. It was very popular and cost us five or ten øre (probably about a penny).

At Saga, where Aunt Reidun lived, the older boys stood for the entertainment. My cousin Odd, the Pederson brothers next door and others were the performers. They were more adventures than the girls, and had scrubbing boards, pan lids and spoons, to accompany their songs.

We paid the same fee for their performance, and were only allowed to go if their concert were held during a quiet period. Some of the songs were made up by the boys themselves, trying to make fun of the enemy. These entertainments were very popular, and made life a bit easier for the children.

Olsen, one of my father's workmates, had a dog called 'Spørran' meaning 'Ask him'. This led to some hilarious situations. If asked, "What's his name?" The answer was 'Spørran'. Some people got angry, accusing Olsen of taking the mickey.

Olsen was a keen fisherman, possessing several fine fishing rods. He also liked a party. One day some of his close friends had gathered in his kitchen with 'Spørran' in attendance. Each had brought a bottle or two of their own variety of home brew. A zinc bath was sitting in the middle of the floor and all was poured into the bath. Some 'liberated' German liquor may well have been added to spice it up. The required number of cups was put into the liquor, whereupon the men squatted around the bath with a fishing rod each and started 'fishing'.

First they had to hook a cup, and then serious drinking could begin, as they fished out the cups and filled them time and again. They all stood as they drank a toast to King Haakon of Norway , at present residing in England; then it was a toast to the Allied forces, to our Russian neighbours and, last but not least, a toast to 'Spørran', who was tripping around the floor, tail wagging, as he looked at the spectacle before him.

It has to be said that Olsen was a widower and had no wife to put a stop to such 'silliness' as Mother said when she heard of it. Father just kept laughing when he was telling us the story, and how a neighbour had come in to find the 'fishermen' in various stages of drunkenness.

"What if they had been caught in an air raid?" Mother asked.

"I suppose in their state, they were past caring," Father replied, trying not to laugh any more, since Mother was not amused.

18

Time is running out

The long, light days of spring were approaching, and our time spent in Andersgrotta increased accordingly. The midnight sun was to the Russians' advantage and they made full use of it. A cloud of apprehension and fear hung in the air, as if people knew that the final showdown between the two great armies was near.

To lighten the mood a little, a lot of joking and bantering was going on. A policeman came in to the shelter one day to check on us.

"Are you getting on all right?" he shouted. A chorus of "yes," answered his question.

"Is anyone here pregnant?"

"Yes," shouted somebody from further in through the tunnel.

"For how long?" shouted the policeman.

"About ten minutes!" came the answer, loud and clear.

The place erupted. Everybody was hooting with laughter. Mother and Aunt Margit were wiping tears off their faces as they always did, when they couldn't stop laughing. Because the adults were laughing, the children were laughing too, not really understanding what was so funny.

"Mamma, why are they laughing and who is pregnant?" I enquired, still connecting pregnancy with the stork.

This only brought on more laughter and tears, but no answers, and I was none the wiser, but I resolved to ask Aase when I got a chance.

The Germans began to dig trenches between some of the houses around Haugen and nearby Haganes. This worrying development was discussed in our kitchen one day. Father was frowning.

"Kirkenes is a fortress already; they must mean to take a stand here. What are we going to do?"

"You know that Aslaug and Ragnvald will take us in again."

"I know, Borghild, but the danger is that when the Germans withdraw from the front, they have to come through Tårnet and Karpbukt. The Russians will stop at nothing to catch up with them, and we shall be in the firing line again."

"I want to stay with Aunt Aslaug," I said, knowing that I should not interrupt their conversation, but remembering the comforting presence of her and her family and the animals.

"I want to go too," Sonja said, "then we won't have to spend so much time in Andersgrotta. It is horrible there!"

"Hm," Father said. "If we go to Jarfjord, we shall be in much greater danger than the last time we stayed there."

Finally, the decision was taken to stay in Kirkenes, for the time being.

Sonja and I were bored. The schools were closed, and we had nothing to do but to stay close to the house and wait for the next air raid. The bomb shelter had become our regular meeting place, where we met our friends and attempted to play in any available space.

"Take Heide outside in her pram for a little while. If the alarm goes, take her right down to Andersgrotta." Mother was busy in the kitchen as usual, trying to figure out what to make for our dinner.

Heide was nearly nine months old now. She smiled and did some baby talk when we played with her. She was really lovely, and we adored her.

Two of the girls from a house nearby, who had been playing hopscotch outside their door, came along to talk to Heide and admire her. Heide just beamed at us, stretching out her arms to be lifted up.

"I wish we had a little baby in our house to play with," said Tullemor wistfully.

"So do I," agreed her sister. "But I don't think our mother would want one just now, with the war and bombing all the time."

Moments later, the alarms started up, joined by the sound of fast approaching aircraft. Heide got frightened and started to cry as we ran with the pram towards our house. Unn and Tullemor disappeared, and Mother came running out of the house as the sound of the first explosions reached us. She grabbed Heide, shouted to us to follow and ran into the house. Following close behind her, we got down on the floor where our mother was trying to protect Heide, and Sonja and I crowded in as close to Mother as possible.

The attack had happened so suddenly that we didn't have time to run to Andersgrotta. Instead, we crawled as far as possible in under the kitchen table, hardly daring to breathe. As usual I had my fingers in my ears, trying to shut out that awful noise of cannon fire, aeroplanes and exploding bombs. The attack seemed to go on for ever. When it was all over, we remained on the floor, while Mother thanked the Lord for saving our lives yet again.

Sitting by the kitchen table another day, looking out at the square, I spotted Mrs Hansen, with a saucer in her hand, heading towards our house. She was a tall woman, with her thick hair pinned in a bun at the nape of her neck. She walked in a strange fashion, as if perpetually leaning forwards.

"Fru Hansen is coming to borrow from you again," I informed my mother.

"Oh, not again," she said, "She always needs something."

All the women on the square borrowed from each other, some more than others. There was a knock at the door and Mrs Hansen shuffled in head first, somewhat breathless.

"I am in a hurry in case the alarm goes again," she gulped, trying to catch her breath.

"Oh sit down, Fru Hansen," my mother said. "There's nothing we can do about it anyway. I have just made some coffee. What about a cup?"

Mrs Hansen accepted the invitation and sat down.

"If we survive the war," she started, as Mother busied herself with the coffee cups.

"If we survive the war," she said again, "it should not be necessary to go around borrowing from each other all the time. There is very little to get in the shops now, even with the coupons."

"We are all in the same boat, Fru Hansen, and besides, when this is over, we may not even have any shops left. What will we do then?"

I never knew Mrs Hansen's first name. People were called by their surnames, the women were known as Mrs Whatever and their men were called, as in this case, Hansen, not Mr Hansen.

"What can I help you with this time?" Mother asked.

"If you have any flour, I could do with two or three tablespoons for my gravy," sighed Mrs Hansen.

"I don't have much but I will lend you some." She took Mrs Hansen's saucer and made for the pantry where she kept flour and other things that she couldn't keep in the kitchen.

"Tusen takk" (a thousand thanks), said Mrs Hansen gratefully. "You will get it back as soon as I can get some more on the coupons."

They chatted on about the war for a while, and what they would do if we survived the war. Presently Mrs Hansen said goodbye and left.

"I don't know what to make for dinner today. It has to be salt fish or herring soup. There are no potatoes left either." There was exasperation in my mother's voice.

The thought of herring soup got me going.

"Can I go and see Gunhild, Mamma?" I asked. Gunhild stayed quite close to Andersgrotta. Besides, we might visit Aunt Camilla, I thought. She might give us something nice to eat.

"All right," she answered hesitantly, "as long as you run right to the shelter if the alarm goes."

Luckily, Gunhild was at home, and her mother told me to come in. Gunhild was pleased to get company and brought out a favourite board game. Her little brother toddled up to me with a ball.

"Do you want me to play ball with you?" He just beamed, and the three of us sat on the floor for a while, rolling the ball back and forth, before resuming our board game.

Gunhild's mother was cooking dinner, fried turnips and potatoes.

"Would you like some dinner with us?" she asked.

The thought of herring soup made me accept the offer, even though their dinner was not very exciting either.

After dinner, Gunhild asked her mother if we could visit Aunt Camilla, who stayed right across the road.

"You can go," she said slowly, "but don't stay too long. She might be tired and want to rest. And remember, if the alarm goes, run to Andersgrotta!"

Aunt Camilla opened the door when we knocked.

"Oh it is you two," she said, pleased to see us.

"Jesus said I would get visitors, come in come in." Closing the door behind us, she urged us to sit down, which as usual was difficult as her house was so cluttered. However, Aunt Camilla made room for us by clearing away books from two chairs.

"I can't offer you anything to eat today," she sighed unhappily. "Are you hungry?"

"We have just had dinner," Gunhild told her.

"Oh that's fine." She smiled and sat down, chatting happily about what Jesus told her to do every day, and then asked us what we were doing.

"Jesus says that it will not be long now till the war is over," she told us. "You'll see." She thought for a while, and then continued, "We might have to leave Kirkenes at first, but we will survive and come back."

"How does he know this?" I ventured.

"Because he knows everything. Does he still not speak to you?" We both shook our heads.

"I daresay he does," she said, "but you are not listening to what he is saying." She chatted on, sometimes to us and sometimes to Jesus. After a while she announced that she was tired, and could we come to visit another time? We agreed, and reassured that we would survive the war we departed, having enjoyed the visit even if there was no cake or biscuit to be had.

The herring soup was waiting for me when I arrived home, but as I had already eaten, I escaped the ordeal of eating the 'Soup' that day.

Later in the spring, I was out around Haugen one day, hoping to see some of my friends – when the two alarms in the town started up. The sound of fast approaching aeroplanes, and anti-aircraft guns starting up, added to the tremendous noise of the sirens.

I was already running towards Andersgrotta, when I heard gunfire close by, and felt the air moving as bullets whizzed past the left side of my head.

Frightened, I immediately dropped down flat on my stomach, pausing for a moment before starting to crawl towards Andersgrotta. I didn't dare lift my head, but kept on crawling on my stomach the rest of the way. As the dog fights raged in the skies above, someone was shooting wildly from the trenches nearby. After several pauses, wondering desperately what to do, I finally reached the entrance to Andersgrotta, where a man grabbed me and pulled me inside.

"The Germans are definitely getting rattled; otherwise they wouldn't be shooting so recklessly from the trenches." Father was alarmed at this development.

"They may have been drunk," said Mother, with disgust.

"Or very frightened," Father added. They were really worried. I could so easily have been killed that day. The question of getting out of the town came up again.

"The place is crawling with Germans; it is dangerous everywhere, including the roads," he said, gloomily.

He had to go out again, while Mother busied herself making up a food parcel for our next trip to Andersgrotta. The rest of us huddled together in the kitchen, ready for the next alarm. Aase was still working, but it was clear that she would not be working much longer.

The Germans, who had frequented our house, were absent. They did not have time for visits and Father was delighted. That was the only good thing about our situation, he would say. We seldom saw Peter now, only when he came to visit Aase and Heide. But he was clearly a worried man. Very serious, and speaking rapidly to Aase, as suddenly as he appeared, he was gone.

During June and July, the air attacks increased in ferocity, as wave after wave of Russian aircraft attacked in their hundreds, bombing and shelling German installations, shipping, the towns of Vadsø, Vardø, Berlevåg and others around Varanger fjord, and the East Finnmark coast. The long-range gun batteries at Kibergsneset – not far from our family in Kiberg – were repeatedly attacked. And the attacks continued, as regular as clockwork, day and night.

We practically lived in Andersgrotta now, only coming out for food and a change of clothes. The fear that the adults could no longer conceal rubbed off on us children.

"How long can we survive this relentless war?" and "when will the Allies be here to free us?" were questions often repeated.

19

Homeless and destitute

Rumours of Allied landings in Europe had been circulating. No one knew for sure, but people were hoping and praying that the rumours were true – and that our nightmare existence would soon end.

One day, in early July 1944, hundreds of people had gathered in Andersgrotta, all having moved in as far as possible towards the centre where the three tunnels met. A hushed and fearful silence surrounded us, with only short, whispered exchanges of words.

Suddenly, a tremendous rumble, like thunderclaps, shook the shelter from above – and as the shockwaves were transmitted down through the tunnel, the lights went out. A collective scream erupted, swelling through Andersgrotta, as panic broke out.

I couldn't breathe. I felt faint. Sonja had the same experience. People were pressing from all directions and we couldn't see anything. Luckily, we were close to Mother when the bombs fell on top of us. She managed to push Sonja and me in towards the stone wall, trying to shield us. She was screaming at the top of her voice:

"Stop, stop, stop, will you! You are hurting the children!"

Other mothers joined in, and soon a voice was shouting from the direction of the nearest entrance:

"You are all safe. The entrance is clear, don't panic, calm down, calm down!"

Gradually the noise and panic subsided, but we were all in shock. Sonja and I were crying, as were most children around us. We could hear the sobs and the sniffles, even if we couldn't see anything. Mother held on to us, and managed to get voice contact with Aase, who shouted back that she and Heide were all right.

When finally the all clear was relayed to us later that day, people were guided towards the entrances by guards with torches. Aase and Heide had been closer to the entrance, and hadn't suffered too much when panic broke out.

Stumbling from the darkness of the tunnel into bright sunlight was a blinding, albeit sobering experience. A strong smell of smoke filled the air. Slowly picking our way through rubble up the hill to Haugen, we looked around in disbelief. The Haugen we knew and loved was almost unrecognisable. It was a beautiful summer day, but wherever we turned there were ruined houses and smouldering fires. The destruction seemed to be widespread, with smoke curling and rising from ruins where houses had been.

Our house was still standing, but only just. The house diagonally across the square from us was gone, blown off its foundations. The house across from our kitchen had burned down.

Bergeton Johnsen's house, opposite our main entrance looked as if it had been lifted and twisted on its foundation. Its wall facing the square was gone; the staircase to the second floor was hanging out through the opening at a crazy angle and all the windows were gone, as well as their front door.

Turning her attention to our own house, Mother was muttering to herself utterly shocked,

"Dear Lord what's to become of us?"

Aase put her arm around Mother, and Sonja and I grabbed her hands, trying to comfort her as we studied what was left of our home.

The steps and the landing had disappeared, and the outside door was missing. We walked slowly around the house, which was semi-detached.

The whole house was in a sorry state. Where there had been windows, there were now only gaping holes. The walls were peppered by shrapnel and there were signs of fire having been put out. The Wara house, our first air raid shelter and an important part of our playground, was still standing, but only just. Slowly, we made our way back to our own house. Around us, our neighbours were moving in a daze, just like us, looking at what had been their homes, shaking their heads, not sure what to do next.

After a while Father appeared, dirty and dishevelled. We ran to meet him, sobbing with relief that he was still alive. He had been out with other fire fighters through it all, he said, finding shelter in ditches, bomb craters and behind sheds.

Looking for planks, he soon had a makeshift approach to our house set up. Very carefully, we walked up the planks and into the house.

Stunned, we tried to take in the destruction of our home. The outside door had been torn off its hinges and hurled onto the kitchen door – both had landed on top of the iron stove in the kitchen. A massive hole had replaced the kitchen window. There was no sign of the curtains, only a few minute traces stuck into the torn wood.

The floor was covered by a thick layer of pulverised material, which had been all our dishes and food, and probably the window as well. The kitchen table and chairs, along with rest, had been turned into rubble. One cupboard door, left on the wall and peppered with holes, was swinging slowly from one hinge.

Mother made her way to the pantry, where she kept most of our food. The pantry was situated off the small hallway. The contents there were pulverised as well. Nothing was left to eat or drink, not even one cup intact. The bedrooms were in ruins too. It was as if an army of rats had torn up the bedclothes, with the beds and other furniture destroyed beyond repair. A sideboard with dishes lay face down, with all the dishes broken and the sideboard full of holes. Here too, the windows had gone. Through the partition wall, we could now wave to our neighbours, the Nordhus family. Our upstairs rooms had fared no better.

Had we been in the house when the bombs fell, we would not have survived, Father told us. We were now destitute (that is what Mother said). All we had left was the clothes we were wearing.

"I think Stalin has decided for us," Father said, heavily. "We have to leave now."

Mother was looking at Aase, stroking Heide's hair.

"You have to take Heide and come with us, you know."

"What about Peter?" she moaned.

"What about him?" Father said brusquely. "If it hadn't been for him and his like, we wouldn't be in this situation."

"That is not true!" Aase shouted.

Mother stepped in and stopped what could have developed into an almighty row.

"Shut up Aase, and see what you can find for Heide. I am sure you can get word to Peter that we had to leave."

Sonja and I were told to look for any bit of clothing that was not torn to pieces, while she and my father discussed the next step.

The truth was that there was nothing left intact. But we gathered together the least damaged clothes, and Mother picked out what was possible to mend. Anything at all which might be of use was made into bundles. Father decided to go to the Company to see if he could get some dried fish. The company had stores hidden away for this eventuality.

He brought back dried fish and some dried milk for Heide. The damage to the town, he told us, was enormous. More than one hundred houses were gone, or damaged beyond repair, in just one attack. He didn't know about civilian casualties yet, but many Germans had been killed. Ships in the harbour had been bombed or sunk. German barracks and stores were bombed, but attempts at destroying the heavily built defence batteries had only been partly successful.

"The sooner we leave the better," he urged. "After the tremendous attack on the town earlier today, we should be able to get out of here before another attack follows. I have told the fire fighters and the Company where we are going and, if at all possible, I will be back."

His bicycle in the basement was intact, as was Heide's pram, which had been in Andersgrotta. But before we left, we had a last look around the house, our home for as long as I could remember. Father loaded as much as possible on his bicycle, Aase put Heide in the pram – anything else was put on top of the pram. Mother, as always, held on to her large handbag, where she kept family photos, two Bibles and papers. Sonja and I were given a bundle each to carry.

The midnight sun was at its highest, with twenty four hours of daylight. Escape under cover of darkness was therefore impossible. Ahead of us lay a 24 kilometres long and hazardous walk. But there was no choice, we had to get out.

And so, with our bundles, bicycle and pram the six of us left, joining the exodus of people heading out of town on a nice summer day in 1944, walking into an even more uncertain future.

Some people on the road were pushing carts with their few belongings, such as a mattress, bedclothes, pots and pans. Others had wheel barrows, and many more, like us, who had lost everything, were travelling light.

Father had prepared some of the hard-dried unsalted fish by softening them up with the back of an axe. This makes it possible to tear pieces off the fish to eat, without cooking them first.

On the way to Jarfjord that day, we chewed dried fish and drank water. The fish is actually very good, especially when you are hungry and have nothing else to eat. Even little Heide got a piece to chew on. When we heard the planes coming on their way to Kirkenes, everybody left the road, hiding among the dwarf trees. The Russians, however, didn't bother us at all. Civilians were not their targets.

After a while, the columns of people were thinning out. Many of them were heading off in other directions, to family or friends. Not many were walking the long road to Jarfjord that day. We stopped a few times at different houses along the way, so that Aase could get milk warmed for Heide and change her nappies. This gave us all a chance to rest our legs.

How and when we got to Aunt Aslaug's house in Jarfjord that day, or night, I can't remember, but I do know that we were all exhausted when we arrived. Aunt Aslaug and Uncle Ragnvald welcomed us into their home, as they had done before – giving us food and something warm to drink. Torgunn was pleased to see us again too – and, warmed by their hospitality, we were finally able to rest and relax. The house and the people – which we had left more than a year earlier – were again there for us; only this time, we arrived on their doorstep homeless and destitute.

German signpost in Kirkenes during World War II.
Photo: courtesy of Kalle Wara.

Kirkenes 4th July 1944. After a massive bomb attack the town is being
evacuated – Sørvaranger Museum. The German Bundesarchive.

Kirkenes is burning. September/October 1944.
– Sørvaranger Museum.

Remaining houses put to the torch by the retreating German army. Oct. 1944.
– Sørvaranger Museum.

The end result of war. Remains of the stone houses below Haugen after the liberation by the Russian Army 25th October 1944
–Sørvaranger Museum.

The rounded steps in the foreground are all that is left of Pettersen's Bakery. 25th October 1944.
– Sørvaranger Museum.

Section of Kirkenes in the early 1940s, looking towards the entrance of Bøkfjord. To the right in the foreground the German 'Soldiers Home'. Photo: Edvardsen. – Sørvaranger Museum.

25th October 1944. Same section of Kirkenes as above, after the final destruction of the town.
– Sørvaranger Museum

20

Dangerous Journey

Aunt Aslaug and Uncle Ragnvald somehow found room for us all in their house in Jarfjord. As soon as we were safely settled in, Father returned to Kirkenes, feeling that he was still needed both at work and with the fire fighters.

Sharing the kitchen worked very well, with young and old lending a helping hand. Peter came to visit when he had a chance, and Aase was now pregnant with their second child. One day there was a heated exchange between them. With the imminent Russian invasion, he would soon be on the move. But what would happen to Aase and the children? Whatever his answer was, Aase turned around, grabbed a mirror off the wall, and smashed it over his head. Peter sank down on to the nearest chair, with the frame of the mirror around his neck, on the verge of passing out. Mother grabbed him, to stop him falling off the chair.

"That temper of yours will get us all into trouble," she said crossly, as she was picking glass out of Peter's hair and scalp. "I am surprised that he comes back to you after the way you treat him."

"What will become of the children and me?" cried Aase.

"You know that we will help," soothed Mother.

Peter, groggy after the encounter with the mirror, had to go. Amazingly, Aase followed him out.

After a while she returned, announcing that Peter wanted her and Heide to move in with him at Storskog. Speechless, Mother stared at her.

"Surely you are not going!" she cried, shocked. "The Germans are already starting to move away from the front, and the Russian planes will be after them every day. Don't expose yourself and Heide to even greater dangers than we are already facing!"

But Aase sat down and cried. She grabbed Heide, who was sitting on the floor, put her on her knee and held her tightly.

"I love Peter, and have to go with him wherever it takes me," she said in a very low voice and tried to wipe away her tears.

Sonja and I got very upset by the thought of Aase leaving with our darling Heide. My eyes brimming with tears, I put my arms around Aase pleading:

"Please don't leave us and take Heide away."

"Listen to Mother," said Sonja. "If you stay, we will help to look after Heide, you know."

Aase tried to smile. "I know you will, and I shall miss you too, but I shall have to think about it first and then decide."

That night we went to bed in a gloomy and sombre mood. Aase and Mother were whispering to each other, but I couldn't hear what they were saying, and soon fell asleep.

The story about the stork had worn a bit thin by now, and I had already made the connection between a growing stomach and pregnancy.

"How did the baby get into Aase's stomach, Sonja?"

"It must have something to do with Peter. He is Heide's father, you know."

"It can't have anything to do with food like the last time," I speculated. "We don't have much food and I don't think the Germans have much either."

She looked at me pityingly. "You really are silly. I don't think food has anything to do with it, besides they won't tell us. But I don't think the stork has anything to do with it either."

Perhaps she knew something I didn't, but she wouldn't say any more and I was no wiser than before.

A week or so later, Peter came for Aase and Heide. We all cried and hugged each other, and my mother tried again:

"Can't you at least leave Heide with us?" But Aase answered in a tight voice:

"You know I can't do that. She is our daughter, and Peter wants her too."

With that she grabbed Heide, turned her back, and hurried away to Peter, who was waiting in a car. Mother was wretchedly unhappy to see her daughter and granddaughter go – but there was nothing she could do to stop them. Complaining to her cousin didn't help much either.

"Aase has chosen her life with Peter, Borghild. You can't force her to come back. You have to let her go."

"How can she know what she is letting herself in for? And what of little Heide?" wailed my mother.

Soon after our return to Jarfjord, I met my old school friend, Anny Johnsen, in the local shop. Because of the developing war situation, we only met at random. At that time the Germans were badly in need of more transport, and were requisitioning horses. Years later, Anny related to me the episode of a bad tempered horse on a neighbour's farm.

When the Germans came for the horse, some of the neighbours had gathered to watch. The owner removed the horse's muzzle and threw the reins to the German soldier. The horse bolted, viciously biting the unfortunate soldier, and galloped off with him hooked to the reins. The locals had watched this episode with glee, feeling that they had got their own back in some small way. This incident had indeed lightened their day!

Uncle Ragnvald's horse Elsa had already been taken, along with the horses in Karpbukt. I didn't see the Germans coming for her but Uncle Ragnvald was very unhappy at losing his dear horse.

In the following weeks, the German traffic to and from the border was stepped up. Every day columns of vehicles, artillery and troops were passing by. A German defence post and troops camping in Karpbukt made it very dangerous for our cousins living nearby.

Torgunn happened to be there one evening, when two Russian

planes – presumably on the way home – must have spotted the Germans and came hurtling down with their guns blazing, shooting at everything in their path. Guri (a member of the family in Karpbukt), took one step back as a hail of bullets narrowly missed her, going through the wall into the room where her two small boys, Terje and Arnulf, were in bed. The bullets passed over the boys and out the other wall, leaving them frightened but unhurt. Guri's husband Solmund, who had recently died, was my mother's cousin.

Torgunn didn't realise at first that she was hurt. Only when she felt something wet running down her arm and side did she discover that she had been wounded. Her arm had been torn open from shoulder to elbow. After first aid to stem the bleeding and bandage her arm, the family asked the Germans if they had a doctor in their unit. Luckily, a doctor was found, but he only had time to improve on the bandage, advising them to get the wound stitched as soon as possible.

After the hospital in Kirkenes had a narrow escape during a bombing raid, doctors and patients had moved to Sollia at Storskog, which was about halfway to Jarfjord. Torgunn needed help urgently and with a bit of luck, they were able to get her to Sollia, where her arm was stitched and given a proper bandage by Dr Palmstrøm. With many patients and little medication he could not keep her there and had to send her home. Everybody was on the move, with the expected invasion by the Russians just around the corner, and Sollia (a former children's home) was not a safe place to stay either.

Meanwhile, the war between Russia and Finland had reached a climax. Tired of war and the large loss of life, the Finns signed a peace treaty with the Russians on the 2nd September 1944. This would have a profound effect on the Finnmark people in the months to come. The conditions of peace were hard. Finland was to pay large sums of money for reparations. The wedge of land between Eastern Finnmark and Russia would revert back to Russia, and the borders would be redrawn. The order to get the German army out of Finland in two weeks was perhaps unrealistic. But, if necessary, the Finns had to take up arms against their former ally and force them out.

The new commander of Germany's large Mountain Army in the Arctic was General Lothar Rendulic. He had been appointed, when General Dietl was killed in an air crash over the Alps, after a trip to visit Hitler in June 1944. Plans for two escape routes from Finland into Norway in the north were already on the table. One route was over the border to Karasjok – a Sami settlement south west of Kirkenes – leading to highway 50 where the German withdrawal from Kirkenes would come. The second route was along the Swedish/Finnish border to Lyngen in the County of Troms, where the Germans would take a stand. Both routes would be used.

But Hitler refused to let Rendulic withdraw his large Mountain Army from Finland. They were there to protect the nickel mines in the north of Finland for Hitler's arms factories. Rendulic's Mountain Army consisted of 200,000 soldiers, with tens of thousands of horses, thousands of tons of equipment and stores, and a large number of prisoners.

Not until 2nd October did Hitler finally relent and give his permission to withdraw. In the meantime, the German army was attacked by their former allies, the Finns. As Rendulic's Army retreated from northern Finland towards the border with Norway, they left burned-out towns and villages behind. But when their order came to join in the destruction of Finnmark, as well as in the hostage-taking, Rendulic protested. He and other generals couldn't see the point of that. However, they had to back down and follow the orders from Berlin.

One day in August or early September, Father arrived to see how we were getting on and to bring some food. His face looked grim, and he was visibly upset. The reason soon became clear. As he was crossing the bridge at Elvenes, he had heard desperate cries. Staying out of sight, he got off his bicycle and crept closer to see what was going on. A guard was beating up a Russian prisoner, who was on his knees on the ground. Other guards and prisoners were nearby. As Father watched in helpless anguish, the terrible cries of pain and agony of the prisoner cut into him like knives. Unable to watch any more, he buried his face in his hands. What could he do to help? Sadly, there was nothing he could do. Intervention would certainly have got him arrested, and the prisoner's fate would have been the same.

"I am sure the man was dead," said my father heavily. "When the guard was finished with him, the prisoner lay still on the ground."

"Why such terrible brutality?" whispered my mother, deeply shocked.

"Brutality towards the prisoners has been going on all the time, but it looks like they are getting more careless now." Deeply troubled by his inability to help, Father could not be comforted.

It was now late September. Father was back in Kirkenes, and Mother constantly feared for him, Aase and Heide. One day she could stand it no longer. She put on a coat and hat and was ready to leave. She had already discussed the situation with Aunt Aslaug.

"I am going to Storskog to see how Aase and Heide are getting on," she said. "You two are staying here with Aunt Aslaug."

Sonja and I protested. "Mamma, we want to come too." But our mother was adamant.

"You are staying here with Aunt Aslaug."

With that she was off. We watched her disappearing from view.

"I am going after her," I said, putting on my coat and shoes.

"She will be angry," warned Sonja. "Besides, Aunt Aslaug will not allow you to go."

"Don't tell her then," I shouted as I ran out the door. I ran till I saw my mother not too far away, then I slowed down to keep up with her at a distance. I knew how dangerous it was to be on the road now and somehow thought I could protect her. It did not take long before she discovered me. She stopped, and tried to get me to go back, but I just stood there, and when she started walking again, I followed. After repeating this several times she gave up, saying grudgingly:

"All right, you better come with me then. Do you realise how far it is to walk?"

I shook my head.

"It is about 12 kilometres."

The distance didn't worry me. I was afraid that something might happen to her. So we walked on.

"If we hear German vehicles or Russian planes, we shall hide among the trees," she said.

Sure enough, after about twenty minutes walk we heard German vehicles coming up behind us. They were heavy goods vehicles coming from the front on their way to Kirkenes. We slipped away from the road and down a slope, hiding among the trees until they had gone.

Back on the road again, we continued walking. A little later, the heavy drone of aeroplanes alerted us. We knew by the sound of the engines that they were Russian. On their way to Kirkenes, they constantly attacked German vehicles on the road. Again we slipped away from the road. This time we hid behind stones built up around a telephone pole. Crouching down – trying to make ourselves invisible – we didn't move until the sound of the planes died away. Only then did we pick ourselves up, venturing back to the road again.

"You shouldn't be here," Mother said. "It is too dangerous."

This didn't deserve an answer, so I kept quiet. She became talkative.

"If we survive the war, everything will be different. We shall be a happy family again; you and Sonja will get a good education, and we shall have plenty of food to eat and a nice house to live in. Wouldn't that be great?"

I agreed, but could somehow not imagine it ever happening to us. While we pondered this nice utopia, more vehicles were catching up with us. Once more we left the road to take refuge among the trees. Lucky for us, no planes were there to attack the German column. When they disappeared on their way to Kirkenes, we moved back to the road again to continue towards Storskog.

It is difficult to calculate how long it took us to walk to Storskog, considering the numerous times we had to leave the road to hide. However, it was still daylight when we arrived. On our right, the ground rose gently, with a narrow track leading up towards a small group of wooden buildings nestled between the birch trees. This was where Aase now lived with Peter and Heide.

As we started up the slope to Aase's house, a column of German vehicles caught up with us. Unfortunately for us and the Germans on the road, a number of Russian planes arrived on the scene at the same time.

Mother and I sprinted up the hill to Aase's house and burst in through the door. The abiding picture I have from that moment is of little Heide standing there holding on to a chair, with her pregnant mother nearby. Now a little more than one year old, Heide looked frightened.

With planes screaming past as they dived to attack the column on the road, Aase grabbed Heide and threw herself on the floor, covering Heide's body with her own, while Mother did the same trying to protect me. The planes were flying so low that from my position on the floor I observed through the window the body of a plane whizzing past.

The noise of the shooting and the explosions was deafening. We all crawled under the kitchen table for some extra protection. I had my fingers in my ears, but the noise was still horrendous, and I could see tears rolling down Heide's cheeks while her mother tried to comfort her. When it was all over, we were just glad to be alive.

It was later discussed why the Russians did not shoot up the house we were in and the other houses nearby. But perhaps they had seen us running up the hill, and thought these were private houses.

A while after the attack was over; Peter arrived to see if we were all right. He was white-faced and very shaken as he told us how many German soldiers had died during the attack, mentioning some of his friends by name. He talked about how it had become too dangerous to stay there now, and that they soon would be moving on.

Mother pleaded with Aase to take Heide and come with us, but she refused, and as far as I understood, Peter wanted her with him. Through it all, I played with Heide and held on to her, unable to accept that they would soon be gone.

There was not much daylight left. With the sun setting it would soon be dark, and we had to get ready to leave. We cried and hugged each other, frightened of what might lie ahead for us all. Reluctant to leave, we lingered a little longer. It was now dark outside and after a last kiss for Heide and Aase, we had to go. Peter offered to guide us past the carnage on the road and see us on our way and Mother accepted, afraid of what we might encounter and of being stopped by German sentries.

Peter escorted us until the road was clear. He could not come any further, he said, wishing us well as he shook hands with my mother. With a wave of his hand and 'Auf wiedersehen', he was gone. What we didn't know was that we would never see our dear little Heide again.

We walked in silence for a long time. Because Mother was crying, I was even more afraid for Heide and Aase.

It was very dark now, with no moon and no lights anywhere. We stayed close to the side of the road in case someone on a bicycle might run into us. Eventually Mother stopped crying.

"Stay close to me," she said. "We may yet have to hide among the trees if any vehicles come past."

So we walked on in a dark and sombre mood, matched only by the blackness around us.

In due course we reached 'Aule Brae', named after a family who lived nearby. As we started down the brae we heard horses with a cart approaching from behind. The horses weren't moving very fast.

"Let us stay behind them and hold on to the cart," Mother suggested. "We'll be safer that way."

In the darkness we couldn't see the driver, but felt comforted by the presence of him and the horses.

Walking down the brae in the middle of the road, holding on to the cart, I suddenly sensed something behind us. I gave my mother such a push towards the side of the road that she fell into the ditch as I dived in after her, landing on top of her.

"What in heaven's name are you ..." she started to say. A split second later, a mighty crash broke the calm of the night, and we could hear, but not see, the horses rearing up on their hind legs, whinnying with fear, and setting off at a gallop down the road for all they were worth.

After we got up and were brushing ourselves down, we realised what had happened.

"You know," said Mother, "that was a car coming down the hill with the engine switched off and no lights on. No wonder he crashed into the back of the cart!" Pausing she exclaimed: "We could have been killed!" She turned to me then and put her arms around me. "Do you realise that you have just saved our lives?" she asked.

As we walked on we held onto each other tightly, or rather Mother wouldn't let go of my hand, as we walked close to the side of the road.

Eventually we arrived home late that night, exhausted, emotionally and physically – but we were safe, to the relief of Sonja and Aunt Aslaug, who both had been extremely worried. As I was falling asleep that night, I could hear my mother sobbing quietly into her pillow.

21

Will we survive?

I never found out what Father thought of our expedition to Storskog, or if he even heard of it at the time. There were plenty of other things to worry about. The noise of war was getting closer, like a distant faint thunder carried on the wind from the east. Again we were caught in the middle, between the fleeing Germans and the pursuing Russian Army, which was getting closer every day.

In the early hours of 7th October 1944, the Soviet Army in the north set in motion a major offensive on the German lines along the entire Litza front, as far as the Fisher peninsula at the Barents Sea. Well trained, prepared and ready, they had waited for the order to attack. The attack was launched on land, in the air and by sea. Over 97,000 troops of the Soviet 14th Army with the help of their North Fleet and Air Force were ready to push the 56,000 strong German 19th Mountain Corps out of their northern territories. The Allied convoys to Murmansk, in spite of heavy losses, had been instrumental in helping to equip the Soviet Army. The ships had brought aeroplanes, tanks, guns and other supplies for the war effort.

During the autumn of 1941 the Germans had fought their way to Litza, but after their disastrous offensive in the spring of 1942, the frontline had remained static. In the following three years the Germans had reinforced and increased their positions along the front, set up stores, built bridges and improved roads. They were intent on protecting the nickel mines in the north for Hitler's guns and ammunition factories – but their dreams of taking Murmansk had faded. The Russians had fought hard to keep the Germans at bay and now the tide had turned, as the Soviet Army was storming towards the German lines. The Soviet North Fleet put soldiers ashore on the coast, while Russian planes attacked from the air.

The battle which followed was hard and bloody. Desperately fighting back, the German Army was gradually pushed closer to the Norwegian border. Unwilling to give in, they tried to hold on, but to no avail. As they retreated, they attempted to destroy stores and supplies, but did not always succeed, to the delight of Russian soldiers, who benefited from extra ammunition, fuel, and even abandoned food supplies. Casualties on both sides were high. The commander in charge of the Soviet assault was Kirill A. Meretskov, who was to be appointed Marshal of the Soviet Union after his victory in the north.

As the retreat of the German Army gained momentum, a constant stream of vehicles and soldiers passed through Jarfjord day and night. They must have been short of vehicles, as groups of soldiers began to appear on foot.

Now in the early days of October, the snow was late in coming. The weather was exceptionally mild; the dwarf birch trees had long since shed their leaves, leaving little cover for escaping soldiers at the mercy of Russian planes overhead.

It was clear, however, that we could not remain on the east side of the fjord much longer. The usual topic of survival had changed from "If we survive the war" to "Our only chance of survival is to get across the fjord and escape into the hills."

Sonja and I listened to their discussions and were old enough to understand the acute danger we were in. "Surviving the war" had taken on a much more sinister meaning, after the many close brushes we had had with the unthinkable. We were all worried, and afraid of what was still to come.

The weather stayed fine in October 1944, and my 10th birthday was approaching fast. Sonja would be 13 years old the following

February; that is "should we survive the war," as the saying went.

Many types and sizes of bombs were used during the attacks, including incendiary bombs. In the days leading up to the invasion, an incendiary bomb fell on a nearby house, occupied by an old lady. Unable to get out, she died in the resulting fire as the house was engulfed in flames.

Father had come to stay with us now. No longer allowed to extinguish the fires in Kirkenes, his fire fighting days were over. The fire engines with all their equipment had been confiscated. When the firemen protested, the Germans drew their guns and ordered them to leave or be shot. Reluctantly they left, but not before they had observed German soldiers moving in to the remaining houses with bottles of petrol, presumably in readiness for the final destruction.

Pay packets did not matter anymore. Society, as we knew it, had broken down. The shopkeepers had left, and all trade had ceased. There was nothing to buy. Bartering, which had started early in the war, changed to the more urgent need of helping each other, as most people now had little to barter with.

Posters were plastered everywhere, encouraging people to take up an offer to evacuate with the Germans when they retreated. But the buses made available had few passengers on board.

Bjørnevatn, at approximately 10km south of Kirkenes, was home to the Company's iron ore mines and tunnels. It was still linked to Kirkenes by rail, but no longer used for transport of iron ore. Instead, it served as a link for German soldiers and their supplies.

A small freighter had found its way to Kirkenes with about two tons of dried fish, just before the firemen were dismissed. The firemen were instrumental in getting it unloaded and somehow got it on the train to Bjørnevatn and onwards to the tunnel. The fish helped to keep the tunnel people from starvation during the final battle and beyond.

The Company had prepared their tunnels with large numbers of bunk beds, up to three high, in readiness for the invasion. The tunnel was filling up now, as more and more people, with nowhere else to go, found their way there. In total about 3,500 people moved in to the tunnel. Families hung up sheets or set up boards, attempting to make their own little area as private as possible, before settling down to wait for the battle that they knew would come. Cattle, sheep, dogs and cats were brought into a side tunnel. The inhabitants included ten heavily pregnant women. Luckily, an excellent midwife was at hand. Nelly Lund was about to be kept fully occupied.

The Germans were too busy to interfere. Elsewhere in Sørvaranger, people literally dug themselves into the ground, avoiding where possible the mainstream of the German retreat.

Kirkenes was burning. Night after night we stood silently outside the house in Jarfjord, watching the sky turning from pink to red, as what was left of our town was slowly and painfully destroyed. The order from Berlin was to burn and destroy everything, and as the Germans fled from the wrath of the Russian Army, they did just that.

One day, during the second week of October, a unit of soldiers on foot stopped at our place and started to set up camp around the house. Father and Uncle Ragnvald looked on with disbelief. They tried to speak to the Germans, but were roughly dismissed. The soldiers were tired, demoralised, and some were drunk. The war was lost, and they were on the run. By sheltering around a private house, they may have hoped that the Russians would not attack them. The fact that they were putting us in great danger was not important. The rest of us stayed indoors. Father and Uncle Ragnvald came in and sat down with the women to discuss our situation.

"We have to get away right now," said Uncle Ragnvald. "You know that shelters are ready in the hills on the other side of the fjord for this eventuality."

"I know," my father said, "and I agree. If the Russians spot the Germans here, they will attack us."

"As you know," continued Uncle Ragnvald, "I have a small rowing boat hidden near Karpbukt." He turned to his wife. "Aslaug, pack what you can and what we can carry. But remember that the boat is small. You and Borghild can decide what essentials to bring."

The women nodded their agreement.

"We should all put on as many layers of clothes as possible," Mother suggested. "At least what we are wearing does not have to be packed. The children will be able to carry some things, but Torgunn should watch her arm and take it easy."

Torgunn, however, would have none of it.

"I can carry with my good arm," she protested, and we all smiled at her.

She had been very brave throughout her ordeal and never complained.

"If we only had Elsa, she could have helped us," Torgunn said sadly.

Elsa the horse, however, had long since been confiscated by the Germans. Father started to get up from the table, and the others followed.

"Let's start packing," he said.

I don't know what they packed, but in the middle of discussing what to take and what to leave, the unmistakable sound of aeroplanes rapidly grew.

"Come on, get down into the cellar," hissed Uncle Ragnvald.

Father was already opening the hatch on the floor.

"Hurry, hurry," he shouted, as one after the other filed down the stairs as fast as they could. But I refused. I was terrified of the confined space down there, with no way out. Panicking, I tried to get into a bedroom to hide. Father caught me and carried me to the hatch, forcing me down the steps to the basement while I cried hysterically.

"You must understand that it is more dangerous upstairs than here," he soothed as he held his arms firmly around me.

But I was not at all convinced. I knew that a direct hit on the house would kill us all. I was trapped, and there was nothing I could do about it. The only way out was through that hatch on the kitchen floor.

The room in the basement was quite small. It had a bench seat along the back wall, with a small window high up on the wall behind us, just above ground level. On the end wall, at right angles to the bench and in line with the path of the river below the house, a shelf unit was attached to the wall, where Aunt Aslaug kept her milk. Barely able to take it in, I caught sight of the two very familiar china bowls – each about two thirds full of milk.

Terrified, we were all crouching on the bench seat with our backs to the stone wall, trying to make ourselves as small as possible. Engulfed in an all-consuming fear of the inevitable, I now, finally, understood what "If we survive the war" really meant. We were all going to die right here in the basement. Our parents, with their arms around us, could do no more to protect us.

The planes must have been circling quite low overhead, because the noise of their engines seemed to fill the little room. From the outside we could hear the Germans shouting, and shots being fired. Suddenly, above all other noise, we heard the all too familiar whistling of bombs coming closer and closer, and there was nothing we could do about it – just sit there paralysed with fear, praying that the bombs would not hit us. We virtually did not move nor breathe.

When the explosions came, they temporarily lit up the room through the small window on the wall above. The noise was ear shattering, but the most amazing thing of all was Aunt Aslaug's two milk bowls. When the shock wave struck, they were lifted up, and floated off the shelf into the room as if on an invisible air cushion, hovering for a moment before crashing down in front of us on the stone floor, showering us with milk and broken china.

Mesmerized, we just sat there for a few moments, hardly able to believe that we really were still alive. Then we all began to move, shaking off milk and fragments of the china bowls.

"All our milk is gone," mourned Aunt Aslaug aimlessly.

"Never mind the milk," said her husband. "Thank God we are all still alive!"

My father was moving towards the steps.

"We have to get out of here and get moving," he urged. "Time is not on our side, and the planes might be back."

One by one we climbed up the stairs to the kitchen, not particularly surprised at what we saw, as our family had seen it all before. The kitchen floor was strewn with shattered glass from the windows, broken dishes, pots and pans, and battered furniture. All the windows in the house had been blown in, and shrapnel had penetrated the house through the wall facing the blast.

The mess in the kitchen was tidied up first. Then Father and Uncle Ragnvald set about boarding up the windows as best they could.

There is no doubt that the bombs were aimed at our house, spotted from the air because the German soldiers had set up camp there. No other targets were nearby. Luckily, they had fallen on the slope below the house, thereby reducing the full impact of the blast. Had they fallen on even ground as close as they did, the house might well have been blown off its foundation, and it is unlikely that we could have survived.

The adults busied themselves with packing.

"We need blankets and pillows," said Mother.

"And towels and some extra clothes," said Aunt Aslaug.

"If you get the bundles sorted out, I will tie them up," offered Father.

"We can't leave the cows," said Uncle Ragnvald "and we can't take them with us. What are we going to do with them?"

There was no answer to that problem.

"It is getting dark now," he said presently, as we were moving about trying to pack. "I rather think we have to stay here overnight and set off with first daylight; the planes will not be back tonight."

The women grudgingly agreed.

"We must speak to the commandant and tell him what we are planning to do, just in case of any problems," Father said thoughtfully. "The cows can be released and chased into the woods as we leave." (The people in Karpbukt had already walked their cows around the fjord to the safety of the other side). "At least that gives them a chance," he added.

Torgunn's parents nodded, but Aunt Aslaug had tears in her eyes. She loved her animals.

"What is the world coming to," she said unhappily. "Everything is wrong. We are losing our home and our animals, and we have done nothing wrong."

Mother tried to comfort her.

"You know we are all in the same boat," she said, putting her arms around her cousin. "We have to be strong for the children, and help each other to get through this ordeal."

But gloom hung over us all, as we prepared for our final night in this house, which was their home and where our family had found sanctuary when we needed it most.

Uncle Ragnvald and my father went out to speak to the officer in charge of the unit camped outside.

"Get out as early as possible," he advised. "We will not stop you or your cows," he promised.

That night we did not sleep much and my mother held on to her large handbag for dear life, even in bed. In it she carried all our family photos, her Bible and some small heirlooms from her parents.

At dawn the next morning we were ready. Torgunn, Sonja and I tried to take some toys with us, but were only allowed one small toy each. I put a small teddy bear in my pocket, Sonja took a small ball, and what Torgunn took I have forgotten. She was older than us, at least sixteen at the time.

What remained of food in the house was packed. Bedclothes were rolled up and tied with string. On the way out, we all carried bundles and pans with the lids tied on – packed with dishes.

It was a fine morning. The Germans did not interfere as we set off down the road. Father and Uncle Ragnvald went into the byre, tied ropes around the necks of the two cows and led them after us. The Germans ignored us. When we were out of sight of them, the men untied the ropes and tried to chase the cows into the woods. But the animals just stood there looking at us, as if wondering what we were up to. The men then took a piece of wood each and smacked their rumps, shouting at them. That got them going! They disappeared in among the trees at full speed.

"I hope they are not trying to get back to their warm comfortable byre again," Aunt Aslaug said. "If they do, we shall not see them again."

"We have other things to worry about now I am afraid," Uncle Ragnvald commented. "The cows just have to take their chances."

The cows meant a great deal to me too. Through all the hours I had spent with Aunt Aslaug in the byre, I had become very fond of them and of her.

"Don't worry," I said to her. "You will get them back, you'll see." She smiled at me and stroked my hair.

"To think that this is your 10th birthday," she said, shaking her head. "You should have had a cake and a birthday party!"

Well, at least she had remembered my birthday, but I could not remember ever having had a birthday party or a cake.

"When the war is over," said Mother, "we shall always have birthday parties." She had omitted to say, "If we survive the war."

Life with parties and no war seemed an impossible dream, as we now were fleeing for our lives yet again.

Luckily, there were no passing vehicles when we reached the main road. We hurried along the 300 – 400 metres to Karpbukt. There was a buzz of activity going on in the German camp. Our other relatives had already fled over the fjord. We were not stopped as we made our way stealthily to the beach, following Uncle Ragnvald to a clump of trees where his boat was hidden, camouflaged by branches.

While the men busied themselves checking the boat and getting it into the water, the rest of us waited anxiously, watching the sky as well as listening for approaching vehicles. For the moment at least, it was quiet.

Presently the men beckoned us to come. Our belongings were handed over first, then one after the other we were helped onboard. My father pushed the boat out and jumped in, while Uncle Ragnvald manned the oars. Aunt Aslaug sat in the bow with Torgunn. Mother, Sonja and I had a little more room in the stern.

The men rowed as fast as they could. Normally, one should expect to cross the fjord in less than an hour, but our route was set diagonally and would take a little longer. We were all looking anxiously towards the hills, where the Russian planes would appear. On the shore behind us we could see the Germans moving about. After a while we began to relax. The shoreline was receding behind us, and we had covered about one third of the distance across.

Then all of a sudden, skimming low over the hills and approaching fast, Russian planes were closing in on us. There were at least four of them. Father and Uncle Ragnvald stopped rowing.

"Get down," they shouted to us. Pushing us down, Mother tried to protect us with her body. Aunt Aslaug did the same with Torgunn, as one of the planes headed directly for us.

"Dear God have mercy on us!" cried Mother helplessly, as the plane began to circle over the boat. I tried to push her away but she held us down. We were all terrified that the Russian would attack us.

Father and Uncle Ragnvald sat still at the oars looking up. They knew that we were at the mercy of that Russian pilot. I managed to look up from under my mother's arm, and saw the plane turn and set off towards the shore to join the others, dipping its wings from side to side as it went – almost as if trying to tell us something. The rest of the planes were already busy shooting up the German defences on the shore behind us.

"Thank God for saving our lives again," uttered my mother in a strange, tearful voice. I am sure we had all prayed silently to God for help, grateful to the Russian pilot that he had taken time to check his targets and did not attack innocent civilians.

The men resumed rowing again.

"She is not going to forget this birthday," said my father, smiling at me. They were all relaxing now, smiling and wishing me a happy birthday! It was the morning of the 14th October 1944, my 10th birthday, somewhere in the middle of the fjord, hopefully on the way to safety.

22

The Hole in the Ground

After the harrowing events leading up to the incident on the fjord, we arrived safely on the other side. The boat was hauled ashore, hidden among trees and covered by branches. Our belongings were shared among us, before we started to climb away from the shore towards the single track road. The road was only a few kilometres long ending at Haga, a small settlement with two dwelling houses and some farm buildings.

My maternal grandmother was born there. Haga got its name from her grandfather, who came up from the south to settle there in the 19th century. Through my mother's parents we had relations on both sides of the fjord. Aunt Reidun and her family had come to Haga as refugees, and we went to Karpbukt, where some of my maternal grandfather's family had settled.

We were now on the north-west side of the fjord, with only a few crofts and the occasional log-cabin scattered along the road. The German presence here was greatly reduced, and those we met let us pass.

Haga was not our destination though. Three or more 'bunkers', dug out and prepared for this eventuality, were spread out in the hills. The men knew where they were going and led the way to our next 'home'. Now and then we paused to take shelter among trees, when we heard or saw planes approaching. From there, we watched the shelling of Karpbukt and Tårnet, and dog fights over the fjord, shuddering at the thought that only an hour or so earlier we had been there.

Presently, we arrived at the point where we left the road and headed up into the hills. It was not particularly steep, and after a little while we arrived at our next shelter. Sonja and I were curious, and had no idea what to expect. Not a house of course, but perhaps a tunnel leading to rooms under the ground? As we soon found out, it was neither.

Our underground shelter, or 'bunker', as it was called, was basically a hole in the ground. Rough steps led down into the 'bunker', where a hatch concealed the entrance. I looked at our new 'home' with fear and trepidation. This hole in the ground with a hatch on top reminded me too much of the basement of the house we had left this morning. However, reluctantly following my mother down the steps, I discovered that it was quite spacious.

The floor was covered with wooden boards laid on tree branches; the earth walls were lined with silver birch trees wound tightly together; the roof construction was tree trunks covered with corrugated iron sheeting on the outside, and camouflaged with turf.

A deep shelf across the room was the sleeping quarters for all the children. The adults had to sleep on the floor. A ladder was leaning against the shelf. Wooden benches were placed along the walls, and a small iron stove sat in a corner, with a narrow pipe piercing the roof to the outside. The families had brought bedclothes, whatever food they possessed, and cooking utensils. Cooking had to be done at night as smoke from the pipe could be spotted from the air.

'The Bunker' was now shelter to 25 men, women, and children as the war in all its fury raged around us.

Life in the bunker was very restricted, and people had to make do as best as they could. The Germans looked in occasionally to keep an eye on us but otherwise left us alone. Due to fear of being spotted from the air, the men only moved from the bunker to fetch water from a nearby river.

The noise of war had become part of our daily life – only now it was getting worse by the day. The shelling from the guns on both sides had grown louder; the planes came and went every day, bombing and shooting at the enemy. Dog fights in sky were a daily occurrence – and so it went on and on. The noise was horrendous. The men took it in turns to keep watch at night. I often sat on the floor, my back to the wall and with my fingers in my ears, trying to keep out the noise. I was hoping and praying that one of the shells – which often came close – would not hit the bunker. Torgunn, Sonja and the other children grew restless in our confinement, but had to put up with it like everyone else. Now and then we would play little games or invent stories. Somebody got us to sing quietly together if the German guard was out of earshot – but mostly we sat around waiting and hoping …

The adults never seemed to tire of starting their conversation with "If we survive the war". However, it had now become interspersed with "If we survive the winter" knowing with increasing certainty that there would be very little shelter to find when the Germans had had their day.

An Arctic winter without adequate shelter was a bleak prospect indeed.

Food and survival were the main topics of conversation. At the moment we were not starving, but had limited food supplies. The big question was: when would food supplies filter through to reach us? The autumn had been unusually mild, with very little snow – but this could change at any time now, bringing snow and hard frost.

Mother worried constantly about Aase and Heide. Aunt Aslaug tried to comfort her, saying one day:

"Please don't worry so much, Borghild. Aase and Heide will have gone away with Peter by this time. They might even be on a ship going south."

This did not help at all.

"If they are on a ship they might be bombed or torpedoed," wailed my mother.

Of course, hearing this, Sonja and I went to our mother and put our arms around her.

"I don't want them to be dead," I cried.

Sonja, being nearly three years older than me, said firmly: "They'll be all right Mamma, you'll see. After the war they will come back to us."

Grabbing our hands, Mother tried to pull herself together.

"I hope you are right and that we will see them again," she said quietly to Sonja, as Aunt Aslaug nodded wisely.

Later on, I saw Father whispering to her. No doubt he was worried about them too, perhaps especially for Heide, whom we all loved dearly.

After about a week in the shelter there was a growing excitement in the air.

"It will not be long now," I heard one of them saying.

"What will not be long now, Pappa?" I enquired, tugging at my father's sleeve.

"The Russians are coming any time now," he said smiling. "And then we will be free and can get out of here!"

What this freedom meant I was not quite sure.

"Are we going back to Uncle Ragnvald's house then?" I asked.

"That depends," he replied quietly. No further explanation was forthcoming, as everybody started talking at once.

"Hush, be patient, the German guard is still here," someone said.

Early next morning, however, the Germans were gone. Father reckoned they had moved out before 7 am. The men ventured out cautiously and looked around. No German soldiers were to be seen in the immediate vicinity. The gunfire had subsided a little. We all followed on up the stairs and out, squinting to get used to the daylight. It was great to be out breathing fresh air again. However, after a little while outside, we reluctantly went back in again. It was still not safe. We were now in no-man's-land between the Germans and the Russians, and had to stay put. The men were anxiously keeping watch at the entrance to the bunker, talking quietly to one and other.

As the day wore on, the tenseness, and a certain nervousness of the adults, rubbed off on the children. We all sat quietly on the bench seats in the bunker, waiting, for what? There was no talking; only one or two men ventured outside at a time.

Then, about three o'clock in the afternoon, the stillness in the bunker was broken by foreign voices outside, followed by two Russian soldiers descending the stairs into the bunker – their guns at the ready. They looked around, counted us, then smiled, and said something in their own language before turning to climb up the stairs.

Father and the other men were already welcoming the Russian soldiers, smiling and slapping their backs. Cautiously getting out of the bunker, the rest of us gathered around the soldiers, trying to show that they were welcome.

I stayed close to Mother, not knowing what to make of it all. Looking around, there seemed to be dozens of soldiers spread out, with their guns ready to shoot. The Russian who appeared to be in charge of the unit spoke some Norwegian. On hearing that the German soldiers had moved out early in the morning he barked out his orders, and the soldiers began to move away.

"Stay where you are for the time being," he advised. "You are not safe yet." With a salute and a smile he was gone.

Unable to believe that our little patch of Norway had just been liberated, we just stood there, looking at the receding backs of the Russian soldiers till they disappeared from view. Then, as if touched by a magic wand, the adults started dancing around, behaving like the Jarfjord calves coming out of the byres in spring. The men and women kissed each other and slapped each other's backs – and as if that was not enough, they congratulated each other as well.

"What is wrong with them?" I said to Sonja, "It is nobody's birthday today."

"They are very happy now that we are free," Sonja informed me.

Freedom, I knew, was very desirable. But what did it really mean? To me it had no shape or form. Almost all I knew was war, bombing, shooting, planes being shot to pieces in the air, people killed or maimed – and each time we were forced to move on, our possessions had dwindled.

The Norwegian national anthem was now in full flow and all the children had to join in. Father lifted me up in the air and hugged me, and then it was Sonja's turn. It seemed to me that everybody hugged everybody else, laughing and smiling. Well, if this was 'Freedom' it was probably all right, I thought to myself.

Mother had moved away from the crowd, standing with her back to us. I went up to her and looked at her. Tears were rolling down her face, as she looked at me with a faraway expression.

"Thank God that we are free now," she said quietly, "but I wonder how it is with Aase and Heide."

"Please don't cry Mother. If we ask God to save them I am sure he will."

She looked at me strangely.

"Yes of course we must pray for them." But she looked very sad. 'Freedom' had not made my mother any happier.

'Freedom', however, had lightened the mood and made the other inhabitants of the bunker happy. There was much excited talk about where we could stay when we left the bunker. Uncle Ragnvald and the others worried about their houses in Karpbukt.

"Judging by the fires we have seen from there, it is unlikely that any of the houses in Karpbukt are still standing," he said heavily.

"When it is safe, we must row across and see what is left," someone else said.

"That will have to wait for a few days yet," Father said thoughtfully.

"First we must find out if there are any buildings still standing around here that we may be able to use, before the cold weather sets in."

The women wanted to talk about food.

"Where can we get food supplies?" one of them asked. "What we have left won't last much longer."

"From the sea," suggested another. "There is always fish in the sea."

"Judging by the explosions from bombs and shells in the fjord, there may not be much to get." Uncle Ragnvald was serious. "Aren't you all forgetting that mines might be a problem too?"

The discussion went on for a while until Aunt Aslaug, ever practical, brought the discussion to an end.

"Let us go inside and see what we have for our evening meal. An early night will be good for us all." She turned, and started down the steps, followed by the other women.

On the 18th October, after requesting permission from Moscow, the Russians had pursued the retreating Germans into Norway. A large force had crossed the border to the east, near Tårnet, moving towards Karpbukt. Other Russian units had crossed into Norway at Pasvik and Neiden. The Russian North Fleet landed soldiers on the outer shores of Jarfjord. It was one of these troops of soldiers which had found us that afternoon. We had arrived at the bunker on the 14th October, my birthday, and now, eight or nine days later, it was still not safe to leave the shelter. For the rest of the day of our liberation, the men kept watch, and nobody moved far from the bunker.

The following night the men again took turns in keeping watch. The planes still came past in waves to support the land troops, as Russian soldiers fought their way towards the inner end of Jarfjord, on their way to Kirkenes.

The following day it was quieter. The gunfire had become more distant, but the planes still came past on their way to attack and harass the retreating Germans.

After some discussions, it was decided that three of the men should make their way down to the main road to see what they could find out. My father was one of them, and I immediately wanted to go with him.

"No, you cannot come today," he said, "It is not safe, and besides, I want you to stay here and keep your mother and Sonja company."

This was not a particularly interesting option, but I knew when to back off. Followed by a chorus of 'be careful' from the women, the men left.

On their return several hours later, there was good news and bad, as we all gathered around to hear what they had found out. They had walked towards the inner end of Jarfjord to see what houses were left. People they met told them that there were no Germans left in Jarfjord, but that hard battles had been fought the whole way, with many casualties left where they had fallen. The houses on the north-west side of the fjord were largely intact, but nothing much was left on the other side – much as the men had expected. They were also warned to be on the lookout for mines and other explosives, cleverly planted and camouflaged by the Germans before they left.

Near the inner end of Jarfjord, the men had seen a farm still intact, and had stopped there to approach the owner regarding somewhere to stay. The farm-house was full of homeless people, who had shared the family's underground shelter and had nowhere to go either. However, the owner, Mr Bugge, said that they had a farm bothy which our group could use until other shelter was found. After having seen the building, the men gratefully accepted. The bothy was just one long room, and we would all have to sleep together on the floor again – but it was vastly better than the bunker, and besides, it was possible to cook there.

The news of better accommodation lifted the spirits in the bunker. However, as darkness was closing in, it was decided to spend one last night in our shelter before leaving the following day.

Dawn next morning saw in another fine October day, with the sun low in the sky. In less than a month the sun would disappear from view for two whole months. It was as if God himself had taken pity on us, by keeping the snow and frost at bay.

After a small bite to eat in the morning, we packed up our belongings, such as they were, ready to leave. The bunker had been a life saver for us, and our final shelter before the invasion. The Germans had kept checking on us, but left us unharmed; the Russians had liberated us, and now we were on our own.

After a last look around, and with no regrets, we left, grateful to have survived the war, but walking towards an uncertain future.

23

A Loaf of Bread

Our next shelter, the farm bothy, was enthusiastically praised by the women. At one end it had a small kitchen with table and chairs. Two windows added to the feeling of light and space. No matter if we all had to sleep together on the floor again; we were used to that by now. Things were improving, and we now had a much better place to stay than the bunker we had just left behind.

So life moved on. The children were able to go outside to play, but with strict orders to stay close and don't touch anything. The danger of mines and explosives was very real. Distant explosions and gunfire could still be heard, and the planes were still passing overhead. The sound of aircraft engines was enough to send me darting for cover, with fingers in my ears. It didn't matter how many times my parents told me that this was no longer necessary – I still ran for shelter for a very long time.

The fear of low flying aircraft overhead never left me. In time, however, I learned to curb the feeling of rising panic that became so ingrained during the long and tough years of war. I was not alone in this respect. Most children were left traumatised, with haunting memories, never forgotten.

Bad news reached us on the day we moved in to the bothy. Lina, who looked after the animals on a small farm, had been shot. We had occasionally bought milk there when Aunt Aslaug didn't have enough.

The farm was owned by a family from Kirkenes, who were in their shelter when they smelt smoke. The Germans had set fire to the buildings. Looking out cautiously, they discovered that the byre also was ablaze.

"Oh, the animals," moaned Lina. She loved the animals, and before anybody could stop her, she was out of the house, throwing caution to the wind, running towards the byre to free the animals. Before she reached the byre, a shot rang out, hitting her in the head and killing her instantly. She crumpled and fell to the ground as the stunned onlookers watched – filled with grief and anger – unable to help. German soldiers were near, some needing little excuse to pull the trigger. And so the buildings kept burning ...

In our bothy, the news was received with sorrow and dismay.

"How many more?" said one woman bitterly.

"Let us hope that everyone responsible for these atrocities gets what they deserve," thundered my father angrily.

Murmurs of agreement were spiced up with what the various people would like to do to the Germans, if they had the chance. Many of the women had tears in their eyes – and looking at Aunt Aslaug I knew she was thinking of her animals.

Our first day of 'Freedom' was coming to an end, and the women were making the floor ready for our new sleeping quarter. There was no 'shelf' to climb up on here, just the floor for everyone. But no one complained, and why should they? We had 'Freedom' and we were alive!

The men sat around the table talking.

"Tomorrow we must try to reach Karpbukt," I heard Uncle Ragnvald say. "We have to find out what has happened there."

"If the rowing boat is still where it was left, and the Germans haven't destroyed it, we could row across," agreed my father.

"What about mines?" asked Aunt Aslaug, joining their discussion.

"Three of us could go, two rowing and one lookout," suggested another.

"Let us first see whether we have a boat and then decide,"

commented Uncle Ragnvald. "It may well be that we have to walk around the fjord, which will take longer, but is probably safer." With that settled, they moved on to other topics.

"There is talk of getting able bodied men together to remove all the casualties," said one of the men.

"Of course," Father said thoughtfully. "We must all help. The Russians are still too busy fighting the Germans, and good luck to them."

"Mamma," I whispered, "what are casualties?"

My mother looked at me in exasperation.

"So many questions you have, child, questions you should not have to ask. Go to sleep now and don't worry about anything." As an afterthought she added: "After all, we have Freedom now."

That word 'Freedom' again did not help me to find out about casualties. So I turned to Sonja whispering my question to her. She in turn had found out from Torgunn that it meant dead bodies, soldiers killed and maimed in the final battle around us.

I was not surprised to hear that many soldiers had been killed and were lying where they fell. Engulfed in the invasion with all its horror, it was a miracle that we were all still alive. At least that's what I heard my father say, so it must be true. There had been many near misses for us all, but somehow I could not imagine myself as a dead casualty. God must have heard our prayers and saved us, I decided.

Rumours that Kirkenes was free reached us the next day, but could not be verified.

As the Germans retreated towards Kirkenes, they blew up the roads, and in many instances planted mines in the craters before moving on. Russian soldiers in the front line soon found that out to their cost; some died as a result, before they learned to watch out for the craters instead of driving right over them.

Ammunition stores were blown sky-high as the German retreat continued. When the one closest to Kirkenes exploded, the streets in the town were peppered with debris and spent cartridges. Fuel depots set ablaze resulted in fireballs and a red sky for days, whereas the coal stores kept burning for many weeks. People's homes and farms were put to the torch, along with stores of hay and straw for the horses. Worst of all, the Germans set fire to or blew up their own food stores.

The vital bridge connection over Pasvik River at Elvenes was blown up and then booby trapped, as the Germans put up a surprisingly strong fight there towards the end.

The solid ring of defence around Kirkenes proved hard to break. The Germans doggedly fought back, refusing to give in. But the superior Russian tactics, in co-operation with their air force, were unstoppable.

A burned out and devastated town met the Russians, as they finally broke through the German defences and freed Kirkenes on 25th October 1944. What had taken the Germans four years to build up in the north was swept away by the Soviet Army in about three weeks. It was undisputedly an enormous achievement.

Our once prosperous little town of about 4,500 inhabitants was now in ruins. Many of the Company's buildings and factories had been severely damaged or blown up. At the harbour the piers were literally reduced to firewood. The population had fled.

In Bjørnevatn, the 3,500 people sheltering in the Company's mines were freed by the Russians in the morning of 25th October. By then, some of the tunnel dwellers had died, and Nelly Lund, the midwife, had helped ten new babies into the world during the invasion.

The German soldiers in Sørvaranger, with their Russian prisoners and Norwegian hostages, were already moving west on the main road (highway 50), with Russian soldiers in hot pursuit. Others fled in waiting ships.

From another direction, the Soviet plans to cut off the retreating Germans at highway 50, by coming in over Neiden, had failed. Their vehicles and tanks had faced enormous difficulties negotiating the rough terrain in that area. Fierce battles were fought at Neiden, where the Russians caught up with the last of the escaping German column. But the bulk of the German Army had just time enough to escape.

Surprisingly, the Russian pursuit stopped at Tana, on the Varanger peninsula. They had their orders, expecting Norwegian and Allied forces to take over. Unfortunately this did not materialise in time to stop the destruction of Finnmark. The Germans, upon discovering the Russian halt at Tana, made the most of their new opportunity. With more time to evacuate the population and take hostages throughout Finnmark, they rounded up people along the coast, in the hills, in caves and even turf houses, forcing them to join the German retreat.

In Jarfjord we were still ignorant of what was going on. Uncle Ragnvald, with two other men, found the rowing boat intact and got safely to Karpbukt, whilst Father and some other men went to a meeting to decide where to bury the 'casualties'. Mother desperately wanted to go to Storskog to look for Aase and Heide but was advised to wait another day or two before setting off.

Returning from their trip to Karpbukt, the men reported that all the houses had been burned. Father and the others came back to say that they would all meet the next day to start the task of collecting the dead for burial in one field, as a temporary solution.

Food was now becoming an urgent problem, and what could be done about it? With the German food stores destroyed, and no shops or supply lines to turn to, we were in real danger of starvation.

Uncle Ragnvald and his party had managed to retrieve some dead fish, which were floating in the sea with their white bellies up. They had kept a few of the freshest, gutting them and washing them in the sea. Father looked at the fish, poking at them as he always did to determine how fresh they were.

"Well," he said, "they are soft but still smell all right. Let us cook them and see."

Soon we all sat down to a dinner of fish, courtesy of Russian bombs or shells, and a few potatoes from a nearby farmer. A decision was taken that night to approach the Russians for food as soon as possible.

It may have been the next day, or the day after, that three Russian schnell boats (landing craft) came steaming in through the fjord and landed on the shore. About 5 or 6 of us children were playing nearby when they arrived. We drew back, but stayed to see what would happen. The ramps came down, and some Russian soldiers moved ashore – cautiously looking around. Slowly we drew nearer, till we were on the beach, but kept our distance from the boats.

After a little while a man came ashore. He was tall and had very short fair hair. Coming towards us, he stopped when he saw that we became uneasy. Then he pointed at us and the nearest boat. We didn't move. Next he beckoned to us with his finger and pointed at the boat again. We began to move, as one, nearer to the boat. He turned and walked towards the boat, and we began to follow. When he stopped, we stopped. He turned and smiled at us, and beckoned again. With curiosity getting the better of us, we followed him as he began to move up the ramp.

We had no idea what he wanted but let him help us on board one by one. He was very friendly, talking in Russian as he showed us around the boat. After that, we followed him down some stairs into what looked like a kitchen. A number of soldiers were sitting around a table finishing their meal. They were looking at us while the man said something to them. I suppose we must have looked very thin and scraggy standing there, with poor clothing and worn out shoes or boots. Perhaps we even looked hungry.

The tall fair Russian with the nice smile fetched a large white loaf, and a green enamel dish nearly full of butter. As he began to cut thick slices of bread and put butter on them, we were watching him with wide eyes and open mouths, not daring to believe that this might be for us. One by one, each of us was given a slice of bread and butter, and immediately began to eat. I was last in the queue. The big Russian lifted me up, gave me a hug and patted my head, then put me down again. Then he put the rest of the loaf on top of the butter in the green enamel dish and held it out to me. I looked at the big Russian and then at the other soldiers, unable to believe that they would give me such a wonderful gift. Then they all smiled and spoke, pointing at the dish and then at me. I hope that I had the grace to say thank you, as I accepted the dish.

The Russians laughingly helped us ashore, waving as we left, and we waved back. I couldn't get home fast enough, never touching the bread.

Bursting in through the door to our new 'home' shouting:

"Mamma, Mamma, see what I got from the Russians!" made them all gather around me. Half of that large white loaf was left and the enamel dish was at least half full of butter. They were all delighted.

"Let us make coffee," said my mother, "and we shall all have a piece of bread and butter."

Of course they didn't have real coffee, but some substitute they called coffee. Soon we had a small party going, where everyone enjoyed this unexpected and very welcome gift from the Russians.

The rim of the green enamel dish was bent outwards to form a wide lip. It was a bit battered, with bits of enamel missing, but we kept it for years. Sadly, it disappeared during a period when I was away from Kirkenes. In all my life since that October day in 1944 I have never received anything more precious than that wonderful gift from a Russian soldier – of bread and butter in a green enamel dish.

24

The Dead and the Living

A friend and I strayed too far from the house one day and came across a dead soldier, lying on his back in a hole blown out by a grenade. We couldn't see his head, which was possibly covered by sand – but by the look of his uniform, it was the body of a German soldier. We hurriedly backed away and ran home, saying nothing about it in case we got into trouble.

Two mighty armies had clashed in a deadly battle where thousands of young soldiers lost their lives – Germans and Russians alike. In the heat of battle, their bodies were left where they fell. The men had already started the gruesome job of collecting the bodies for temporary burial. The graves would be marked with wooden crosses for identification.

In the meantime, my mother had slipped away, making her way to Storskog to look for Aase and Heide – after first asking Aunt Aslaug to keep an eye on us. Even when Father told her that she wouldn't find anything, Mother still persisted in her quest to find out what had happened to her family.

She hadn't walked very far when, coming around a bend in the road, she almost tripped over a dead soldier. The back of his head was missing. On the verge of fainting, she forced herself past, taking deep breaths and swallowing hard. Knowing Mother's habit of fainting at the sight of blood, she must have drawn on divine strength to keep going. All the same, she had noticed a wedding ring on the man's finger.

Another family had lost its husband and father, she thought sadly. Continuing on her way to Storskog, she averted her eyes from other bodies – still to be collected for burial – trying to stay calm by taking deep breaths.

At Storskog, she discovered that the houses where Aase had stayed were all burned to the ground. The Germans had gone, and with them Aase and Heide. Filled with despair, she turned and made her way back again, still not knowing whether her daughter and granddaughter were dead or alive. When she passed the soldier with the back of his head blown off, someone had covered him with sacking.

Rumours were circulating that a nearby German field hospital had been burned down with its patients inside. Father wanted to investigate. Informing Mother where he was going, he was getting ready.

"I want to come too," I said.

"No, no," said Mother. "You are staying here with me."

Father looked at me thoughtfully.

"She can come with me," he said. "She has seen so much already, and may as well learn all the realities of war."

My mother was not convinced but gave in, and so we set off with my hand firmly in his. Sonja was not at home, or she too would have come with us. It was not far to walk.

On the way there we came past three dead horses. They were lying on their sides close to the road. One of them looked like Elsa, but when questioned Father said that it was not Elsa. He had a good look at the poor horses.

"They have worked them to the bone and left them to die, when they were no longer able to work," he said angrily.

"They" presumably were the Germans, but I didn't say anything more, seeing how upset he was. So we carried on walking, till we came to the ruins of the field hospital.

The building had been long and narrow. All that was left now was the foundation and a lot of rubble. As we began walking slowly past the ruins of the building, my father suddenly stopped to take a closer look.

So I looked too, and, startled, began to realise what I was seeing.

Burned bodies were lying there, two and two together; they were charcoal grey in colour; their heads were small and featureless, the arms and legs short, with hands and feet missing. The scorched bodies were resting on top of each other, leaning slightly to one side.

Father was muttering to himself under his breath.

"They have been lying in bunk beds too sick to be moved and when the building burned, they fell to the beds below and fused together. How terrible!"

Moving along, we saw more burned bodies. He looked at me.

"Do you understand what you are seeing?"

I nodded. "'They are dead and burned casualties."

"How do you think this happened?" he asked, studying me.

"Someone set fire to the building," I replied. After all, we were used to hearing that the Germans set fire to our buildings.

"Hmm," he muttered, "but this was their building."

Standing there – looking at the ruins of the field hospital and the charred remains of the bodies – he held my hand and continued talking to me.

"You are only ten years old, and all you have known in your short life is war, destruction, and death. But the war will soon be over, and a new life of peace and freedom will begin again. Then we can build new houses, schools and hospitals, and hope never to see war again."

I listened, but could somehow not imagine a future without war.

"Where are the Russian prisoners?" I asked.

Looking grim he turned and pointed towards Kirkenes.

"The Germans took them away when they fled. Many of them will not have survived. They were too weak from starvation, hard work, and not enough clothes to keep them warm."

"I wish the Germans had left them. Then we could have looked after them," I said, thinking about the Russian prisoners and the pretty toys they made for us children, feeling very sad. Father agreed but added,

"What could we give them to eat; we have nothing ourselves and no houses to live in."

"But we would not have kicked them and beaten them with guns," I persisted. "We would have been good to them."

Looking at me he nodded slowly.

After a last look at the ruins with the burned bodies, we left, making our way home; my father deep in thought and I, holding his hand, thinking that we were very lucky to be alive and not dead and burned casualties. Even now, after all these years, the picture of the bodies burned together two and two in the ruins of that field hospital is as clear in my mind today as it was then.

Father continued to help bury the dead soldiers, and during the early days living in the bothy, I sometimes saw German uniforms and helmets strung up in the trees.

Because of the mines and other types of explosives – camouflaged and left by the Germans – accidents were inevitable. Children were warned of the dangers and told not to stray away from the house, and not to touch anything.

The first accidents we heard of happened to the sons of the local school teacher. The older one picked up something which exploded, tearing away some of the fingers on both hands. Then the younger brother found another device which also exploded, but he was luckier and only burned the inside of his hands. Other accidents followed, leaving many children dead or maimed for life.

Food shortage was acute and famine became a real threat. We were often hungry, but there was little or nothing to eat. My father walked for miles in search of food for his family. He always came back with something, often from the Russians.

Blown up and burned, the ruins of German food stores were scavenged by people looking for tins that might still contain edible food. Surprisingly, the food in tins still intact could be eaten. And so a different battle for survival was unfolding.

Our Russian liberators, when approached, helped as best as they could. Without their help, widespread starvation could not have been averted. The whole civilian population was in the same boat, lacking food and shelter. With the weather getting colder, snow and frost were expected at any time. But another three months would pass before food supplies from the outside world reached us.

Of no particular interest to the Germans, the west side of the fjord had been left largely intact. All the same, the area had been patrolled regularly by German soldiers, who had retained a presence there. The reason for not burning the houses here may have been that the Russians came over the border to Jarfjord more quickly than expected. Running out of time, the Germans abandoned the burning and fled.

In the overcrowded bothy, families did their best to live with each other at such close quarters. Soon, however, they all started to look for alternative accommodation.

My mother approached a distant relation, asking for help. Their house was too small to accommodate our family – instead we were offered the use of a shed a bit away from their house. It was extremely basic, but would at least be a roof over our heads. The offer of the shed was accepted, and my father went to work to make it habitable.

After saying goodbye to our co-inhabitants in the bothy, one day in November 1944, we collected our few belongings and started walking to our next shelter.

25

The Shed

I suppose we had been lucky to secure the plank shed as our next 'home'. The shed, however, was empty, and very basic. My father got some nails and the loan of a hammer from the neighbour. Soon he had two beds made with planks and bits of wood, one for Sonja and me and one for themselves. There was just enough room to move between the beds. Straw mattresses were made to fit the beds. Our bed clothes were those we had brought with us from shelter to shelter. A table and four stools were quickly knocked together with more bits of wood.

To complete the new accommodation, our neighbours gave us a small wood burning stove to cook on, with a pipe serving as a chimney. There was not room for much more. The shed had no insulation, but hairy sheets covered the plank walls. One tiny window, single-glazed, let in some light. Luckily, a small porch sheltered the door into our new 'home'.

Mother took one look at it and sighed.

"How are we going to get through the winter?" she asked, with tears in her eyes.

"Like everyone else, make the best of it," said Father roughly.

Sonja and I said nothing. We had already detected the tensions between them, but I at least, did not understand the reasons for it. So we moved in, and tried to make the best of a bad situation. I missed the warm presence of Aunt Aslaug and her family. They had been allowed to remain in the farm bothy when everyone else moved out. It was not until 1947 that the family finally moved back to Karpbukt, where Uncle Ragnvald had built a new house – close to the site of their old one.

During November the weather got colder. Ice began to form on the fjord. It was very cold in our shed, in spite of keeping the iron stove going with wood. That winter, it was so cold at times that we would stand in front of the stove, turning around slowly trying to keep ourselves warm. Ice formed in and around the corners of the shed, and most of the time the window was a solid sheet of ice.

We were short of everything, including clothes. Washing clothes was a major problem. As washing powder and soap were unavailable, the clothes had to be washed in warm water from the stove and hung up on a clothes line between two trees, where they immediately froze solid.

When the small river nearby froze over, we had to melt snow on the stove to get water. It takes an awful lot of snow to get a pan-full of water so, in order to get enough for cooking and washing, we carried in endless amounts of snow.

Winter seemed to go on for ever. The days passed slowly, each much the same as the previous. A daily routine evolved. To get out of a relatively warm bed in the morning (we had quilts filled with feathers) and into that freezing room was an effort. Getting our clothes on as fast as possible became a competition between Sonja and me, in order to get the best position at the stove. As we turned slowly around in front of it with clattering teeth, trying to keep warm, we were already wondering where the next bit of food was coming from.

Father did a marvellous job. Starting in the morning by getting the fire going, he was soon away looking for food. He always came home with something. It could be a bit of bread from the Russians, a drop of milk from a local farmer or crofter, or a bit of salt fish or herring.

Society as we knew it no longer existed. There were no shops, no bakeries, and no supply lines leading to Finnmark. Everything was razed to the ground, except for a few houses or huts here and there. We were totally dependent on the Russian Army for food, and our survival. They did not let us down, but helped as much as they could. They shared their food with the civilian population as far as possible; they dug up and made safe mines and other explosives; they repaired roads and bridges, and when they left us in September 1945, the areas they had occupied were in a far better state than they found them in October 1944.

Although our corner of Finnmark had been liberated by the Russians in late October 1944, the rest of the country was still under German occupation. We were effectively separated from the rest of Norway until the capitulation of Germany in May 1945.

As Father was constantly out searching for food, Mother stayed home keeping an eye on us to make sure we didn't stray from the shed. Sonja and I got very bored in our continued confinement because we had no books or games to pass the time. Sometimes we met up with the boy across the road and had snowball fights. This often ended in tears, as he was very good at hitting his targets (us) very hard.

One day, not long after we had moved to the shed, Mother decided that we would walk to Haga to check on Aunt Reidun and her family.

The two houses at Haga were full to capacity with homeless people, all related to us in some way – many from Karpbukt. They had been in hiding in another 'bunker' in the hills during the Russian invasion. Uncle Edvard had in fact been in charge of the construction of the bunkers. Sonja and I enjoyed seeing Ruth and her brother Odd again, while Mother was chatting with her sister and the others, discussing food shortages, housing and having survived the war.

Thick ice had formed on the fjord now, and fishing was impossible until spring. German U boats were still a threat in Varanger fjord, where little or no ice formed. Some traffic had already started up across the ice between our side of the fjord and Karpbukt. Father had been forced to leave his bicycle behind when we crossed the fjord in October. He had hidden it well, he said, and hoped it was still there. For now the bicycle was of no use in the snow and he decided to wait till nearer spring before crossing the ice to look for it.

Christmas arrived, cold and dark. With the sun well below the horizon in mid-winter, this was the darkest time of the year, with only a couple of hours of twilight. We had no Christmas tree, no presents, and as usual very little food. Supplies would not reach us for another six weeks. Instead, we huddled together around the fire trying to keep warm, eating whatever Father had managed to scrounge for us that day. Our parents tried to tell us that at least we had 'Freedom' and things would improve. Sonja and I couldn't see that this 'Freedom' had brought us much, as we were hungry most days, but we didn't say anything to make our parents even more miserable. To round off Christmas Day we made an attempt at singing Christmas carols before going to bed. Our memories of a 'normal' Christmas, with nice food and presents under the tree belonged to a distant past.

Slowly and painfully, the long dark days of winter passed. The shed was very cold, no matter how much wood father packed into the stove. Only by standing very close to it could you feel a little heat.

Our parents were often bickering. She was pining for Aase and Heide, and he would say that Aase had got what she deserved, but what a shame for Heide. So Mother cried, and Father looked angry. I suggested that we should pray to God to keep them safe. After all we always used to pray to God before, didn't we? They looked at me strangely, and stopped bickering for a while.

One day, my father came home with a story which startled us all, and served as a grim reminder that there was still a war going on. Near the sea, on the east side of Jarfjord, a few chalets had been left standing, apparently too far from the road for the Germans to have time to set fire to them. Mrs Johnsen, a middle aged woman, lived in one of the chalets. In her porch she kept boots, and a large heavy winter coat. One morning, as she was bustling around in her kitchen, she heard a noise and went to investigate. A Russian soldier was retrieving her coat from a hook on the wall, when he was interrupted. He gave her a startled look and – before she could do anything to stop him – ran off with the coat under his arm.

Losing her only winter coat was more than Mrs Johnsen could tolerate. She gave chase, but soon lost track of the soldier. Determined to get her coat back, however, she walked to the Russian camp and complained to the officer in charge. Asked if she could recognise the soldier, she said that, yes, she could.

The officer assembled his soldiers, and asked her if she could identify the thief. Mrs Johnsen confirmed that she could and pointed to the soldier. To her shock and utter disbelief, the officer pulled out his gun, and shot the soldier dead right in front of her and the other soldiers present.

This unexpected turn of events left Mrs Johnsen speechless and in shock, as she stumbled away from the camp, the coat forgotten. She had only come to retrieve her coat. But the officer in charge may have wanted to set an example to his soldiers.

Mrs Johnsen kept running until she arrived at the house of a friend, where she collapsed on a chair, crying hysterically. Eventually her friend got Mrs Johnsen calmed down enough to hear her story. News travels fast in a small community, and consequently, any more thefts by the soldiers went unreported. It was said however, that some of the front-line soldiers were former criminals given a chance to fight in the Red Army. If they survived, they would have their sentences quashed. But if they transgressed – as may have happened in this case – no leniency would be shown.

With the return of the sun in late January, the days began to lengthen, giving us a little more daylight every day. By early February 1945 the first supplies reached us via Russia; brought by the convoys which did such a marvellous job during the war, in spite of the many ships sunk on their way to Russia. Depots were set up to distribute food, so that each family would get something, according to the size of the household. This lightened the mood in the shed.

We had a feast the first time Father came home with tins of soup, which was orange in colour and had meat and vegetables in it. I never forgot the taste and smell of that soup. It was absolutely wonderful (a far cry from mother's herring soup!). Following the soup were small white biscuits in a square shiny tin with a small round lid on the top.

For Father, there was a tin of tobacco which smelled like prunes, and some cigarette paper. How pleased he was that, finally, he could have a real smoke! Life got a bit easier after that. But the next food supplies to reach us did not arrive until April, when we again got tins of soup, some biscuits and, to our delight, a little corned beef.

Supplies of clothes had come from America via Murmansk. Mother brought Sonja and me to a depot where we got dresses. I got a dress in a beautiful burgundy colour with short puffed sleeves and wide elastic holding the waist together. Sonja got a lovely blue dress with small white flowers. To top it all, we got nice hats to go with the dresses. We had not had new or fancy clothes for as long as I could remember, and were both very excited about it all. But Mother was not struck with the hats.

"It's not hats and summer dresses you need, but warm hoods and jackets," she said, exasperated. But Sonja and I were delighted with our new clothes, parading back and forth in the limited space of the shed with our dresses and hats, while Father looked amused, and Mother had to smile too.

The Russians had a large camp near the inner end of Jarfjord. They showed great consideration for the population. Any accommodation still standing after the invasion was left to the civilians; the Russians themselves slept outside in tents all winter. Without their help, widespread starvation could not have been avoided in a population already worn out by war and shortages, and ultimately left with nothing in the face of an oncoming Arctic winter.

Large fires lit up the Russian camps, and sitting around the camp fires in the evenings, the soldiers were singing their beautiful haunting songs. Sometimes a balalaika would accompany their songs. Groups of children gathered at the outskirts of their camp fires to listen. One of their songs went something like this:

> Bela Russia agranoia
> Okraina saladoia
> Asha sha sha sha maladoia
> Systraniemis de krana krasi.

I don't know what it means, and the spelling is probably wrong, but that is what it sounded like. Another beautiful song was about 'Sten Karasin', a pirate on the Volga River.

The month of April saw the beginning of the spring thaw. By May there was still some snow on the ground, but small green buds were already appearing on the birch trees. We often saw Russian soldiers searching for mines, using sticks lengthened with metal wire like fencing wire. It must have been effective, because piles of mines grew at the side of the roads as they were defused and made safe.

A new and unexpected problem was facing us now, with the warmer weather. The hairy sheets on the walls of the shed turned out to be home to masses of insects (wall-lice), which seemed to crawl out when we were sleeping, and drop down on us to bite and suck blood. They became such a pest that my father had to take out the beds and everything else, tear the sheets off the walls, and burn them. The backs of them contained generations of insects, skeletons, eggs and young insects. The adult insects were reddish brown in colour, and the size of a child's finger-nail.

"To think that we have lived here all winter with millions of insects," my mother said shuddering with disgust. The insects bit her more than us.

"If it hadn't been for the warmer weather, they would still have been hibernating," my father replied. "They are not going to suck any more blood out of us."

During the winter, Father had walked over the ice to Karpbukt and found his bicycle. After carrying the bike back, it had been stored in the porch. He brought it out now, pumped air in the tyres, and made the bike ready for use. Disinfectant was needed for the shed and he set off to see if it would be possible to get some.

Several hours later he returned, telling us that he had cycled to Bjørnevatn, where he had been able to get some from the Company's store which, amazingly, had not been blown up as intended.

Father set about painting disinfectant on the walls, ceiling, our beds and anything that might still harbour the insects. After that we all helped to carry in the beds and the rest of our things. He had cured the insect problem, but we could see daylight between the planks, which were now the only barriers separating us from the outside. Luckily, we were now into spring, with the severe winter frost behind us so we managed well enough delighted to be free of the insects.

The Russian pursuit of the German Army had stopped at Tana, to the north-west of us, but still in east Finnmark. Earlier in the winter, news of forced evacuation and hostage taking throughout Finnmark had filtered through.

"When are our own soldiers coming to help, and where are the rest of the Allies?" Father was asking gloomily.

"Who knows the answer to that, with the whole world at war," Mother replied. "Surely it cannot go on much longer. There is a limit to what people can suffer."

"That limit is fast approaching. Think about all those who are hostages to the Germans, herded south like cattle. It is still going on, and what of us? Can we survive another winter like this?"

They fell silent, and Sonja and I looked at each other. It was not often that we saw our father as gloomy as this. He usually made light of things to keep our spirits up. After all, we had 'Freedom', and therefore everything was supposed to be all right, wasn't it? I thought about suggesting that we could all pray together, but somehow couldn't bring myself to say anything, either about our 'Freedom' or praying together.

"At least we are into spring now, with the ice breaking up and summer just around the corner," Father said eventually. "We might soon be able to get some fresh fish."

Even I, who had seen enough of salt fish and herring to last for years to come, thought fresh fish would be a welcome addition to our meagre diet.

26

Sollia Hospital

During the winter I had been troubled by severe bouts of tonsillitis. Our poor living conditions may well have been a contributory factor. As spring was approaching, my throat got worse, and I had problems swallowing. Mother decided to take me to Sollia Hospital at Storskog to see a doctor, whilst Sonja went with Father on his daily forages for food. With no transport available, our only option was to walk.

Protected by the surrounding hills, Sollia sits snugly among tall slender silver birch trees on a sloping hillside, slightly back from the main road – only 300 metres from the border crossing into Russia.

The large two storey building was erected in 1930 by the Sami mission, as a refuge for children suffering from tuberculosis. It had a capacity for approximately 30 children. After heavy bombing in June 1944, the hospital in Kirkenes was damaged and had to be evacuated. The Sami mission at Sollia agreed to move out, and the hospital took over the building. An operating theatre was made ready, and there was room for 25 patients. Now the only civilian hospital in Sørvaranger, Sollia and its patients had survived the heavy fighting during the German retreat.

Today Sollia, with its chalets and modern restaurant, is a popular destination for tourists.

Eventually we arrived, only to discover that the waiting room was full.

Sitting there waiting our turn, we listened to how other people had survived the invasion. Some now lived in the burned out basements of their former homes. Corrugated iron sheets, planks and anything they could find had been used to make roofs over their basements. Turf and snow were good fillers for openings and holes. Others lived under upturned boats set on posts, with walls made of turf, earth, and snow. The lack of food had been hard on everyone – but all praised the Russians for their help and support.

The conversation turned to accidents, especially among the children. A few days ago, two boys had been brought in, badly hurt. As it turned out, my mother knew both families, whose sons were about my age. The boys had found an explosive device, and put it on a chopping block. While one held on to keep it steady, the other hit it with a hammer or a stone. The resulting explosion threw them off their feet, tearing off both Odd's hands at the wrist, while Alf lost an eye, had his mouth torn open nearly to his ears, and lost most of his teeth.

We still had some time to wait, and Mother decided that we should visit the boys. A nurse followed us to the room where Odd's mother sat beside her son's bed. She rose to her feet and thanked us for coming, inviting us to sit down. While she told Mother how the accident happened, I was studying Odd. His eyes were closed and he was very pale, his bandaged arms were lying on top of the blankets. Because his hands were missing, the arms looked curiously short.

Alf's head and face were almost completely covered in bandages. Looking at them both, I wondered how anybody could manage without hands, eyes, and teeth. The teacher's son, who had lost some fingers or parts of fingers on both hands, was lucky I thought – at least he had his hands and some fingers to use. Soon Mother got up, saying that it was time to get back to the waiting room, so we said our goodbyes and wished them well.

After some time, we were called in to the legendary Dr Palmstrøm – legendary, because he stayed with his patients through thick and thin throughout the war, always doing his best for them in the face of adversity. The stories of him were legion. One in particular, I think, puts the man in a nutshell. When the infectious diseases were at their worst in 1943, and the hospital and other buildings were overflowing with patients, Dr Palmstrøm was called to a house where a young teenage boy was very ill. The doctor diagnosed acute appendicitis and decided to operate immediately, as time was running out for the boy.

The boy was put on the kitchen table and his mother had to stand by to assist Dr Palmstrøm. During preparations to operate, the air raid alarms sounded. The boy's father was forced to leave his wife and sick son, to take their other children to the bomb shelter. Undaunted, the doctor started to operate as the attack got under way. The operation was successful and the boy recovered.

Dr Palmstrøm was much loved for his kindness and for his fearless battles with the Germans to get the extra medicines, and equipment needed for his patients. He was larger than life, a tempestuous man who, after having been forced to evacuate to Sollia with his patients and staff in 1944, refused to leave the new 'hospital' with his patients, even when the Germans ordered them out. The Germans intended to burn the building, but no matter how the soldiers threatened and waved their guns, Dr Palmstrøm refused to budge. Where would they go? Where would he carry his patients? Outside among the trees? The Germans grudgingly backed down and moved on, aware that the Russians were not far behind.

Now I was here at Sollia, sitting on a chair in Dr Palmstrøm's office, facing him. Mother had come in with me, and sat nearby. After asking her a number of questions, he gave me a thorough examination.

"Hmm," he said, shaking his head. He turned to Mother.

"Her tonsils are very swollen and infected. This in turn makes swallowing difficult. As you know, medicines are in very short supply. I could send you home with a few tablets for her and something to gargle with, but the chances are that you will be back with her very soon."

Thinking it over for a minute he looked at me and turned to my mother.

"I suggest that we remove her tonsils here and now. She can stay here for three nights so that we can keep an eye on her, then you can come back for her."

Mother looked startled, and I didn't like the sound of this development at all.

"If you think so Doctor, I shall leave her here with you," she said then.

Dr Palmstrøm was not one to let the grass grow under his feet. Turning to my mother again as he rose, he said briskly,

"You can see her in the ward when it is over."

To me he smiled saying, "Don't worry, little girl, you will not feel anything and your throat will soon heal up."

Mother gave me a hug and told me not to worry, which was useless advice, as I was already very worried about this development.

My worries turned to alarm, when two nurses came in, starting to tie my legs to the legs of the chair and my body and arms to the chair back. When the tears began to roll, the two nurses were very nice to me. They patted my hair and face, telling me this was necessary in case I started to move during the operation. They were to stand on each side of me to support me and hold me still.

Dr Palmstrøm didn't waste any time. He came bustling in with a steel dish holding long injection needles. Another dish held something that looked like long scissors bent at an angle at the point. I took it all in, unable to believe that this was really happening to me. After all we had only come hoping to get some tablets!

"We'll soon have you on your feet again, little girl, don't you be afraid," he smiled. But afraid is what I was.

"Open your mouth," he said.

I was too frightened to do anything other than obey – and as one of the nurses held my mouth open, Dr Palmstrøm went in with the long needle for the first injection. Then he put another injection in the same tonsil. The second tonsil got the same treatment. By now I was crying and retching. Tears were rolling down my face and my nose was running. The nice nurses wiped my face, doing their best to soothe me and calm me down. After a while my throat was numb. I couldn't even swallow.

Dr Palmstrøm came back again and positioned himself in front of me.

"It will soon be over," he said kindly," but you have to sit very still. Do you understand?" I nodded.

"Good girl," he said. "Open your mouth again."

I obeyed, and as one nurse kept my mouth firmly open and the other one held my head still, Dr Palmstrøm put those long scissors down my throat and started cutting one of the tonsils away. I could feel him cutting it out, but there was no pain. I relaxed a little. Suddenly the scissors came out with a round lump of what looked like a meatball covered in blood.

"There." he said cheerfully, "that's the first one. It was not so bad was it?"

This did not merit an answer and besides, due to the situation I was in, I was unable to say anything at all. Grabbing the scissors, he was ready for the next one.

"Open your mouth again and let's get the other one out."

So I opened my mouth again, and with the help of the two nurses I got through the next few minutes a little better. Soon another lump of meat came out with the scissors, and with it I was spitting blood as well. The nurses were drying my tears and face, and I was given a little water to rinse my mouth. Now they set about untying my arms, legs, and body from the chair, and getting me to my feet.

Dr Palmstrøm stroked my head and said kindly,

"You did well, little girl, and will soon be fine again."

The nurses led me to a room shared by other patients, where a bed was ready for me. Mother came rushing in, having anxiously wandered around waiting for me.

"How are you?" she inquired, clearly worried. I pointed to my throat.

"Of course you will not be able to speak," she realised. "Is it sore?"

I nodded vigorously. She stayed for a while, holding my hand, saying that I would be fine and that three days would soon pass. But soon she had to leave for the long walk home.

The next day my throat was very sore, but gradually it became easier to swallow. I had to gargle regularly with salt water, drinking only water and thin soup. After three days, Mother came back for me, and I said goodbye to Dr Palmstrøm, the nice nurses, and my other newfound friends.

Before we left, we visited the boys who had had the accident. While my mother chatted with their mothers, I just sat quietly watching them.

Closing one eye and hiding my hands, I tried to figure out how it would be to see with one eye and to have no hands. Seeing with just one eye was not easy, I decided – but how would Odd manage to dress himself, or eat, or pick up anything, without his hands? The thought of the situation these boys were in, just by picking up an explosive, made me realise that the warnings from our parents not to touch anything suspicious were very much justified.

Sonja and Father were very pleased to see me when we arrived back. It was now spring and we could spend more time outside, or walk to Haga to visit our cousins. Ruth and Odd were always happy to see us, and when I related my experiences in Sollia to them they didn't believe it at first. Ruth kept teasing me about the episode with my father's helmet, and I threatened to bring my father next time so that he could do his old acrobatics with her. Sonja, who was thirteen years old now, was more interested in talking to the boys than playing with Ruth and me. But we enjoyed the trips to Haga, and my mother was happier after those visits.

Aase and little Heide were in our thoughts every day. Were they still alive, and what had happened to them? As yet no communication south was possible, and especially Mother suffered the agony of not knowing.

On the fjord the ice was breaking up now, and thawing fast. Soon it would be possible for the boats, which had escaped the German destruction, to go fishing. A neighbour had promised to take Father fishing. That really pleased him. Apart from the possibility of getting fresh food for us, he genuinely liked fishing.

That summer the fjord was boiling with shoals of saithe, to such an extent that at times it was possible to stand with a landing net and scoop fish into the boat. For the people in Jarfjord it was like manna from heaven, with fresh fish and livers giving us much needed nourishment, and a new lease of life.

News of the capitulation of the German Army reached us sometime in May 1945. The war was over. The much talked about 'Freedom' was now a reality all over Norway. News of large scale forced evacuation of Finnmark had filtered through, but not many details as yet.

My mother had friends in Vardø who owned a log cabin, still intact, on the east side of Jarfjord.

"If we could borrow or rent their cabin, we would have much more room," she said.

"Surely life can only improve now that the war is over." Father was pleased at the prospect of better accommodation.

He decided that we should all try to get to Kirkenes to see what was left, and possibly get a message sent to Vardø. But would Mother's friends still be there?

We set off early one morning, walking towards Kirkenes. On the way we got a lift from a passing Russian vehicle, arriving at Kirkenes sometime in the forenoon. Stunned by the sight that met us, we stopped.

Looking around, all we saw were ruins in every direction. Chimney stacks rose up from the ruins like accusing fingers pointing at the sky. With tears in our eyes we began moving towards Haugen, where we used to live. Other people were moving around too, just as shocked and bewildered.

The houses on Haugen had gone. Father began to dig in the ruins of our house, and found a large lump of metal, which was the remains of an ornamental solid brass shelf my mother had brought from Vardø. I spotted what was left of my ice skates, twisted and destroyed but still recognisable. Sonja found the metal Santa base for the Christmas tree, but they would never support another tree. Tears were rolling down my face now. I had loved the Santas, and now, like everything else, they were destroyed too. Mother tried to comfort me.

"We will get another Santa tree holder," she said. "You'll see."

But I didn't believe her. Where would we get that from? We had nothing at all any more. After a while Father stopped digging through the ruins. It was pointless, he said, and regretfully we moved on.

Some houses between Haugen and the sea had been built of stone blocks or mass concrete. Attempts at burning the houses had failed, and the use of explosives had only been partially successful.

These houses could be repaired and put to use again my father said after a good look at one or two of them.

Only a handful of houses were left standing around the town. A/S Sydvaranger, the iron ore company, had suffered widespread damage, but the railway line to Bjørnevatn had been repaired, and now served as a transport link.

Before we left, we walked down to the piers. They, too, were reduced to rubble and firewood. Luckily for us, a small fishing boat from Vardø was tied up there, and Mother got a message sent with them with the request to use the log cabin. When we returned to Jarfjord later that day, we were able to travel on the railway to Bjørnevatn and walked home from there.

Eventually we heard from Vardø that we could move into the log cabin known as 'Vallehytta'. Our parents were delighted, and therefore Sonja and I were pleased too.

The following day we set off to look at our next accommodation. It was not so far to walk, perhaps two to three kilometres. The cabin was very close to the sea, and even had a small rowing boat in a shed. The kitchen had a table and chairs, and a wood burning stove, and the two bedrooms were complete with beds. How wonderful! A small well of spring water added to the feel of almost luxury. Now we were all really delighted!

Moving in didn't take much effort. There was not much to carry except bedclothes, some utensils, and our clothes, not forgetting Mother's handbag with our family photos and, last but not least, the green enamel dish which I had got from the Russians. Having said our thanks and goodbye to the owners of the shed, we left it with relief, closing a chapter we would rather forget.

It was summer now, and Father tried out the rowing boat, which was leaking a bit – but he soon had that fixed and put it back in the water. Oars had been found too; so the three of us rowed along the shore exploring the area. He came across some fishing gear as well, and was soon fishing for small saithe which, at the time, were plentiful. Sonja soon got the hang of fishing, and Father showed her how to take the fish off the hook and gut them. Mother was delighted with the fish. Our diet was still strange, however, and depended on what else Father managed to get for us.

One day, after we had moved to the cabin, he came home with a young Alsatian puppy given to him by a friend. Sonja and I still missed Lappi and were happy to get a new dog to play with. It would learn to look after us he said. Soon he started cycling to Kirkenes, making contact with his employers at the iron ore company. The Company was now making an effort to assemble the workforce in order to get things moving again and to plan the way ahead.

By the end of the summer, Mother had somehow found out that Aase and Heide were alive and living in or near Oslo – and that Aase had given birth to another little girl at the end of December 1944. They were all well. We were delighted to hear the news, although Father passed no comment.

September saw yet another change to our lives. The Russian soldiers, who had liberated us and helped us through the winter, began to march back over the border to Russia. Sonja and I were very disappointed not to have been able to wave goodbye to them. Voicing my disappointment to Mother, her answer was:

"We didn't know when they were leaving, and it is a long way to walk to Storskog. We might also have come on the wrong day, you know."

The subject was closed, and we knew when to back off.

Afterwards, sitting on the steps outside, Sonja and I were talking about the Russians.

"The toys and rings we got from the prisoners were all destroyed in the fires." she said. "It would have been so nice to have something left. When I grow up I would like to visit Russia," she continued, turning to me, "and what about you?"

"Can I come too?" I asked.

Laughing, we ran down the steps, and headed for the sea shore to look for shells and pretty stones.

27

Forced evacuation

News of the forced evacuation of Finnmark had filtered through during the winter. This is a brief account of that evacuation – an important part of Hitler's final plan for the north.

The Soviet Army had retaken their territories in the north and liberated eastern Finnmark as far as Tana. The German Air Force could no longer bomb Russian towns and villages in the Arctic from airports in Norway. The Red Army had finished what they set out to do, and their guns fell silent on 6th November 1944.

Casualties had been high on both sides. The battle to clear the German Army out of Russia's Arctic territories and eastern Finnmark cost the lives of more than 15,700 Soviet soldiers. More than 2,100 died on Norwegian soil. During the withdrawal from northern Russia and Finland into Norway, the German losses were over 22,000 in dead, wounded, and prisoners.

In the wake of the battle, the roads were littered with burned-out vehicles, equipment, blown up tanks, and guns. At the roadside dead horses were looking sightlessly towards the sky. Along the way, fallen soldiers from both sides were left where they fell, until the fighting subsided and the dead could be buried. Smoking ruins were all that was left of the once peaceful communities.

The lovely forest of dwarf birch trees, lining the road between Jarfjord and Kirkenes, was shot to pieces. The white wood of broken trees was pointing to the sky or clinging grotesquely, by a whisker, to the stumps they had once sprung from. Many years would pass before nature had repaired the scars of war in the once beautiful birch forest.

The Russians had expected Norwegian and Allied troops to take over the pursuit of the German Army in Finnmark. When that did not happen at the expected time, the door was left open for the Germans to follow Hitler's orders to the letter.

On the 28th October 1944 Hitler had decreed that the retreating German army would enforce the evacuation of the entire population of Finnmark. Earlier attempts at voluntary evacuation had failed. Quisling had sent two of his right hand men, Jonas Lie and Johann Lippestad, to persuade people to leave, but few had taken up the offer. Those who decided to flee from the increasing air attacks had already gone. A scorched earth policy was to be implemented throughout Finnmark, leaving nothing for the pursuing Russian Army. Power stations, electrical installations, telegraph communications, roads, and bridges had to be demolished or blown up. No sympathy for the civilian population would be shown.

"Take them by force if necessary," was the uncompromising order.

Hitler's senseless policy shocked many German leaders. The sheer enormity of forcing the entire population of Finnmark (about 70,000 people) out of their homes, onto the roads or into the holds of ships, in wintertime, was staggering. People would suffer, but would also be a liability to the retreating army, they argued. An estimated loss of 25% to 40% of the evacuated people, in winter conditions, was entirely possible, should forced evacuation become a reality.

General Nicholas von Falckenhurst, and others, wrote to Hitler asking him to reconsider his decision. Their requests were turned down, and Josef Terboven, who was fully behind Hitler, had got his way. Von Falkenhorst was relieved of his duties in Norway, and atrocities in all their horrors were unleashed upon the people of Finnmark.

The decree came too late to force the people of Sørvaranger into evacuation. With the Russians so close behind, the retreating Germans had already gone, leaving a scorched and desolate land behind, strewn with mines, explosives, and booby traps. The majority of the population had taken refuge in the Company's mining tunnels in Bjørnevatn, where about 3,500 people were sheltering. Many, like us, who had been forced to leave early when our homes were bombed, were hiding out in the countryside, where many people had literally dug themselves into the ground.

As the Germans withdrew from Sørvaranger, people on the north side of the Varanger fjord, fearing forced evacuation, had already fled into the hills with their animals – hiding out in turf houses or caves. Before leaving, some hid their valuables by burying them in the ground or in sand pits. From their hiding places in the hills, local people watched as their homes and farms were put to the torch. Luckily, the byres were often damp, and the flames fizzled out. After they were liberated by the Russians, people returned home, repaired their byres and moved in to share the shelters with their animals.

Kiberg and one or two other fishing villages were spared, possibly because time ran out, or perhaps orders were ignored. Bugøynes, a fishing village at the inner end of Varanger fjord, was left untouched. A German commander went against his orders, and spared the village. When he came back to visit after the war, he was greeted as a hero by the locals. These incidents, however, were the exceptions. But there are stories of Germans who, resenting what they had to do, practically said sorry, but explained that they had to obey orders. Generally, however, their orders were followed to the letter.

With the realisation that the Russian army had halted at Tana and was no longer in pursuit, the Germans took their time rounding up the civilian population throughout the rest of Finnmark. As forced evacuation became a reality, people feared the worst, but still could not quite believe that this would be their fate, or that their homes would be burned.

Indeed, the Germans didn't have things all their own way. With the help of local Norwegian officials whom the Germans thought could be trusted, a deal had been negotiated with the Sami people for the purchase of their reindeer herds of about 70,000 animals. These were to be used for transport and food for the German army on the way south. The Samis were asked to move west with their herds to specific points, where they would meet up with the Germans. But the Samis, with encouragement from the same Norwegian officials, saw their chance and moved east, escaping with their animals under cover of fog. They had completely outwitted the Germans – their herds were intact, and only a small number of Sami people were forced into evacuation.

Telecommunications, electric installations, roads, and bridges were blown up, as people were forced to join the retreating German army. Minefields were laid, as well as mines hidden along the roads. Large Sami villages, such as Karasjok and Kautokeino, did not escape either, and they too were destroyed.

The journey across Finnmark was tough. People suffered terribly on the long treks, with little shelter from the biting wind and bitter cold of the treeless tundra. They had only been allowed to bring what they could carry. The columns of escaping Germans were many kilometres long, snaking across the Finnmark plateau with their vehicles, prisoners, and Norwegian hostages. The Germans were very thorough. If they suspected that people were in hiding, small patrols returned a day or two later to capture them in a second round-up.

Many prisoners-of-war did not survive. Worn out, cold and starving, often unable to rise again to continue the journey after a break, their fate was sealed by a bullet or a rifle butt. How many died this way, and were left lying by the roadside, is unknown.

Around the coast, German patrol boats played havoc with the fishing communities. Some fishermen had scuttled their boats to prevent confiscation. Others, who had kept their boats, were now forced to use them in the evacuation. With their passion for order and method, the Germans systematically visited every fishing village and township from Vardø to Hammerfest and beyond, forcing people out of their houses and on board waiting ships, while their homes burned. (Båtsfjord was an exception and was overlooked). Many, who had fled with their animals, returned too soon, only to be caught by surprise when the patrol boats unexpectedly reappeared. Those who were not caught were hiding out in more inaccessible and well hidden caves and earth houses. There they survived for weeks or months in the Arctic winter, under atrocious circumstances, often longer than necessary, as they did not know that the war had ended until they were found by their own people.

And so farm by farm, village by village, and town by town was laid waste. An estimated 45,000 to 50,000 people were evacuated or forcibly taken hostage. Many of the approximately 20,000 civilians left in Finnmark and North Troms County by May 1945 were living either in the areas liberated by the Russians or – as in the case of North Troms County – in caves and earth houses in the hills or on islands.

Desperate to get away from the bombing in Kirkenes, a family friend with her two daughters had returned to their native Vardø in the summer. When it, too, was extensively bombed, they fled to Mehamn, a small fishing village on the coast with about 800 inhabitants. Unable to get further south, the evacuation caught up with them there. One day, a German patrol vessel came into the harbour at full speed. Armed soldiers leapt ashore with their guns drawn. The inhabitants, unwilling to go with the Germans, were rounded up.

A German officer addressing the crowd stated that they would be better off following the Germans than to remain and be mistreated by the advancing Russians. Our friend's oldest daughter, looking at the officer, remarked:

"We prefer to take our chances with the Russians. They can hardly treat us any worse than you have done."

The officer's face reddened, as he smacked her across the face.

"You better watch your mouth," he spat. He waved his gun and pointed to the boat.

"Get on board!" The villagers had no choice but to board the German vessel, and were ferried out to a larger ship anchored offshore. From there, they watched in disbelief as their homes were put to the torch, and their village razed to the ground. Upon arrival in Tromsø they were put ashore to be transported south by other ships. Whilst ashore, they discovered to their delight that the German battleship *Tirpitz* had just been sunk. Surviving German sailors were milling around, some with dazed looks on their faces, as if they could not believe what had happened.

Two German ships, *Karl Arp* and *Adam Binder*, became notorious for their treatment of the evacuees. *Karl Arp*, a 4,500 ton German freighter, was detailed to pick up evacuees in Indre Billefjord, a small port in Porsangerfjord. The ship was slowly filling up with evacuees from east Finnmark – many from as far as Tana, about 100 miles to the east. Most were exhausted by their rough journeys across Finnmark. Many had been waiting for days or weeks in warehouses and barracks at different stops, while the round-up of the population continued. Irrespective of their age or state of health, Hitler's policy did not allow consideration and respect.

The ship's hold was soon filled to capacity, with 1900 people packed together like sardines in a tin. Wooden boards covered boxes of ammunition in the hold. A layer of straw covered the boards, which was to serve as a communal bed for 1900 people. With such a dangerous cargo, they could not even light a match.

Toilet facilities for the 1900 people were limited to two makeshift toilets at the deck's railing, open to the elements from below. The result was that the wind often carried discharged toilet paper up into the air and back on deck and, it was said, even into the soup pots on deck – where a field kitchen was catering for the evacuees. A small portion of bread accompanied the soup each day. There was very little water for the evacuees, and what was available had been contaminated.

As the ship finally got under way, people were afraid – afraid of being torpedoed, afraid of moving in case their place was taken when they came back – and deeply worried at what lay ahead. There was so little room in the hold that they could not even stretch their legs.

First seasickness struck – then dysentery and typhoid. Scrambling up the ladders to the deck and the toilets was an ordeal in the cramped, overcrowded conditions.

Disease spread quickly and, as the days wore on, armies of lice moved from person to person. With sickness and diarrhoea taking hold, people were sick were they lay, into the hay or straw. Unable to eat, they were finally too weak to fight their way up the ladder to the toilets, and let their waste go where they lay, adding even more misery. The stench and conditions became unbearable. During that appalling journey, some people lost their minds, and others died.

When the ship finally arrived in Tromsø, the shore authorities were denied access, in spite of several attempts at getting on board. They were told brusquely that all was well on board. However, at least the deceased were put ashore. Soon the *Karl Arp* was under way again, with Narvik as its destination.

Unbelievably, the German plan had been to march the hostages to a camp some distance away from Narvik. Instead, 95% of those on board were too sick to walk anywhere. Firemen and the Red Cross became involved in bringing the sick people ashore. Many of the volunteers had to put on gas masks before entering the hold. One young woman with a baby in her arms was so weak that she stumbled on the gangway, losing her baby overboard. In the darkness, the baby could not be found.

The sick evacuees were brought to hospitals and other buildings, where they could be treated and cared for. Families in Narvik came forward, offering to take in evacuees even when they had little room to spare. As Narvik had been under siege in 1940, they had some idea of what the evacuees had gone through.

When the next shipment of 1200 hostages arrived at Tromsø in *Adolf Binder*, under similar circumstances, representatives from the local authorities bluffed their way on board, claiming special permission from a higher German authority. Amazingly, they were not asked to show any papers. When the hatches were opened, they stepped back, appalled by the stench. Forcing themselves to go down the steps to the hold, conditions were far worse than expected. After heated discussions with the Germans, they were allowed to bring about ten or twelve of the very sick ashore for hospital treatment, but their relatives were denied permission to accompany them. As with *Karl Arp,* the ship then continued on its journey south. From Tromsø, and Narvik, the evacuees were sent further south, many as far as Oslo.

The persecution of people in Finnmark and North Troms County did not stop until the end of the war. The Germans did not give up easily, hunting for those they knew were in hiding. Many atrocities took place in the last months of the war, both on humans and animals, as demoralised and brutalised soldiers, who were often drunk, took out their frustrations on the innocent.

One incident happened when a family of four ventured out of hiding, thinking that the Germans had finally gone. Looking for food, they were taken by surprise when a German patrol boat appeared, approaching the shore at speed. As they ran back up the hill, the Germans opened fire. The woman and her two children were hit, but in spite of their injuries they managed to escape. The soldiers did not find them and the family survived.

Another small group on the coast were similarly taken by surprise by a German patrol boat. They ran, and, out of sight of the Germans, managed to dig themselves into a deep pile of seaweed at the beach. There they lay hidden for nine hours, not daring to move, while the German soldiers roamed the waterfront and the area, knowing that the Norwegians couldn't have got far. In the end the Germans gave up and left. Very cold, stiff and wet, the people crawled out, hardly able to move, but they had survived. Not all the hunted were so lucky.

Atrocities against animals also beggar belief. They were often used as targets, and shot at as they tried to escape. In one incident where the cows had been shot at, the animals dragged themselves down to the sea and, with their heads hanging down, bellowed in pain as their intestines floated in the sea around them. Their heartbroken owners were appalled at what they were witnessing, but were utterly powerless to intervene. Any intervention against a drunken German soldier would have been suicidal. In another incident, petrol was poured over the backs of sheep and set alight, sending them into the hills like living torches.

On the Finnmark plateau, small groups of people fled on skis. Some were caught; others escaped. Casualties were inevitable among those who, caught out in snowstorms, lost their way and wandered around for days until their food ran out and the weakest began to die.

Of the 45,000 to 50,000 people evacuated by force, an estimated 200 to 300 people died. But the exact number is not known. Some were buried in Tromsø, some in Narvik and others elsewhere. Neither the German estimate of 40% casualties nor the Norwegian Nazis' estimate of 25% loss turned out to be correct. One reason may be that the boat journeys to Narvik only lasted about one week, although most of the travellers had been on the move for weeks before boarding the ships. Another reason may be that those who were evacuated south in their own fishing boats, or on local freighters, had a better chance of survival by bringing a few belongings and some food. It could also be that people in the Arctic – toughened by a harsh climate and hard work – had a little extra to draw on, giving them an edge in the final months of their degradation.

The total destruction of Finnmark, with the displacement and harsh treatment of its people, was unparalleled in Norway during the Second World War, involving more than 70,000 people in a county larger than Denmark

As the Allies prioritised Europe, the small Norwegian forces, when they arrived, were too little, too late and had little impact on the last months of war. The Germans had already done their dirty work, and Finnmark lay stripped to the bone.

28

Red Cross to the rescue

Our new home, the cabin by the sea, was a huge improvement from the shed of the previous winter. There was much more room, and we had proper beds to sleep in. Sonja and I rowed back and forth along the seashore, exploring the bottom of the shallow water and enjoying our newfound freedom. Due to the many accidents involving children and explosives, some of them fatal, our movements were very restricted. But as it turned out, with the twists and turns of life, destiny was soon to take Sonja and me far away from our new home.

A rumour reached us that Sweden was offering to help families in Finnmark through the Swedish Red Cross organisation *'Rädda Barnen'* (Save the children). The offer was to provide foster care in Sweden for deprived children from the devastated areas, while temporary shelter was sourced for the remaining people of Finnmark in a bid to avoid the hardship of the previous winter.

The children would be looked after by Swedish families from October 1945 until May 1946, where they would receive proper food and care. At first, our parents wouldn't hear of putting our names on the list.

"I don't want you two to go away to another country for a whole winter," said Mother, and Father agreed.

"After all, the war is finished now, and new houses will be built for us," he said.

But with an Arctic winter lurking around the corner, new houses were still just a distant dream. Soon the list contained hundreds of names, as people considered what was best for their children. Both Sonja and I thought this would be a great adventure. All we could think of was a nice warm place to live, with new clothes, proper shoes, good food, and no insects in the walls!

Most of the children we knew were going. Caught up in the excitement of it all, we kept nagging at our parents to allow us to go. Eventually, they relented and put our names on the list. What no doubt tipped the balance in our favour was weighing up the bleakness of our present existence, against a winter in Sweden with proper food and care.

The old coastal steamer D/S *Dronningen* was chartered to provide transport for the children to Narvik. Because the sea around the coast was far from safe from mines, two mine sweepers were assigned to escort the ship. By sailing during daylight hours only, it was considered reasonably safe. In Narvik we would board a train for the onward journey to Sweden.

Mother did her best to make our clothes presentable for the journey to Sweden, and Father made bags for our few belongings. However, we were disappointed to hear that our cousins Ruth and Odd were not going to Sweden.

On the morning of the 9th of October 1945, we found ourselves in Kirkenes, ready to board D/S *Dronningen* along with 323 other children. Young volunteers from the Norwegian Red Cross accompanied us and looked after us on the sea journey to Narvik. There, the Swedish Red Cross took over the responsibility of getting us safely across the border to Sweden. Each of us had four or five labels around our necks showing our names, our parents' names, where we came from and where we were going.

Saying goodbye to Mother and Father was hard. We all had tears in our eyes, and with promises of being good and to write home, we boarded D/S *Dronningen* for the first leg of our journey.

October is a cold, dark month in the Arctic, the midnight sun with all its light and promise left well behind, and the long, dark winter looming ahead. It was cold the day we left, with low ominous looking clouds and a carpet of snow covering the ground. The sea was choppy, dark, and threatening. A large crowd had gathered on the pier, where families were saying goodbye to their children.

As the three hundred and twenty five children flowed up the gangway, I tried to turn and wave to my parents, but wasn't sure if they could see me. Suddenly I felt like running ashore and never leaving them again. But instead, I was carried along the deck with the flow of children, unable to turn back. I spotted Sonja and stayed close to her.

When D/S *Dronningen* slowly backed away from the pier, we crowded the decks, waving. Families and friends seeing us off waved frantically back. As Kirkenes became smaller and disappeared behind us, we were all a bit subdued. Some of the smaller children were snivelling, with tears running down their faces. The nice Red Cross carers were there immediately to comfort and care for them.

We were led inside, where we got our first dose of lice powder sprayed over our hair, and inside our clothes. After this surprising start of the 'adventure', the young women looking after us brought us to our cabins. Eight children had to share a four berth cabin, two for each bunk and not much room to sleep. Luckily, Sonja and I shared one of the bunks. Stacks of small boxes lined with tinfoil were set up at each bed. They were there we were told, in case we were seasick. It had not occurred to me that we might get sick on the journey. But as it turned out, the carers had their hands full when most of us got seasick, and they had to carry out the sick boxes. We learned that the bigger boys had to sleep in the hold of the boat on beds of straw, with blankets to keep them warm.

How to put on life jackets in an emergency was next, demonstrated to us by our carers. When we showed alarm at this development, they told us not to worry. All ships had to follow this rule.

Because the ship sailed during daylight hours only, the journey took four or five days. I was very seasick for three days.

"I wish I was dead," I wailed. "I want to go home."

Sonja tried to help me as best as she could. Unable to eat, I stayed in bed most of the time, being homesick as well as seasick. She was not seasick, and told me that it was pointless to be homesick.

"Soon we'll be sheltered by many islands and the sea will be calm," she said.

"How do you know that?" I moaned.

"The Red Cross women told us that the Captain had said so."

"When will we be in Narvik?" I muttered, sick and exhausted.

"The day after tomorrow, but you'll soon be better now," she said confidently. I didn't believe her. The next day, however, was calm and I began to feel better.

On deck later that day, the fresh air helped to revive me, and I looked around curiously, seeing land all around us. We were sailing through a narrow sound, with houses dotted on little islands, some quite close to the shore.

It had been a bad trip. Most of the children had been very sick. Some were sick in their bed clothes. The bigger boys in the hold did not fare better. After a while they had not been able to crawl up the ladder to be sick over the railing or to empty their own sick boxes. The toilets were overflowing and the crew had a busy time trying to clean up and clear the toilets.

The ship was stinking. The journey to Narvik on board D/S *Dronningen* was only memorable for how bad it was. The volunteer helpers did their best, but some of them had been sick too. Those who were not seasick had been helping out as much as possible.

Definitely feeling better now, I was suddenly hungry, and went in search of something to eat. Lisbet, one of the carers, led me to the dining room and fetched milk and sandwiches. Good! After little or nothing to eat for days, I was very hungry.

On our last day onboard D/S *Dronningen,* I was finally able to meet up with the girls I knew from Kirkenes. Most of them had also been seasick. Since we would arrive in Sweden the next day, we all wondered and speculated about our foster families, hoping that they would be nice to us. Sonja continued keeping an eye on me. After all she was nearly three years older and I was glad to have her around.

Having brought us safely on the perilous journey from Kirkenes to

Narvik, D/S *Dronningen* was tied up at the pier when we woke up on the final morning. As instructed, we washed and dressed, before assembling in the dining room for a last meal on board.

A final unpleasant surprise was in store for us when we gathered on deck ready to go ashore. On the pier in Narvik, spectators had gathered to look at the 'children from Finnmark'. Lined up on deck in two lines, we were moved forward one by one. On each side of us two people were standing at the ready, dousing our hair and inside our clothes with lice powder, to great amusement of the spectators on the pier.

Red faced and embarrassed, we tumbled into the waiting buses, relieved to get away from the prying eyes and laughing faces.

Narvik had been the scene of the last big battle for freedom in 1940, and it showed. Curiously, looking through the bus windows, I observed that it had, however, survived much better than Kirkenes.

The rest of the trip was uneventful. As the train sped across the border into Sweden, the landscape changed. The rocky hillsides of Norway gave way to great forests, stretching in all directions. Tall conifers whizzed by the train as it hurtled deeper into Sweden. In stark contrast, the bare landscape of Finnmark has very few trees, only patches of dwarf birches here and there. Pasvik Valley in Sørvaranger is the exception. Bordering Finland and Russia, it has some fine pine and spruce trees.

Upon arrival at our destination in the north of Sweden, we were quarantined in a camp at Kusfors for the next one to two weeks.

Kusfors turned out to be a small village, with two large refugee camps close by. The camps had originally been set up for civil defence purposes. During the war, they had been used to accommodate Allied pilots making emergency landings in Sweden. German deserters had also stayed there. A large number of refugees from Finland occupied one of the two camps. The other, designated for us, was designed to hold 1000 children. A high barbed wire fence separated the two camps.

We were the first Norwegian children to arrive, followed by two additional shiploads from Finnmark of 250 to 300 each. The camp was laid out like army barracks, with small wooden buildings designed to take about sixteen children and one carer each. The sleeping quarter was one big dormitory filled with bunk beds. The boys and girls had separate quarters. Our carer was called Anna.

The buildings had been given fancy names like Teddy Bear, Sugar Mountain, Dolls House, Haystack and Snow House. Sonja and I, along with fourteen other girls, were placed in 'Sugar Mountain' (Sukkertoppen). I had been allocated one of the top bunks and fell out of it on the first night. Hearing the noise, Anna came rushing in. Luckily, there were no bones broken, just the shock and some developing black bruises.

The next day was my 11th birthday. No one knew about it except Sonja and, to my great disappointment, the day passed unnoticed. On my last birthday we had been on the run; on this one I was in a camp in Sweden where nobody took any notice. Did Mother and Father remember my birthday, I wondered. Then, thinking of Aunt Aslaug, I brightened. I was sure she would remember it!

Getting to know our way around the camp, we found that there was a building for everything: There was one where we got our meals; one where we bathed and washed; one was a sauna and one was a hospital.

As the days passed, each in turn was taken to a doctor's office, where we got weighed and measured. We were tested for tuberculosis and other illnesses. Those of us who still had head lice got another dose of lice powder. Some children had illnesses which required hospitalisation. All had to be vetted before being sent out to the Swedish communities.

Meal times were the best part of the day, when we assembled at the dining room building. Picking up a tray each, we queued for our meals at a counter. Different, but good was the children's verdict on the food. The meal times were good for another reason. It was routine, something to hold on to in a new and strange world. Here we struggled to understand what our Swedish carers were saying, in a new language, not so very different from ours – but different enough to create misunderstandings. Though all of us had come out of the war traumatised in one way or another, the resilience of children carried us through – and so we settled in to our new life in the camp fairly well.

Soon it was made clear to us that all the younger children would be in the first group to be sent to their foster families. I realised, to my horror, that I would be separated from Sonja, who was my only link with home. Anna told me in her lovely Swedish tongue that I would be well looked after and not to worry. Telling that to a child of the war is not much help. Worry and fear were second nature to us.

The big day arrived, and the departing children were assembled at the railway station. Sadly, I had to say goodbye to Sonja before leaving the camp, not knowing when we would see each other again. She smiled and said to me:

"Remember what Mother and Father said and be good."

With tears in my eyes, I turned and followed the others. So far the Sweden trip hadn't turned out to be much of an adventure!

Many of the Swedish carers accompanied us to our destinations. At every station a crowd had gathered. One of the labels we carried around our necks had the name and address of the foster family. As children got off at their destinations, I saw people moving from child to child, examining their labels till they found the right one. Their credentials were checked by the carers and the child handed over.

By this time I was thinking even less of our 'great adventure'. We were like packages sent by post to be collected. Perhaps there was no other way of doing this but, standing there with the other children at the railway station in Öjebyn, I felt helpless and lost.

Some people came forward and began to examine our labels. A small round woman appeared and looked at mine. Suddenly, to my surprise, she gave a shriek and ran away, only to reappear with a family of three, a man, a taller woman, and a boy two or three years older than me. The tall woman examined my labels and obviously found their names there. She smiled and said something to me, and before I knew it she gave me a great hug. One of the carers came over to confirm who they were and handed me over to them.

As simple as that.

I had difficulties in keeping my eyes off the woman's hat. It was black and sat like a cloche on her head with what looked like a large birds nest sitting on the top, tilting slightly forward. It may have been the height of fashion in Sweden, which I knew nothing about anyway, but I had never seen anything like it.

The family had brought a push sledge, indicating that I was to sit on it. As we set off for their house, they were chatting away, smiling at me – and I had no idea of what they were saying.

And so began the next part of my 'adventure' in Sweden.

29

Evacuee in a foreign country

Öjebyn was a small country town in northern Sweden, near the larger town of Piteå. It was well spread out, with a small town centre surrounded by farms and crofts. In the old part of the town a surprising number of small wooden houses stood fairly close together in rows. They were very old, and mainly used at religious gatherings like Easter and Whitsun, when their owners moved in for the holidays.

Following the strange meeting at the railway station in Öjebyn, Nanny and David Johansson became my foster parents in Sweden. They asked me to call them Aunt Nanny and Uncle David. Their son Rolf, about three years older than me, was nicknamed Rolle. Unsure of what to make of this new member of their household, he ignored me and kept his distance for a while.

My new foster parents turned out to be nice people and very good to me. I got a room to myself, which was a novelty I never had before. Perhaps coming here was not such a bad idea after all! The language, of course, was a drawback and caused problems at first. Many words have totally different meanings. The cooker was called 'spis' which in Norwegian means 'eat'. The Swedish word 'rar' means sweet or charming, but in Norwegian it means unhinged or not of sound mind. 'Pitbonska', their dialect, was sufficiently difficult for Swedes from other parts of the country to struggle with. Small wonder then that I had no idea what they were saying.

The first trip with Aunt Nanny to the local Co-op ('Konsum' in

Swedish) was mind boggling. Supermarkets did not exist in those days, but this Swedish shop was like something out of this world. I stopped inside the door and just stared.

The shop was bursting with light, and had gleaming glass counters, where shop assistants in white jackets were moving around serving the customers. A lovely smell of freshly baked bread and buns filled my nostrils, as I stared at the glass counters. Behind the glass I saw meat, cheese, and all sorts of other delicacies. They had milk, bread, buns, and crisp breads. Catching my eyes in particular were cakes, chocolates, and sweeties. The shops in Kirkenes were never like this, and here, no one was queuing. I was overwhelmed. It was the nearest to heaven I had ever come – only the angels were missing!

Aunt Nanny was speaking to me, but as I had no idea what she was saying, I just looked at her. She then pointed to the chocolate counter, and I nodded. The shop assistant put some caramels in a bag and chocolate in another. The caramels were chocolate coated and became an immediate favourite. To think that they had all this food in Sweden and we had very little food and no shops at home! I suddenly wished that my mother and father could have been here to see all this.

Uncle David provided pen and paper one day so that I could write home, and Aunt Nanny came with me to the post office to get a stamp and put the letter in the post box. Keeping up a stream of conversation on the way, she looked at me now and then as if expecting an answer. As most of what she was saying meant nothing to me, I either nodded or shook my head, hopefully at the right places. But she just laughed and said what I took to mean that 'I would soon learn'. When we were out together, people often approached us asking about 'Flickan från Finnmark' (the girl from Finnmark). Aunt Nanny always put a protective arm around me, telling them my name, and since I didn't know at first what they were saying, I kept quiet.

Because of the broken communications in Norway, and especially in Finnmark, a letter could take two to three weeks to get to Kirkenes. I often wondered where Sonja was and wished I could see her or talk to her – but a month or so would pass before contact was made.

Soon after arriving in Öjebyn I was enrolled at the local school. By attending school and listening to my foster family, I began to pick up the language and make new friends. Although my education had been very erratic, and at times non-existent, I enjoyed my time at school in Sweden. In particular I enjoyed geography, with reading and writing Swedish a close second.

During Swedish lessons we learned about the great writer Selma Lagerlöf, whose book, 'The Wonderful Travels of Nils Holgerson' was read in class. The book made a great impression on me at the time and spurred me on to read other books in Swedish. My circle of friends expanded as I began to speak the language better. One of my best friends that winter was Gerd. She lived close by, making it very convenient for us to visit each other. Her mother was very friendly, and encouraged me to come as often as I liked.

Like all their neighbours the Johanssons had a phone in their house. One day when Aunt Nanny answered the phone, I could hear her getting excited.

"Yes, yes, she is here," she was saying, "yes she is fine." Turning to look at me while speaking, she beckoned to me to come to the phone.

Puzzled I moved towards her. Handing me the phone she said, "It's your sister. She wants to talk to you."

Carefully I took the phone. I had never spoken to a phone before. Aunt Nanny pushed the phone to my ear.

"Speak to your sister," she whispered.

"Hello," I tried.

"Hello, is that you, Bjarnhild," came the voice out of the phone. It certainly sounded like Sonja. Getting a bit bolder I said:

"Yes it's me, where are you?"

"I am in Landafors beside Aunt Irma and Uncle Svante," she answered. I realised she was talking about her foster parents but had no idea where Landafors was.

"Where is it?" I asked.

So she told me that it was in the middle of Sweden, near the coast. Her foster parents were Irma and Svante Hanson, who had a small son called Bo. She also told me that she had remained in the camp about a week longer than me, before being sent south by train with other children. Her foster family was very nice and she was pleased to be with them.

Aunt Nanny took over, to speak to Sonja's foster parents, and it was decided that we would keep in contact and talk on the phone from time to time. Sonja's foster parents had tried hard to find out where I was, but had found it difficult to get the information from the authorities.

The unexpected call from Sonja had made me very happy. What I now was looking for was my first letter from home. It came a week or so later. My mother wrote that they were fine and happy to hear from us both; relieved also that we had arrived safely and were now settled down with our new families. After contact was established with my family, I felt a lot happier, and started to enjoy my time in Sweden much more.

Christmas was looming, and Aunt Nanny announced that she and I were going to bake biscuits, buns, and 'Christmas bread'. Baking in Norway during the war had been non-existent, apart from my mother's struggle to bake bread with poor quality flour.

I looked forward to it with great anticipation. When Aunt Nanny put on an apron and tied another one on me, I got really excited. She put white head-squares over our hair, and with a mischievous look on her face started chanting: 'Now we look like real bakers, real bakers, real bakers'... as she took my hands and danced around the kitchen wiggling her hips, making me do the same. Uncle David burst out laughing, while Rolle looked disgusted and made for the door.

"Why can't Rolle bake with us?" I asked, looking at the closing door.

This created another burst of laughter from both of them.

"Oh never mind him," said Aunt Nanny, wiping her eyes. "He wouldn't be seen dead in an apron."

Aunt Nanny was a good teacher, and saw to it that I learned the whole process of baking biscuits. The large kitchen table, sitting in the middle of the floor, served as a baking board. Soon we were cutting out ginger men, stars, and other shapes. We made biscuits with almonds, and we made butter biscuits. Uncle David sat in his favourite chair, smoking his pipe while watching the proceedings. In between instructing me, Aunt Nanny was singing. I don't know what she was singing, but she liked to sing while she worked.

The first day of the great baking experience came to an end and was announced a great success. I entirely agreed. We all had a taste of the finished products, before they were packed in air tight tins for storage until Christmas.

Just before Christmas, we baked Christmas bread, which was made with yeast. It was sweet and contained raisins. When risen and kneaded again, it was cut into three lengths and pleated like a woman's hair. I struggled with the pleating and couldn't get it right. Aunt Nanny just laughed and told me to make it round instead. Her pleated bread looked much better – but it was all very good.

Christmas decorations were Aunt Nanny's next target. Rolle and I were sent out to find slim tree branches of a certain length. They were dipped in what must have been a watery type of glue, and then tossed with glittery stuff in different colours. When dried and arranged in vases they looked stunning.

Uncle David didn't escape either. He had to decorate the walls with roll after roll of Christmas scenes. To finish, we all had a hand in decorating the Christmas tree brought home by Uncle David. His job was arranging the lights for the tree. The end result was lovely. But, with a lump in my throat, I remembered Christmas a long time ago with Mother, Father, Aase and Sonja, when our tree was held by a ring of Santas painted in bright colours.

The Swedes were great for traditions, then and now. Over the years, keeping alive the contacts and friendships made in 1945/46, I have learned to appreciate their traditions. It gives structure to your life; it makes you feel safe in the knowledge that some things remain unchanged. I experienced some of these traditions during my winter in Sweden, although at the time I didn't think of them as such.

On Christmas morning we were up at seven o'clock, getting ready for church. I couldn't understand why we had to get up so early.

"Why can't we go to church in the afternoon?" I asked them.

"Because it is 'Julotta' and everybody goes," said Uncle David.

I was still mystified, but said no more.

It was dark outside, with hard frost and quite a lot of snow. Uncle David had his horse and sledge ready and waiting for us. We carried blankets to wrap up in, as we had quite a long drive ahead of us.

The horse was tramping its feet, impatient to move, its breath freezing in the cold morning air. We piled into the sledge, wrapping up, with Uncle David at the front to steer the horse and sledge. Moving off, the crisp, clear sound of the bell around the horse's neck broke the silence of the early morning. Soon other bells joined in, as more horses with sledges carried people to church for the eight o'clock service on Christmas morning.

The church was well lit up outside, and the horses were tied up in rows nearby. When we arrived – leaving our blankets behind in the sledge – people were already moving towards the church. Curiously, I looked around as we found our places inside. It was beautifully decorated, with lots of flowers, candles and other signs of Christmas. Soon the church was full and the service could begin.

The only thing I remember from that service is that I recognised some of the psalms and that the whole thing was lovely, even if I didn't understand all that was said. When prayers were said, I prayed quietly for Mother, Father, Sonja, Aase, and little Heide, hoping they were all safe and well.

Outside the church, daylight had crept in, and people were mingling for a little while exchanging Christmas greetings. But it was too cold to stay for very long. Soon we were tucked up in blankets again, on our way home, to the merry sound of the horses' bells.

Christmas lunch was an elaborate affair. The many dishes for the table, which I was now helping Aunt Nanny to set out, had been prepared beforehand. There were all kinds of herring dishes and salads; meat dishes; crisp breads and other types of breads and buns, including the Christmas bread which I had helped Aunt Nanny bake. Jugs of a special kind of soft drink for Christmas, called 'Tomte brygg', was put on the table. It looked like dark beer, but was surprisingly good.

Soon Ragnhild, Aunt Nanny's sister, and family from Piteå arrived to share Christmas lunch with us. They had a son, Per Ivar, who was the same age as Rolle. (It was Ragnhild who found me at the railway station).

A lively lunch hour followed, with Ragnhild's humour and infectious laughter spilling over on the rest of us. Uncle David moved to the organ and started to play Christmas carols, while the rest of us gathered around to sing along. It was a lovely, enjoyable day – a day to remember always.

30

Going Home

The winter wore on and the language problems became a thing of the past. My stay in Sweden, however, was marred by illness. I caught one cold after another. Then I got measles, followed by ear infections. Something didn't agree with me. Years later, I realised that it was the abundance of rich food my body couldn't handle. After years of little and poor food, I was now in the land of plenty, but my body couldn't tolerate it. At the time nobody knew about allergies, or realised that the effects of such a drastic change of diet could be the cause of all my misery.

The first letter from home with bad news was to tell me that my grandmother in Lofoten had died. She was my father's mother, and had sent us parcels at Christmas before the war. I don't think I cried but I was very sad. I had never known her, and now I never would. It occurred to me that Father would be very upset. He adored his mother, and had always told me how kind she was, promising that one day he would bring me to Lofoten to meet her and grandfather.

I read that we had been allocated two rooms in a house which belonged to the Company, and that my parents had now moved to Kirkenes.

"Great," I thought to myself. "At least we will return to a house in Kirkenes, even if it isn't Haugen!"

The house was one of three houses on the outskirts of the town, on top of a hill behind the AS Sydvaranger works. Strangely enough, the houses had survived the holocaust of the invasion, but only just. Two and a half stories high, with a full sized basement, they had four flats with three rooms each, and two rooms at the top. After necessary repairs had been done, ten families moved in to 'our' house, with two families to each flat. We got two rooms and another family got the third room in our flat. A washroom and store-rooms in the basement were shared by the families. The toilets were outside. My remaining years of growing up were to be spent in that house.

The next letter with bad news was waiting for me one day when I arrived back from school. The only thing I took in from the letter was that Heide had died. Our darling Heide, whom we all had loved and adored, was no more. After Aase had taken her away more than a year earlier, we had all missed her terribly. Bursting into tears, I was inconsolable. Aunt Nanny held me and tried to soothe me. Uncle David did the same. Even Rolle hovered around looking sad and uncomfortable. My best friend Astrid's death had been dreadful, but this was even worse. The war was over, and I had so looked forward to seeing Heide again, and now I never would! It was unbelievable.

When I was able to read the letter again, my mother wrote that Heide had taken ill with what seemed to be a chest infection, and had subsequently died from it. There were so many questions to ask, but no one in Sweden able to answer them. However unwillingly, I had to accept what had happened, and that I was here to stay until spring.

Another letter told me that father had lost the tips of three fingers on his right hand in a work accident, but that he was fine now. Three times I had received letters from home with bad news. But the loss of Heide was by far the worst, and very difficult to come to terms with.

Sonja's phone calls were a great help. She had stayed with our granny and granddad in Lofoten and was very upset about both her and Heide. But life had to move on. The Johanssons were very good and kind, treating me like a daughter, and I, in turn, got very attached to them.

School was a great diversion from my grief. I borrowed books from the school library as often as possible. The geography lessons taught us the names of all the counties in Sweden and where they were. We learned about the towns, rivers, lochs, and islands of Sweden. The history lessons taught us about when Sweden was a great empire, and about King Gustav Vasa. We all liked the music lessons, where we learned many songs and how to sing them together like a choir.

Uncle David was teaching me to play their organ. He had a repertoire of songs which he taught me to play and sing. I enjoyed this immensely. Aunt Nanny would join in the singing to make it great fun – and when her sister Ragnhild visited it became very entertaining. 'Flickan' is getting better, she boomed in her rich voice, clapping her hands.

Rolle had gradually come to accept my presence in their family and occasionally sat down to play a board game with me. At other times he showed me his record collection and played them on their radio gramophone, which sat in a cabinet. Another new discovery, as the only gramophone I had ever seen was the kind you wound up with a handle.

Spring was coming. With the sun climbing higher in the sky every day, the snow had started to thaw. My time in Sweden was about to come to an end.

I could tell that Aunt Nanny and Uncle David didn't like it. They kept saying,

"You will come back to us again, won't you?"

And I would say, "Of course I will come back."

But I didn't know when that would be possible. What I did know, however, was that one day I would be back.

The arrangements for the return journey were similar to those of our arrival in Sweden. We would be picked up at the railway stations and transported directly to Narvik, where one of the coastal steamers was waiting to bring us home.

A few days before leaving, I said goodbye to my teachers and classmates. Aunt Nanny took me to Piteå to say goodbye to her sister Ragnhild's family and to other friends I had made during my time there. Many of my friends promised to be at the railway station.

One sunny day in May 1946 I was again at the railway station in Öjebyn, but this time I was going home. Aunt Nanny had packed my suitcase and put in some extra goodies, like my favourite chocolate caramels. She had also put in sandwiches and fruit, along with my new clothes.

At the station I was surrounded by my foster family and friends. Ragnhild had come from Piteå to wave goodbye to 'Flickan' as she always called me. Aunt Nanny and Uncle David hugged me with tears in their eyes. Rolle offered me his hand in goodbye and hurried off. My friend Gerd was hugging me, and Ragnhild gave me a mighty bear hug telling me to take care.

With tears in my eyes, I turned and got onto the train to join the other children already there. I found a window, and waved furiously to all my Swedish friends and family, as the train slowly picked up speed and left the station. The abiding picture is of Aunt Nanny and Uncle David walking alongside the train, waving to me. I knew I would miss them all, but I also missed my mother and father. It was with mixed feelings that I found a seat and settled down for the journey back to Norway.

The journey to Narvik is a blur, as the train travelled on in its rhythmic fashion, stopping here and there to pick up more children. In Narvik I was reunited with Sonja, who made me feel a step closer to home. We were both delighted, and had so much to tell each other. All the children looked well fed and well dressed, and had a great deal to talk about.

Boarding the coastal steamer this time, no one stood by to douse us with lice powder. So we boarded in a much more dignified manner at Narvik, looking forward to going home. As with the train journey, the passage north on the ship is a blur. The weather was much better on the way north. We were informed that we would arrive in Kirkenes sometime in the middle of the day on the 17th May 1946. Remembering that this is Norway's Independence Day, the children were getting very excited, as the big day approached.

On the 17th May 1946 the ship sailed slowly in towards Kirkenes Harbour, with the ship's whistles blowing to announce our arrival. Other ships lying there joined in with their whistles as we glided towards the pier. Looking at the town, I saw a sea of army barracks and Nissan huts. Little else had changed. The ruins and scars of war were still very much in evidence.

The children were hanging over the railings, straining to see their parents. The piers and streets nearby were packed with people who had turned out to meet us. There was clapping, cheering, and waving of Norwegian flags. When parents discovered their children there was shouting and more cheering. With the gangway in place, we had to line up and vacate the ship in an orderly manner. As the children tumbled onto the pier they were claimed by their parents, lifted up and swung around, hugged and kissed, while everybody talked at the same time, in Swedish and Norwegian!

I spotted my Mother and Father. They were standing with Aunt Reidun and her family, obviously looking for us. When they saw me they came running, and I practically threw myself at them – so happy to see them again. Sonja appeared and we all hugged each other. Very excited I was shouting:

"Pappa, Pappa, I know all about Sweden!" They laughed and I turned to Ruth starting to tell her about Sweden. She too laughed. Puzzled, I looked at them all, and suddenly realised why they were so amused. We were all speaking Swedish!

Father took our suitcases while we linked arms with Mother, slowly walking uphill to our new home, all talking at the same time, trying to catch up with each other's news.

The future was still uncertain, but we had 'Freedom' and we had each other. One year had passed since the war ended.

The Swedish experience was great for most children. But for some it turned out not to be. Some of the older children, especially boys, were used as labourers on farms, and were often neither well treated nor well fed. For them Sweden was a great let-down. But for the majority of us, Sweden was a great place to be. It led to friendships and contacts for life, even through to the younger generations. Both my sister and I returned to Sweden to stay with our foster parents and to work. Many others did the same. Many also married Swedes and settled there, as did my sister. At the end of the war the Swedish people offered us a home and stability when we needed it most. For this we are very grateful.

Epilogue

In the autumn of 1945 Nissen huts (half-moon shaped buildings) and barracks arrived to ease the housing crisis for the coming winter. Shopkeepers returned to Kirkenes to set up shop, and slowly supplies began to arrive. People were picking up the pieces to start again.

The rebuilding of Finnmark was urgent and had to be given priority, but the start was slow. It was not until 1947 that it really got off the ground.

The Marshall Plan, with financial aid from the U.S. was a great help, not only for Norway, but also for other hard hit countries in Europe including Germany. Already in 1946, against government advice, the evacuees from Finnmark began to return home. By the end of 1947 about 90% of those forced into evacuation had returned. That they came back to the ruins of their homes somehow didn't matter. As long as they were free and back home where they belonged, they could start again. But hardship was inevitable, as the rebuilding of Finnmark took many years to accomplish, and continued until 1962.

A/S Sydvaranger, the iron ore company, was so badly damaged that production could not start again until 1952.

Teachers from the south were encouraged (with extra pay) to travel to Finnmark, to help educate the children. We spent our remaining school-years in barracks, but our teachers were excellent, making sure that we got a good education.

My sister Aase lived in a camp near Oslo with her German boyfriend Peter, and their two little girls. A son was born to them in 1945, but their oldest daughter Heide became ill and died in 1946.

When Peter finally was sent back to Germany, he promised to come back for Aase and the children as soon as possible. But after he was reunited with his German family in the ruins of Hamburg, he never returned and sadly, his family in Norway would never know their father.

For Aase life was very difficult. She had to work, and, unable to care for her children, they were put into a home for orphaned children. Aunt Reidun offered to look after my sister's second daughter, and the little girl was brought to Kirkenes. In time, however, Aase had her little boy adopted, rather than to let him languish for years in a children's home.

My sister had paid dearly for her love affair with a German soldier. The only 'crime' she had committed was to fall in love. There is no doubt that Peter was the love of her life. She told me many years later, that when she realised that he was not coming back, she wanted to die. In time, however, she married a Norwegian seaman who, incidentally, had been sailing on a merchant ship with the Allies during the war. Aase's daughter was brought south to live with them. They had one son together. Hers was not to be a long life however. Aase died suddenly when she was only fifty-three.

An estimated 8,000 to 10,000 children with German fathers were born in Norway during the war. Hitler's 'Lebensborn' program encouraged German soldiers to father 'Aryan' children to be part of the super race of Greater Germany. Norwegian woman were acceptable as they were looked upon as blonde, blue-eyed Viking descendants.

Clinics were set up by the SS to take care of the women and their babies. The babies were to be sent to their fathers' families in Germany. But as far as is known, only a small number of these babies were ever sent to Germany. Most of them were traced and brought back to Norway after the war.

Discrimination was widespread. Not only did the women suffer after the war, but their children suffered too, as many people took out their hatred both on the women and on their innocent children.

Many of the children suffered abuse and were traumatised. My niece, Aase's second daughter, suffered because of who she was. The trauma she endured has left deep marks. For her, the support of a fine family has been invaluable.

In later years there have been moves afoot trying to get some compensation for the war children. But the trauma they endured can never be compensated.

In 1950 my mother had a serious stroke and never recovered. She died when she was only fifty-nine. On a trip to Kirkenes in 1952, when Aase came to visit our mother and her little girl (who at that time was well looked after by Aunt Reidun) she and my father finally made peace with each other.

Father suffered periods of alcoholism for many years. After he came to live with us, he gradually recovered, and was very happy here in Shetland, even learning to speak a little English. He enjoyed seeing his grandsons grow up and was able to play with some of his great-grandchildren. Surrounded by his family he died peacefully when he was eighty years old.

In time, my sister Sonja married a Swede and moved to Sweden (close to her foster-family) where she spent the rest of her life.

My cousin, Kurt Vian, spent two and a half years in Sachsenhausen concentration camp in Germany. He survived, and was picked up by the Swedish Red Cross, who brought him and many other Norwegian prisoners back to Sweden in their famous white buses.

My other cousin Kåre, Aunt Margit's son, was arrested towards the end of the war for his activities against the Germans. He was badly tortured during his interrogations. The surrender by Germany in May 1945 probably saved his life.

Odd and Alf, the victims of an explosive device, became my classmates after the war. Odd, who lost both hands, coped very well and had no trouble keeping up with his class work. He used to pick up the pen with his mouth, put it between his stubs and write away as well as any of us. He went on to become a schoolteacher, and in time headmaster. Alf got a glass eye, false teeth, did very well at school and moved south to study law. Kalle Wara survived the war and went on to write a number of books about the war years and his own experiences.

Approximately 100 people from Sørvaranger lost their lives as a direct result of the war. Surprisingly few died during the bombing raids, no doubt due to excellent shelters. Some died trying to get away when the coastal steamers were torpedoed while others were executed or died at sea on merchant ships.

The war had stripped us of everything except our lives, two Bibles and some family photos. Family ties had been stretched to breaking point, and our faith had taken a severe blow. Sadly, we were never to attend the Adventists meetings again. As for me, I will agree with Aunt Camilla – the Lord works in mysterious ways, our lives had been saved, when so many others were not.

During the years of occupation some 80,000 Norwegians fled the country, some in fear of their lives, others to join Allied forces. Many escaped over the border to Sweden; others fled west to Shetland in their fishing boats and became members of the 'Shetland Bus', working as couriers, picking up refugees in Norway and putting ashore agents, radio-operators, weapons and commandoes. Their operations became increasingly hazardous as the Germans constantly were on the lookout for them. However, when the losses of men and boats became unacceptable, three excellent sub-chasers were given to the 'Shetland Bus' men by the US navy.

Their trips to the Norwegian coast increased to include commando raids, and attacks on German shipping and installations. In total almost 400 tons of arms and ammunition was brought across to Norway by the 'Shetland Bus'. The constant raids from Shetland helped to keep alive Hitler's belief that Norway would be invaded by the Allies.

The resistance movement in Finnmark was by its nature difficult. The landscape was vast and bare, the climate harsh. Sweden was too far away, Finland was allied with Germany, which left our big neighbour in the east, the Soviet Union. Many fled east, at times whole families. Those who were trained there as agents for the Russians returned to set up a contact network in Finnmark.

Hiding out in caves and turf houses, the partisans observed German ship movements, U-boats, aeroplanes and other activities, sending coded radio messages back to Russia at great danger to themselves. Their contacts in the communities were invaluable for information, providing maps of defence positions, troop movements and so on. Because of all this activity, the Russians were able to attack with much greater success.

Eleven members of one group were arrested and executed at the outskirts of Kirkenes in August 1943. Their families were transported to concentration camps in Germany. Many other partisans paid with their lives, as they persisted in defying the enemy.

At midnight on 8th May 1945 World War II in Norway came to an end. Following orders from the German High Command, the German forces, led by General Franz Böhme, surrendered their weapons. Hitler had kept approximately 400,000 troops in Norway during the war. Now about 360,000 remained. Norwegian and Allied forces took over, and soon all administration was transferred to civilian authorities.

Thousands of Norwegians were languishing in concentration camps in Germany, or in Norwegian prisons at the end of the war. More than 10,000 civilians had died out of a population of 3, 5 million. The counties of Finnmark and North Troms were left devastated.

Milorg, the highly organised resistance movement in the south of Norway, very quickly had 40,000 of their own people mobilised and armed. King Haakon VII arrived in Oslo on the 7th June 1945, with Crown Prince Olav, his family, and members of his exiled government.

Milorg and its forces, along with other returning freedom fighters, escorted the King and his party to Oslo, to a tumultuous welcome by their countrymen. The King had arrived forty years to the day after Norway had gained its independence from Sweden in 1905. That same day, King Haakon VII was re-instated as King of Norway and given back his powers by British General Sir Andrew Thorne, the Commander in Chief of the Allied forces in Norway.

A coalition government was formed, and led by our future prime minister Einar Gerhardsen (liberated from Sachsenhausen concentration camp) until elections could be held. They faced an enormous task. Prisoner-of-war camps throughout Norway held up to 100,000 Allied prisoners including German deserters – all in a poor state of health. In addition to the considerable German forces in the country, foreign civilians who had been used as forced labour numbered about 30,000 to 40,000.

Disarmed German soldiers were returned to Finnmark to help clear minefields, and to uncover and make safe all types of explosives. But each summer for many years, demolition experts travelled north to clear up the thousands of tons of explosives, mines, and shells left behind. Even today the earth regularly yields remnants of the dead as well as shells and other explosives.

By the summer of 1946 the remaining German soldiers were returned home. Some Russian prisoners wished to remain in Norway, fearing their fate when they returned to Russia. Sadly, the Allied policy was to send all prisoners home, realising too late that some would pay the ultimate price when they returned. About 17,000 prisoners had died in Norway due to appalling conditions, mistreatment and executions. At least 13,000 of them were Russian. All in all, a terrible price to pay for defending one's country.

Sweden was a neutral country in 1940 and chose to remain that way. But neutrality came at a price. They were persuaded to allow the transit of German troops by train through Sweden into Norway and Finland. The transits started in the summer of 1940, albeit against the wishes of the Swedes, who nevertheless submitted to pressure from mighty Germany.

Early transits were quite small, but gradually increased and became weekly runs. The agreement was that German soldiers travelled unarmed through Sweden. On their return journeys, the trains brought back wounded soldiers and those going on leave. By 1943 the Allies put on pressure for an end to the transports. Sweden terminated the agreement with Germany, and the transportation stopped.

But Sweden's role had many facets. The Norwegian border with Sweden, from Narvik in the north to the far south, became an important escape route for Norwegian resistance fighters and others trying to escape. Even the Germans, with all their might, could not effectively guard the entire border.

When fighting broke out between Finns and Germans, following the signing of a peace agreement between Finland and Russia in Sept. 1944, about 50,000 Finnish refugees escaped over the border into northern Sweden. From Denmark a large part of the Jewish population had fled to Sweden, where they were safe and looked after.

The neutrality of Sweden meant that they could communicate with the Germans. Count Folke Bernadotte had talks with Himmler and was able to get permission for the Swedish Red Cross to enter Germany with food parcels, blankets, and medicines. The Red Cross had a fleet of white buses, with large red crosses painted on the roofs to identify them and hopefully avoid attacks by Allied planes. The Danes were allowed to help, and the buses travelled widely within Germany in the last months of the war. Their intentions had been to rescue Scandinavians, but ultimately they rescued about 15,000 prisoners, of which just over half were Scandinavians.

In 1940 Norway had the fourth largest merchant navy in the world. Both the Nazis and the Allies recognised the value of the modern Norwegian fleet. Ignoring Quisling's order to sail to Germany or other neutral ports, the fleet went into service with the Allies. To administer the fleet, the company Notraship was formed with head offices in London and New York. Almost one third of the oil used by the British during the war was delivered by Norwegian tankers. Nearly 700 of the ships were lost, and many hundreds of sailors lost their lives.

In September 1942, the naval vessel *King Haakon VII* was gifted to Norway by the U.S., to be used as an escort ship or sub-chaser. Originally commissioned by the US Navy, it had been launched in April 1942. In the presence of the Norwegian Crown Princess Martha, at the hand-over ceremony in Washington, President Roosevelt gave a moving tribute to the Norwegian people with these famous words:

> "If there is anyone who still wonders why this
> war is being fought,
> let him look to Norway.
> If there is anyone who has any delusions that
> this war could have been averted, let him look
> to Norway;
> and if there is anyone who doubts the
> democratic will to win, again I say, look to
> Norway".

Acknowledgements

This book would not have been written without the encouragement and unfailing support of my husband Hebbie. He always believed that this story should be recorded and, as he bluntly put it "You cannot go to your grave without telling your story." He has been my first and severest critic. In spite of the sparks flying at times, I am deeply grateful for his support and belief in me.

I owe special thanks to Linda Sutherland, who has patiently read and commented on my manuscript in its various stages, and kept me right on certain aspects of grammar and punctuation.

Thanks also to Heather Cooke, tutor for The Writer's Bureau, whose help and advice, especially on presentation, has been invaluable; to Mary Blance of Shetland Radio whose program about my life promoted such an interest in my book, and for her continuing help and encouragement; to David Cooper for his help and support, and for producing the maps included in the book.

A special thank you goes to Camilla Carlsen for her help with my research at Sørvaranger Museum, Kirkenes in 2007, and for providing me with photos from their archives. I am deeply grateful also to Kalle Wara who made us very welcome on our visit to Kirkenes and generously offered me some of his war photos to use as I please. His generosity of spirit shone through, as he told us that he carries no grudge or hate towards anybody, in spite of what he saw and experienced as a slave labourer for the Germans during World War II. Many thanks also go to Thorbjørn Tharaldsen, Bjørnevatn, for his help with some of the local information in chapter 10 – and who is working on his own book from that time.

I was particularly happy to meet up again with my second-cousin Torgunn Østrøm, who provided me with family photos from the war when we, as evacuees, stayed with her family twice; the second time in July 1944 when we arrived at their doorstep, destitute.

I am especially indebted to my great niece Heide Mari Olsen who, at my request, travelled to Shetland to discuss my manuscript. Her words: "The truth has to be told, even if it hurts," made a deep impression on me.

Special thanks go to Anny Johnsen, my old school friend from Jarfjord, for her interest and encouragement and long standing friendship. Her family, like ours, almost didn't make it in that final battle of October 1944. But that is her story. She, like many others up north, could easily write a book herself.

I was lucky enough also to meet other old friends and relations on my trip north. The conversations I had with them, telling their own stories, helped broaden my own memories and verify others. They are as follows: My cousin Ruth Jensen, my cousin Kirsten Seljeseter and her husband Steinar (who have both sadly passed on), my second-cousins Henrik and Terje Borthen, Inga and Idar Rushfeldt, Mary Halstensen, Kirsten Basma Eriksen, and Svea Andersen.

Last but not least I like to thank my sons Dag, Rune and Karl Petter for their continuing interest and support, especially Dag, who regularly logs in on my computer with help and advice and to sort out problems beyond my capacity.

Bibliography

The sources of historic information used in this book are all, but one, of Norwegian origin. The Royal Naval Museum, Portsmouth was consulted regarding the authenticity of my photograph of HMS Devonshire.

Norwegian Sources:

Sørvaranger Museum, Kirkenes.

Sørvaranger Historielag.   (Sørvaranger History Group)
Sørvaranger under 2. Verdenskrig. (Sørvaranger in the 2nd World War)

Norge i Krig. Bind 1 – 8   ('Norway at War'. Book 1 – 8)

Finnmark i Flammer, Bind 1 – 2 ('Scorched Earth', Book 1 – 2)

Nordpå, by Kalle Wara.   ('In the North', by Kalle Wara)

Varanger Årbok 1994.   ('Varanger Year Book 1994')

Festung Kirkenes, by Finn Fløtten. ('Fortress Kirkenes' by Finn Fløtten)

Kirkenes i krigsåra 1940 – 1945 ('Kirkenes in the war years
By Henrik Nordhus   1940 - 1945', by Henrik Nordhus)

Norsk Krigsleksikon.   Norwegion Encyclopedia of
                                 World War II.